Nashua Public Library
3 4517 011108178

W9-BLA-225

SIMPSON

IMPRINT IN HUMANITIES
The humanities endowment
by Sharon Hanley Simpson and
Barclay Simpson honors
MURIEL CARTER HANLEY
whose intellect and sensitivity
have enriched the many lives
that she has touched.

The publisher gratefully acknowledges the generous
support of the Simpson Humanities Endowment Fund
of the University of California Press Foundation.

SOMEPLACE **LIKE** AMERICA

ALSO BY DALE MAHARIDGE AND MICHAEL S. WILLIAMSON

Journey to Nowhere: The Saga of the New Underclass

And Their Children After Them: The Legacy of Let Us Now Praise Famous Men—*James Agee, Walker Evans, and the Rise and Fall of Cotton in the South*

The Last Great American Hobo

Homeland

Denison, Iowa: Searching for the Soul of America Through the Secrets of a Midwest Town

BY DALE MAHARIDGE

Yosemite, A Landscape of Life, with Jay Mather

The Coming White Minority: California, Multiculturalism, and the Nation's Future

BY MICHAEL S. WILLIAMSON

The Lincoln Highway: The Great American Road Trip, with Michael Wallis

Old Dogs Are the Best Dogs, with Gene Weingarten

SOMEPLACE LIKE AMERICA

TALES FROM THE NEW GREAT DEPRESSION

DALE MAHARIDGE

PHOTOGRAPHS BY **MICHAEL S. WILLIAMSON**

WITH A FOREWORD BY **BRUCE SPRINGSTEEN**

UNIVERSITY OF CALIFORNIA PRESS | BERKELEY LOS ANGELES LONDON

University of California Press, one of the most distinguished university presses in the United States, enriches lives around the world by advancing scholarship in the humanities, social sciences, and natural sciences. Its activities are supported by the UC Press Foundation and by philanthropic contributions from individuals and institutions. For more information, visit www.ucpress.edu.

University of California Press
Berkeley and Los Angeles, California

University of California Press, Ltd.
London, England

Designer: Sandy Drooker
Text: 9.5/14.5 New Century Schoolbook
Display: Akzidenz Grotesk
Compositor: BookMatters, Berkeley
Printer and binder: Thomson-Shore, Inc.

Library of Congress Cataloging-in-Publication Data
Maharidge, Dale.
Someplace like America : tales from the new Great Depression / Dale Maharidge ; photographs by Michael S. Williamson ; with a foreword by Bruce Springsteen.
p. cm.
Includes bibliographical references.
ISBN 978-0-520-26247-8 (cloth : alk. paper)
1. Working class—United States—Case studies. 2. Working poor—United States—Case studies. 3. Unemployed—United States—Case studies. 4. Poverty—United States—Case studies. 5. United States—Economic conditions—21st century. 6. United States—Social conditions—21st century. I. Williamson, Michael, 1957– II. Title.
HD8072.5.M33 2011
305.5'620973—dc22 2010053750

Manufactured in the United States of America

20 19 18 17 16 15 14 13 12 11
10 9 8 7 6 5 4 3 2 1

This book is printed on Natures Book, which contains 50% post-consumer waste and meets the minimum requirements of ANSI/NISO Z39.48–1992 (R 1997) (*Permanence of Paper*).

In memory of Terry Magovern, a working man

And to Michael Williamson

You always said
It's the school of life
Tuition?
Everything I make
Graduation?
The day
They put me in a box
Six feet under
Thirty years
Classroom America
Finding all the secret places
Hidden in plain sight
Moving like Agee's spies
"Delicately among the enemy"
It's still out there
Bro'
Waiting
America
A night road
Endless beneath our wheels

CONTENTS

FOREWORD **BRUCE SPRINGSTEEN**

I had completed most of the "Tom Joad" record when one night, unable to sleep, I pulled this book down off my living room shelf. I read it in one sitting and I lay awake that night disturbed by its power and frightened by its implications. In the next week, I wrote "Youngstown" and "The New Timer." Dale Maharidge and Michael Williamson put real lives, names, and faces on statistics we'd all been hearing about throughout the Eighties. People who all their lives had played by the rules, done the right thing, and had come up empty, men and women whose work and sacrifice had built this country, who'd given their sons to its wars and then whose lives were marginalized or discarded. I lay awake that night thinking: What if the craft I'd learned was suddenly deemed obsolete, no longer needed? What would I do to take care of my family? What wouldn't I do?

Without getting on a soapbox, these are the questions Dale Maharidge and Michael Williamson pose with their words and pictures. Men and women struggling to take care of their own in the most impossible conditions and still moving on, surviving.

As we tuck our children into bed at night, this is an America many of us fail to see, but it is a part of the country we live in, an increasing part. I believe a place and a people are judged not just by their accomplishments, but also by their compassion and sense of justice. In the future, that's the frontier where we will all be tested. How well we do will be the America we leave behind for our children and grandchildren.

This was the introduction I wrote in 1995 for *Journey to Nowhere,* Dale and Michael's book telling the story of the losses suffered by American labor in the second half of the twentieth century. *Someplace Like America* takes the measure of the tidal wave thirty years and more in coming, a wave that *Journey* first saw rolling, dark and angry, on the horizon line. It is the story of the deconstruction of the American dream, piece by piece, literally steel beam by steel beam, broken up and shipped out south, east, and to points unknown, told in the voices of those who've lived it. Here is the cost in blood, treasure, and spirit that the post-industrialization of the United States has levied on its most loyal and forgotten citizens, the men and women who built the buildings we live in, laid the highways we drive on, *made* things, and asked for nothing in return but a good day's work and a decent living.

It tells of the political failure of our representatives to stem this tide (when not outright abetting it), of their failure to steer our economy in a direction that might serve the majority of hard-working American citizens, and of their allowing an entire social system to be hijacked into the service of the elite. The stories in this book let you feel the pounding destruction of purpose, identity, and meaning in American life, sucked out by a plutocracy determined to eke out its last drops of tribute, no matter what the human cost. And yet it is not a story of defeat. It also details the family ties, inner strength, faith, and too-tough-to-die resilience that carry our people forward when all is aligned against them.

When you read about workers today, they are discussed mainly in terms of statistics (the unemployed), trade (the need to eliminate and offshore their jobs in the name of increased profit), and unions (usually depicted as a purely negative drag on the economy). In reality, the lives of American workers, as well as those of the unemployed and the homeless, make up a critically important cornerstone of our country's story, past and present, and in that story, there is great honor. Dale and Michael have made the telling of that story their life's work. They present these men, women, and children in their full humanity. They give voice to their humor, frustration, rage, perseverance, and love. They invite us into these stories to understand the hard times and the commonality of experience that can still be found just beneath the surface of the modern news environment. In giving us back that feeling of universal connectedness, they create room for some optimism that we may still find our way back to higher ground as a country and as a people. As the folks whose voices sing off these pages will tell you, it's the only way forward.

SOMEPLACE LIKE AMERICA AN INTRODUCTION

Hobo Kenneth Burr, thirty-five years old, was murdered on December 5, 1984, in Santa Barbara, California. Shortly after, a flier was tacked to trees and telephone poles.

"This is a warning to all tree people," it read. "You are not welcome here in Santa Barbara. I will make life difficult for you. I have a faithful and respected group of citizens behind me. You bastards are low life scum and will not endure. I promise you."

The flier was signed "B. Ware." The phrase "tree people" referred to the homeless men and women who slept in a park under or near a Moreton Bay fig tree, a member of the ficus family with a trunk 40 feet in diameter. This stunning specimen could shade ten thousand people on a sunny day, by one estimate.

A resident unconnected to Burr's slaying had posted the flier, wishing to capitalize on the murder to scare away the tree people. At the same time, cops were "sweeping" the homeless at night to make their lives uncomfortable.

For journalists, this had all the elements of a good story: a town that was a rich enclave, homeless masses, a homicide, mean cops, and a vigilante. Days after Burr was slain, Michael Williamson and I rolled into town with backpacks and sleeping bags.

We quickly ran into the Reds—Wayne, known as "Crazy Red," and Rick, "Regular Red." The Reds were nicknamed because of their hair, not their politics. Not long after we met Crazy Red, who was a Vietnam War veteran, he asked me a question.

"Do you want to know what I think of the War on Drugs?"

"Sure," I said.

"Only way to fight one."

How could I not like him after that? We spent the rest of the afternoon with the Reds. It was a typical day in the life of the homeless. That is, nothing happened. Crazy Red loved to read. He showed us how he got a free newspaper. With a practiced snap of the wrist outside a coffee shop, he smacked a Wall Street Journal *box, and it popped open. He preferred the* New York Times, *but its boxes were more difficult to break into.*

We went to the spot where Burr's body had been found. All that remained of his camp was a torn Bible, a scattered pack of playing cards, and beer bottles.

Come evening, the Reds took us to meet Kelly. We watched her crawl from a wheelchair onto an old couch beneath a bush. We also met Joseph Phillips, sixty-four, and Geraldine Graham, seventy-three, who stood below Chico's Cantina, watching young people dance. The two eventually bedded down with blankets behind a dumpster. They shivered—California coastal nights are a lot colder than you might imagine.

The Reds told us the sweep wouldn't happen for a while. We drank coffee at a diner. Then the four of us unrolled our sleeping bags with other homeless people beneath the spreading branches of the mighty fig tree.

At midnight, commotion: blazing lights, shouts, police moving in fast. Dozens of tree people, clutching blankets and sleeping bags, fled. We ran with them. I looked back at the encroaching phalanx of cops and sputtered, indignant, "How can they do this!? This isn't right!"

Crazy Red looked at me as if I were crazy.

"Where do you think you are?" he asked. "Someplace like America?"

My America is one of iconic landscapes, places of lost dreams and hard-lived lives. The Deep South: abandoned cotton gins and vine-covered shacks of tenant farmers. The Great Lakes region: rusting stacks of ghost steel mills on forested riverbars; the ruins of a Detroit hotel with a rotting piano collapsed on the floor of its ballroom, where one imagines giddy couples dancing away the nights after the men came home from World War II to an industrial America that promised a limitless tomorrow. All through the Midwest and the West: century-old grain silos; telegraph lines that now transmit only the sound of the wind; storm-ravaged homesteads with blown-out windows on the desolate prairie. California's Central Valley: forgotten backwaters where people who evoke the Joads still walk lonely roads flanked by orchards of orange, peach, and prune; the sun-blasted camps of the newly unemployed of 2010, in secret patches of dusty digger pine, just as their counterparts formed the Hoovervilles of the 1930s.

My America is also seen up close in the eyes of its people. They are eyes that speak without words.

Among those Michael and I remember the most: The eyes of a woman who has fallen from upper-class privilege and is now standing in a charity food line are still proud and hurting a year after she lost the big home. A frugal white-collar mom, raising children on her own, works two jobs year-round, in some seasons, three; her eyes fill with tears as she talks about how she is barely surviving. A waitress in her sixties, whose tips are way down, will never be able to retire and believes she'll work until she falls dead; her sleep-deprived eyes gaze into a realm of numbness as she sprints between tables. Unbridled fear is in the eyes of a Latino man, a U.S. citizen, who is terrified of being stopped and once again bloodied by cops who assume that he's undocumented because of his brown skin.

There are so many more, named and nameless, thousands of eyes.

Take a minute and turn through some of Michael's photographs. The eyes you see tell a story of decades of economic assault.

There is something else visible in these eyes: toughness. Study the image of Ken Platt and his son on the cover of this book—both generations epitomize this steel-like resiliency. Or turn to the second section of photographs and look into the eyes of the woman who has just come home with her husband to a little shanty made of blankets strung over wooden poles, hidden in the bushes beside the Colorado River, after she has put in a long night shift working at a casino.

You cannot defeat people with eyes like these.

Some say that Americans are no longer able to stand up to tough times the way the "greatest generation" of the 1930s Depression and World War II did. But this is so very wrong. We are wounded as a culture today, certainly, and many of us are soft, bewildered, made numb by loss. Yet something is going on. We are at the front end of a process. People will rise to the challenge of these hard times. We have a long way to go before the transformation occurs, but it will happen.

I know this because I've been out there looking into the eyes of Americans, some of whom I've visited repeatedly over the decades, listening closely to what has happened to them. There's a lot I don't know. But American working people, I know. Mine is a journey that began in 1980, when I hired on as a police reporter at the *Sacramento Bee.* I was unaware then that I would soon be drawn into the lives of America's economically dispossessed and homeless. At the *Bee,* I met up with Michael Williamson. He was young like me, newly a staff photographer after having spent a few years as a copy boy. Michael would go on to cover this story with me. It's not a story we set out to do. It found us.

By 1982, we were immersed in reporting the recession of that decade, which was then the worst hard times since the Great Depression. (Those days now seem nearly idyllic in comparison.) Over a period of three years, we documented the decline of a steel town; this work became our first book, *Journey to Nowhere: The Saga of the New Underclass*. We traveled around the nation with job seekers by bus, by thumb, in boxcars, and in a rusting 1973 Olds Delta 88. We slept in rescue missions and hobo jungles. We saw, over and over and over, desperation and terror in the eyes of the newly homeless. It was a look we weren't supposed to see in America.

Throughout the next few decades, we continued interviewing and photographing workers, white collar and blue collar, whose lives had been growing steadily worse, despite the glowing economic reports found in the business and popular press. We hit the road for newspaper and magazine articles and for books. Other times, we went just because we felt it had to be done, even if our work never saw publication.

A conservative estimate is that we have journeyed, together and separately, a half million miles by car and freight train around the country since 1980 to experience the material presented in this book, talking with hundreds of people. In 2009 alone, Michael traveled forty thousand miles—twenty-five thousand driving, the rest by air—over four and a half months as he took some of the pictures found here.

THE MARCHING PHALANX

Even though this book chronicles three decades of our work, my passion for this quest is rooted in events and research dating to the 1930s.

Someplace Like America was conceived when I was at Yaddo, the artists' colony, in 2007. In the colony library, I'd reread work by Louis Adamic, who had been at Yaddo in 1931 and 1933. This Slovenian immigrant had faced hard times while he was emerging as a young writer. He traveled a hundred thousand miles around the country between 1931 and 1937 for his 1938 book *My America*. Adamic, though no stylist, had an ability to write about the present as if it were the past; that is, he possessed hindsight in the moment. His forgotten book provides an incisive portrait of a desperate nation.

Adamic raised questions long ago that are valid today, essentially the questions that I want to ask in this work. Do we want to tolerate hunger and desperation, with a large and growing portion of our population living in Third World conditions? Or do we want to care for one another? Do we want to reserve life chances for a very few who are wealthy, or do we desire to be a nation of opportunity, offering a level playing field for everyone?

Adamic wasn't my only inspiration. I've long been a student of the 1930s. As a child, I listened to my elders talk about the Great Depression. I read books—an early one was *The Grapes of Wrath.* When I moved to California, I scoured the Central Valley's back roads, locating landmarks from Steinbeck's reporting for his novels: Weedpatch, Pixley, Marysville, the Tagus Ranch east of Highway 99, which was the Hooper Ranch where the Joads picked peaches. I did a bit of field labor under the hot Central Valley sun.

I studied the Farm Security Administration photographs, including those by Dorothea Lange, who did a lot of work in the Central Valley during the Great Depression. I also befriended Carl Mydans, who at the time was one of the last living FSA photographers.

I met some of the few surviving Dust Bowl migrants, including one who had been involved in a cotton strike that turned bloody when farmers opened fire on unarmed protesting workers. Lillian Counts Dunn was there on October 10, 1933, when farmers' bullets pocked holes in the American flag flying over her head, and strikers fell dead and wounded around her as she shielded her fourteen-month-old daughter at the union headquarters in Pixley. That strike became a basis for Steinbeck's *In Dubious Battle.*

In addition to reading Steinbeck and Adamic, I delved into other books by serious documentarians: Sherwood Anderson, James Rorty, and Edmund Wilson. The fiction of John Dos Passos, especially his American trilogy books, was also influential. I concentrated on works that had been published in the Depression years. To me, observations made in the moment were more valuable, because I wanted to compare the psyche of Americans then and now. In many cases, books written later didn't capture the uncertainty and fear of those times—no one writing during the depths of the Depression knew how things would turn out.

I sparingly quote just a few of these writers, yet all of their voices were in my head as I worked on this book. There are echoes of the 1930s in recent events. That decade's lessons course through this book amid the stories of today's fallen workers.

Of all the writers who influenced me, Steinbeck's voice is among the strongest. In 1999, Tom Wolfe spoke to my students in the Communication Department at Stanford University about his method of operating as a writer. When he approached the reporting of a story, he said, his "Theory of Everything" was "status," or social position. By this, he meant that people are motivated by "group expectations." As he had explained in an interview one year earlier, "How other people view us has an important effect on how we view ourselves."

Long before Wolfe articulated this notion, Steinbeck had elaborated his theory of the "group-man," the idea that people can come together in a "phalanx," an assemblage that can develop its own motives and behaviors—which might be quite different, even at odds, with those of individual participants. From my reading, his concept most clearly applies to authoritarian groups, those with an "iron fist," as he wrote. I think of it as a "marching phalanx" when powerful groups conspire, wittingly or unwittingly, against individuals or social groups who do not wield political or monetary clout. In *The Grapes of Wrath,* for example, the big eastern bankers and local cops were arrayed against farm laborers and dispossessed migrants.

This book is about today's marching phalanx. Again, it's about big bankers and, in some places, local cops. It's also about politicians who don't care about people who can't or don't give them donations. And, once more, it's a story of people and weaker groups caught up in events beyond their control, dealing with tragedy and challenges.

THE VIEW FROM THE AMERICAN STREET

When I first began to think about doing this book, my intention was to give context to the then-raging bubble economy. I knew that millions of Americans were in bad shape and were not sharing the benefits of the alleged boom. Then things took a bad turn in the fall of 2008, when the stock market tanked. I sent my Columbia University journalism students down to Wall Street to cover the story. They half-expected to find people jumping from windows. (No traders leapt to their deaths, even in 1929; that tale of the early crash is fable, or wishful thinking, as historians have documented.)

Now, two years later, officials brag that another Great Depression has been avoided. Yet what has been done for workers and low-income Americans, who have for too long been bleeding? When we look at where most of the help has been directed, it's plain to see that we took care of the wealthy, just as we'd been doing for the previous thirty years. Trillions for the titans. Crumbs for the rest of us.

But have we really averted a crisis like that of the 1930s? The answer, officially, on paper, is yes—at the moment that I write these words. But many rapids (and maybe even a waterfall) appear to lie in wait in the economic river ahead of us. Regardless, I argue that millions of American workers are in fact in a Depression—and have been for some time—and that the overused modern expression "Great Recession" is misleading. In fact, if we applied this terminology to the 1930s, the Great Depression was technically two "Great Recessions," one that spanned the years 1929 through 1933, and another that ran from 1937 to 1938. Between 1933 and 1937, the market and other indicators upticked, a "recovery" that didn't, however, mean a return to pre-1929 conditions. Things regressed after 1936, when

President Franklin Roosevelt backed off on stimulus spending in the face of conservative opposition.

I'm not an economist, but from my street-level perspective, the technical definition of a Great Recession or a Great Depression might mean a lot to Wall Street and banking interests, but it means very little to the jobless and underemployed. These official pronouncements often seem like nothing more than semantics. My Great Recession is your Great Depression if you lose your job and your home. The oxymoronic term "jobless recovery" is an insult to those who have been laid off.

In the past century, the economic experts were repeatedly wrong in the lead-up to the 1929 market crash, and they continued to be wrong through the 1930s as they predicted a turnaround. And they're likely just as wrong now. Who knows what will happen this time? I don't. All I do know is that we should stop relying on the words of supposed experts and should instead listen to the voices of people like those in this book, listen to our own instincts as we try to survive. These ordinary people are the real experts.

This is not a wonky book about government policy or the merits of specific economic remedies. Rather, it aims to describe the human side of where we are today, trapped in an economy whose fruits have been denied to a majority of Americans.

It has taken thirty years of war against working-class Americans to get where we are. It may take a generation to get out of this mess. We are at a cultural and economic turning point. One era has ended; another, as yet unnamed, is dawning. How will it be shaped? As we begin to understand the pointed, painful questions that must be addressed, perhaps we can begin to change.

After a long career as a journalist and documentarian, I'm deeply disillusioned and cynical about our political and business "leaders." They have failed us, repeatedly.

Yet I am ever the optimist about the American people. One thing I've discovered in all these years of hearing Americans talk about their lives and dreams is that collectively we are strong. We are survivors. We emerged from hard times in the 1930s. We will do so again and will begin the long process of rebuilding an economy that works for everyone, but this can happen only if we relearn some lessons about caring for and relying on one another. And relearn we will, for we have no other choice.

OUR JOURNEYS

As Michael and I traveled over the years, we didn't seek out individuals who offered polemics or who were absorbed in politics. We simply listened to Americans who were in trouble because of the economy. In our interviews with workers, some people appeared to be liberal, others conservative, but most were apparently in that amorphous "middle." I can't write with certainty about their politics because we didn't ask about party affiliation. Left, right, center—we didn't care. Our focus was on them as people. (In most cases, they have allowed us to use their real names, although I have sometimes omitted a last name to protect an individual's privacy or have, in a few cases, changed a first name.)

Michael's photographs for this book represent a key story component beyond anything I could ever hope to accomplish in words. Michael is foremost a journalist. Yet, because of his life experience, he understands dislocation and loss at an especially deep level; his work for this book crosses into the realm of poetic intimacy. Michael is a bluesman with a camera. As in our other team projects, some of his photographs are not directly tied to the text—rather, they're separate narratives that enhance the work as a whole. (The occasional photos and document scans that appear within the chapter text itself are ones I have provided because I believe they reveal things words cannot. But these images cannot compete with Michael's photographs.)

The book opens with a series of "snapshots," in words, of America today. It describes the people we met on a five-day road trip in early 2009, from Washington, D.C., to Michigan and into the mid-South. I hope it will serve as prologue to the rest of the book and suggest the lens through which we'll present our entire thirty-year journey. It's important to understand, up front, that the growing disaster we documented in the 1980s remains with us, that the pain we found in those years persists, and that the contradictions have not been resolved.

After these snapshots, the book's narrative is roughly chronological. Part 1 reaches back to the 1980s. Some of these stories from our book *Journey to Nowhere* are being retold in a different and shorter form, with new material, taken from my notes, that I didn't use in that project. You will be introduced to the city of Youngstown, destroyed by the closing of steel mills and the resulting loss of tens of thousands of well-paid jobs. You will also meet former steelworkers such as Joe Marshall Sr. and his son and Ken Platt. I tell their stories to show the forces that sent people on the road, desperately seeking work.

Some of them became homeless. We met Sam when he walked into a rescue mission in St. Louis, his second night on the street with nowhere to sleep. Michael and I jumped on a freight train with him as he headed west to seek work.

In Texas, we discovered Jim and Bonnie Alexander, homeless in a tent with their two children. They had migrated from Michigan after losing their jobs and home, hoping for employment in Texas.

These new members of America's growing "underclass" seemed bewildered, lost and confused in an America they never expected would turn against them. It was a nasty era. Many Americans never escaped its dark grip.

Parts 2 and 3 move into the 1990s and the year 2000. In this period, Bruce Springsteen made a surprising entry into our lives, when he was inspired to write two songs based on several of the people we had introduced in *Journey to Nowhere.* Everywhere in those days we encountered people who had fallen out of the middle class, even in such supposedly good times. Among those we met in 2000 was Maggie Segura, a single working mother in Texas who had been thrown into desperate straits because her daughter was born with congenital health problems that weren't fully covered by her medical insurance. And we saw up close the effects of hunger among schoolchildren in Texas.

Part 4, set in the late 2000s, updates some of the stories from the previous thirty years. We returned to Youngstown and learned the fates of Ken Platt and the Marshall family. We revisited the Alexander family, who had something important to tell us about today's America. And I went back to visit Maggie, who continued to struggle economically, despite working multiple jobs. It's no exaggeration to say that many of these people have been in a Great Depression for the past three decades.

In part 5, we look at other people and places in 2009 and 2010. Michael and I were repeatedly drawn to the apocalypse otherwise known as New Orleans, still unhealed half a decade after Hurricane Katrina. I was in Arizona on the eve of that state's passage of the most repressive anti-immigrant legislation in America. In New York City, I went down to Wall Street and spied on the Big Boys who'd been bailed out with our tax dollars.

Part 6 recounts how some workers are coping with today's changing economy, by becoming self-reliant and by reaching out to build community. There's Sherri Harvel, an African American professional woman and a single mother, who has become an urban farmer in Kansas City. Former pulp mill worker Tim Lapointe, like many Americans, is becoming involved with his neighbors to get through these hard times. Their stories, coupled with the others in this book, epitomize the struggles people are facing today as well as the ways they are fighting back.

People are doing things on their own to survive and even thrive. That's the message of all the disparate characters you will read about.

ABROAD AT HOME

That day and night in Santa Barbara with Crazy Red stuck with me. The reason became clear as the decades progressed.

Many of us who grew up in America between World War II and the end of the 1970s realized, as the 1990s and 2000s came upon us, that the nation of our youth was no longer to be found. Among those born during or after the 1970s, many know that something is amiss, though they have no personal historical context rooted in those postwar years on which to base their concerns.

Crazy Red was a street savant, far ahead of his time. He had never truly come home from Vietnam; his soul remained caught somewhere in the middle, out over the Pacific Ocean. Crazy Red was an outsider who lived on the edge of society, who viewed it from that great distance. He was, as the title of Anthony Lewis's long-running column in the *New York Times* suggests, "Abroad at Home."

So with those words, "Where do you think you are? Someplace like America?" Crazy Red gets to name this book.

Our title is meant as both a statement and a question. Our thirty-year documentation of this nation, in words and photographs, is our statement. And, through the voices of the people we came to know, we ask the question: what do we want to become as we move forward?

SNAPSHOTS FROM THE ROAD 2009

BETWEEN THE 80TH AND 90TH MERIDIANS

The country is reeling. Housing prices, the market, and confidence are tumbling. Awhile back, you'd been called an idiot because you remembered the 1987 crash and kept your 401(k) in a 4 percent money market account; any fool could make a 10 percent return or more on the big board, people said. Now you don't look so stupid, as stock market 401(k)s have lost half their value. Optimism comes in this form: in the most recent month, the nation lost 660,000 jobs, and a business commentator on the radio says it's a good number because a month earlier 740,000 jobs had vanished. Maybe it's a trend. Maybe we've hit bottom. Maybe things are turning around. Maybe the market is going to roar again, and all will return to "normal."

No.

This time it won't be over in a few months.

As you drive in the land of 80–90, a swath of central North America that runs from the Great Lakes due south to the Gulf of Mexico, between Chicago to the west and Pittsburgh to the east, roughly bounded by the 80th and 90th meridians, you listen to radio pundits with a large degree of chagrin, because many people in this region have been in their own private Great Depression since 1980. Some in 80–90 laugh at the losses being talked about on the radio and in the papers—jobs, homes, 401(k)s, pensions. It's bitter laughter, the laughter of vengeance, because they've lived so long with loss. Yet in their next breath, they utter words of hope. It's just how we are, as a people, and you thank God, the deity, or whatever for this. Without hope, we'd all be dead.

Yet sometimes it's difficult to maintain hope in 80–90.

The sound that stays with you in 80–90, in places like Youngstown and Detroit and New Orleans, is the crunch of broken glass beneath feet.

The smell: defecation in the squats.

In some cities, the official flag is plywood nailed over windows. On some blocks, like the ones you see in Columbus, Ohio, there are more homes with plywood flags than without. Plywood, bright yellow and new in the inner suburbs. Plywood, gray and weathered in the inner cities, torn off rear windows by squatters, desperately fragile people who shit in deserted kitchens and hunker from the cold curled up on sheaves of dumpster cardboard in bedrooms where immigrant men and women long ago slept in beds bought with factory wages. Those people of old were workers with machine-soiled hands; no amount of scrubbing would remove that dirt. They dreamed of better lives for their children. Where are those children now? On the coasts, perhaps. Others are in those freezing bedrooms with shattered panes and charred crack pipes in the corners; dreams now come in the night with the flash of a butane lighter to a tube of glass. A dream on that cardboard bed, if only for a moment—

Dreams—

If only life were better—

In a north-to-south tour of 80–90, you're forgiven if you blink your sleep-deprived eyes and forget where you are, because you've been traveling a hard road. Detroit, New Orleans—it's all the same, save for the palm trees. The former's destruction is attributed to "necessary" change, "creative destruction," becoming part of a "global economy"; the latter's ruin is blamed on wind and water. But both blames are skewed, obscuring the reality that the devastation is the result of an error so vast that it took thirty years to form and may take thirty years to be healed. But it must and will be healed.

Everywhere you drive, trees and vines now grow where people once lived. In the one-time steel manufacturing city of Youngstown, forests at the edge of the road are marked by slate and cement stairs every hundred feet or so, stairs that lead nowhere, as if they were graveyard markers for an America that no longer breathes, for a business and political leadership that no longer leads. Huge swaths of Youngstown, Detroit, New Orleans look like scenes from Cormac McCarthy's *The Road;* the apocalypse has come, the end of the world. You enter abandoned houses and buildings. Danger lurks. In Detroit, people smash glass and hammer at the walls six stories overhead in a crumbling train station that was once as fancy as New York's Grand Central; reverberations of destruction echo, and you hurriedly exit.

When you do meet people face to face, some are edgy, crazed. At a sprawling factory site being demolished in Muskegon, Michigan, in a neighborhood where more than 50 percent of the adult men are unemployed, a car that pulls near the mound of rubble prompts a hard-hatted worker to go berserk: he screams, lunges at the surprised driver, and slugs him. In Detroit, when you stop on a corner for a minute, dealers standing nearby whistle with fierce urgency, their eyes rising to a second-floor window where you imagine a rifleman poised with an AK. You speed away, heart racing.

In New Orleans, amid the smell of rot, your flashlight beam doesn't reach the far walls of an abandoned elementary school, where hundreds of children laughed and played just four years earlier. Now you imagine a desperate, knife-wielding killer behind each pillar. The pornography that comforts a lonely squatter is taped next to a blackboard.

Everywhere: wind blows through jagged teeth in window sashes.

Everywhere: gunfire in the night, sometimes during the day. You get used to it, so long as it isn't too close.

Everywhere: you're glad when you get out to a part of the city where life is normal. Yet even in the exurbs, not far from a Starbucks, you see the empty Circuit City and Linens 'N Things big-box locations with FOR LEASE signs in the windows. Word is, more chains will close in the coming months.

And you wonder: what is normal?

The five stories that follow are from a five-day road trip that I took with Michael and documentary filmmaker Ron Wyman in 2009 to find out what constituted "normal" everyday reality for people in the northern and central part of the United States between the 80th and 90th meridians. We did little planning for those five days; our discoveries were largely due to serendipity. These five stories stand out as emblematic of the continuity and intensity of the crisis America's working people confront. It's frightfully easy to find desperation in America today. You simply have to go out there and listen.

ISLAND WOMAN: DETROIT

The house at 3015 Monterey is listed for sale at a price of $1 on www.realtor.com. It has to be a mistake. But a call to the sales agent confirms the price: a buck.

From an aerial view on Google Earth, the Detroit neighborhood looks pastoral, dotted with meadows that have been freshly mown, judging by the tractor wheel tracks running in concentric rings, as if they were farm fields in which hay has been cut.

If only this were true. The meadows, of course, are where houses and apartment buildings once stood. The city now mows the lots a few times each summer; otherwise, in a few short years brush and trees would take over. As we drive into the neighborhood, many still-standing homes are boarded up or occupied by squatters. Here and there are burned-out shells.

We roll up to 3015 Monterey. It doesn't appear so bad in relative terms: some windows are covered with fresh plywood, others have unshattered glass. We peer inside. The two-story house seems solid. It's certainly in better shape than its neighbors: an apartment building with all its windows smashed out, a house in ruins. Winter snows have left them sodden.

Sudden commotion: a large man stands on a porch a block away, waving his arms and screaming. He is displeased by our presence.

"EEEHHH-EEEH-AHHH-OHHH!!!!

"MOTHER-R-R-R-R-R FUCKER-R-R-R-R-R-R-R!!! EEEHHH-EEEHHH-AAH-OHHH!"

"You wonder what a PCP high sounds like? That's it," Michael says.

We ignore the screamer, whose long and piercing screeches continue as Michael and Ron take pictures. Snow falls. I wander into the vacant dwellings on each side of 3015 Monterey. The screamer's howls are muted by the walls: "Eeehhh-aahhhheee-fuck-aaahhhh-owwww . . . "

When I emerge, a car pulls up to a corner house across the street. Only then do I notice the fine dwelling of brick and nicely painted siding, with a fence surrounding a coddled lawn. The home has new front steps. A woman gets out of the car. The screamer, exhausted, falls silent.

I approach the woman and mention that I'm writing about the house across the street that's listed for a buck.

"A dollar!" shrieks Yvonne, a woman of late middle age, who is both suspicious of a stranger and yet eager to talk. "It started at seven hundred dollars!"

After the surprise settles and Michael and Ron come over, Yvonne says, "My husband worked at General Motors for thirty-one years. Says he ain't working for the man no more." Her husband retired in 2000.

They moved into the house in the early 1980s. Detroit was considered bad then. We'd reported from here in 1984 and had found desperation in a neighborhood not that far away, where the infant mortality rate rivaled that of Haiti. But those days seem like good times now that the auto industry is so ravaged.

"We've seen it come and we've seen it go," Yvonne says.

"How's the neighborhood? Dangerous?" I ask.

"I don't care what they're like. We used to know all of them." Now she knows only a few of her neighbors.

"How long has that house been empty?"

"Well, about two years. It's tore up on the inside. They been in and out of there. They been selling drugs. But I don't care. People been doing just everything. I don't care what they do. As long as I take care of mine."

Yvonne looks warmly at the house that she and her husband own free and clear. She notes that all the windows are brand new. They keep investing in the house.

"What do you think is going to happen to it?" I ask her, nodding to the dollar house across the street.

"I don't care! I'm just going to take care of my property. Keep mine looking good. That's it. I don't care what they do anywhere else. I don't care they don't pick up any paper, their lawn's not mowed. Long as mine's looking good. That's it."

Yvonne explains that a huge building housing dozens of residents once sat in the big meadow across the street. "The apartment building has been gone since like '85 or '86. My husband cleans up some of the field," she says, referring to the trash people dump, "so when we're sitting on our porch, we don't have to see it. We just take care of our own."

She looks around at the many empty houses near and far within her sight. Her index finger marks each one, with a story. "That one's boarded up," she says. "The lady, she passed over there. I don't know what happened there—they lost their house. It's just a lot of houses. All of them need to be torn down. I mean, I don't care what happens over there. I'm right here. People ride down the street and say, 'Your house is looking good.' My house *is* looking good. Right here, that's all it is. I mind my own business. That's it. I don't care what nobody else is doing. I go to work. Do what I got to do to keep my property up. Pay my taxes. I don't owe nothing. We don't care what's over there."

We talk for another half hour or so, and these words, or a close variation, punctuate every third or fourth sentence: "I don't care what they do over there!" As we walk away through the ravaged neighborhood, I marvel at Yvonne's tenacity.

"How could she feel otherwise?" Ron notes about the island that is Yvonne's house. "It's all she can control."

She sits on the ground with her back against the food bank's big diesel truck rig, apart from the 223 other people in line, at the Fifth Reform Church in a city in Michigan, on a workday afternoon. The woman has short-cropped blondish hair, and she is well dressed.

Her eyes are downcast. You don't need a shrink to tell you that she's not happy to be here at the mobile drop site for the food bank operated by the Second Harvest Gleaners, part of the Feeding America network.

To her left, on the sidewalk, is a long row of containers, which recipients will use to collect food. The containers had been set out to mark places in line for people who began showing up at 4:00 A.M. to claim a spot. No two containers are alike. There are clothes hampers, tote tubs, plastic coolers, and cardboard boxes—a trail of yellow, blue, green, white, orange, and brown. Some containers sit in children's red wagons. One, a blue clothes hamper, is atop a yellow plastic sled.

Once they arrived, people were each given a number so they didn't have to stand out in the 20-degree air. Most are inside the church now, waiting for those numbers to be called.

These people aren't the street homeless. None of the 224 faces register as being any different from those you'd see in a suburban shopping mall. Conversation is muted. We talk to people and hear essentially the same story from all of them: Most worked for companies that supplied auto manufacturers. They are laid off. Money is tight. Refrigerators are nearly empty. A fifty-six-year-old woman says, "At my age, no one wants to hire you."

But it's the face of the woman seated on the ground against the truck that stands out as somehow not belonging. She marks her isolation by not joining the others inside. We approach the woman when her number is called and she goes through the line. At first, she's reluctant to talk. Then she comes alive; her face is transformed by a smile.

"I had the house on the hill," Sally says. She is the kind of person who laughs easily, even when talking about the bad things that have happened.

Out pour her pertinent facts: She's forty-six, with two children, ages nine and eleven. Sally and her husband had a dry cleaning operation in a city a few hours distant. Business fell off after 9/11. Then a big local company instituted "casual Fridays," and business went down a bit more. Then the auto companies started hurting. This and that—it all cut into the profit margin, to the point of ruin. They lost the business. A year and a half ago, the house went into foreclosure—$100,000 in equity, $300,000 owed to the bank. They have a half million dollars of debt. A divorce is in the works.

"I'm currently on disability," Sally continues. She has no job. No savings. No credit. She now rents a house from her sister in this city.

"We lived an upper-middle-class life. We lost our home and five acres in an affluent neighborhood. And my husband and I couldn't get on the same page, so here I am, relocated and starting over, standing in a food line to help make ends meet."

We mention that when we first saw her, seated against the truck, she seemed to be an unwilling participant in the food bank line. She laughs and admits that of course she doesn't want to be here.

But, she asserts, "this is not outside of your world," as if replying to anyone who might judge her. "This is helping me, and I'm going to keep coming until it gets better. We're mothers. We're going to do what it takes to provide for the kids. I have no credit now. And a lot of debt, which I haven't been able to work out because the divorce isn't final. So I'm just in limbo."

How much does coming to the food bank save her?

"I would say two hundred dollars in meals a month. I use what I get and create my meal plan around it. This is actually not that great of a truck today—"

She laughs sheepishly, looking down at her food. Inside the gray plastic milk carton on wheels, with an extending tote handle, she has four heads of romaine lettuce, two loaves of bread, three four-packs of Dannon yogurt, a half dozen Snapples.

"Sometimes there's a lot of protein and a lot of really valuable things that I wouldn't normally buy, like yogurt."

Sally's children were used to abundance. As she describes it, they were typical upper-middle-class American kids, with a desire for designer clothes, lots of "things." She's trying to get them to understand that labels on clothes don't mean that much, and she has made clothes for them herself. She's happy that the kids no longer live in the rich neighborhood.

"It was materialistic. Everything was brand names. I had to reevaluate my priorities and focus on what is really important to me and the message I want to send to these kids. Definitely, we're closer. I'm hoping that they both have received God as their savior. They now know I do the food truck, get help from a church. And I'm trying to show them that we are a community, and we're all trying to help each other get through this. I don't want them to know all the details of our situation; I don't think they're old enough right now. But I think it's important for them to know that we are victims of this era."

When we ask her about a name for "this era" that she keeps talking about, I expect her to reply with the phrase "a new Depression," or the overused "Great Recession."

Instead, she responds rapidly: "Ugly. It is ugly."

When I press her to explain, she continues, with long pauses as she tries to collect her thoughts: "Because I think that this . . . economy . . . has hit—I still don't think the very well-to-do have been hit enough to realize what has been done to the middle class. I think there has been a merging with the lower class. The middle class has been eliminated. You're either really rich or you're in the poverty level. And I think the government is denying the recession. . . . I think it's been very active for at least five years.

"I agree with the economists that it's going to get worse before it gets better, because I keep hearing about companies going out. I think it's going to bring us back to the—I don't even know what era, what year. But it's going to have people reevaluating their priorities."

Sally doesn't see herself as part of any grand reordering of the American way of life. She just sees herself and her two children doing what they have to do to make it past "this era" in America. She is actually very upbeat. Sometimes she's down, sure—change doesn't come quickly. But she's not really the dour-looking person slumped by the truck. She's busy building a new life.

As Michael and Ron take pictures of Sally, I stand back and think this: her new America is not a nation of an ever-growing GDP. It's not the nation Wall Street wants to see, because Sally's America is not one awash in big bank bonuses based on fake profits and rampant consumerism funded on credit most people can't pay off.

Sally's America is decidedly CEO-unfriendly.

"I have no credit, and I plan to get no credit," Sally says. "My motto now is 'less is more.' I grow tomatoes. Then I freeze them and use them all winter long."

She also grows strawberries, picks wild blueberries, and makes jam. She grows food that is expensive to buy. She would have a bigger garden, but the deer and rabbits do damage. Sometimes the food bank has fruit in bulk, such as cases of pears. She cans them in mason jars, virtually for free. "They cost a dollar seventy-eight in the store. But they are not as good as the ones I can.

"We'll go back to the one-stall garages and the one-vehicle homes," she continues. "Kind of a throwback to the fifties. But with dual incomes. People will use mass transportation more. Maybe, I hope. Maybe it will evolve, and we'll make a greener world. Maybe they'll get out on the bike trails and bike to work. I'm hoping for this city that they get the grant to do turbines.

"It took being here for me to get this. It's been a blessing in disguise. I would have stayed in the house on the hill. I'm going to be a better person. I'm going to be a better mother for it."

THE DANCER: LOUISVILLE

In fifteen minutes, the show will begin. It will mark the death of dreams for some, and the start of fresh dreams for others.

One hundred people wait in the audience in West Hall A at the Kentucky Exposition Center in Louisville. Gray hair or balding domes dominate. Most are men, most are white—just three black faces are present. The couple in the front row stands out: they're young, in their late twenties. Among the crowd, many nervously purse their mouths in anticipation of a process most have never gone through before—bidding at an auction for foreclosed homes, conducted by the Real Estate Disposition Corporation, a firm that sells bank-owned properties.

Some are first-time home buyers keen for a bargain; others are investors. They've gained entry with a $2,500 cashier's check and a promise to put 5 percent down if their bid is successful, which is the cut REDC takes. According to congressional testimony, 2.2 million homes were foreclosed on in 2008; the few dozen homes that will be sold tonight are among that number.

There's a hint of the sense of humor that will pervade the proceedings in the music that booms from huge speakers. Among the songs, two from the *Rolling Stones:* "Between a Rock and a Hard Place" and "Under Pressure."

"It's show business," says one auction official as James Brown's "Living in America" thunders in the hall. "It's been a big show for the last four and a half years. I'm just a carny in a suit."

The carnival barker atmosphere is carefully crafted. The man explains that most people have never been to an auction, and they're nervous. It's the job of the REDC crew to put them at ease, make them laugh—and motivate them to buy houses, in some cases for dimes on the dollar. The Irvine, California–based auction staff travels around the nation, working some twenty-five days a month. They make good money, but the man complains that they're now too busy. Before the bad times started, there weren't that many foreclosures, and auctions were shorter. He had time to go to the beach many afternoons. Now beach time is out—some auctions last a grueling thirteen straight hours.

As I flip through a thick booklet of REDC homes in foreclosure in the four-state region around Louisville, I cannot help but think of the homeless, formerly suburban, families who may be living in tents in two or three years, when the relatives they move in with kick them out, or when they can't pay rent. We saw it in 1983. Things aren't there yet, but we can expect to see it again in 2011 and maybe beyond.

When I ask about these families, the auction official quickly responds: "Nope. No guilt at all. I feel sorry for the guy who lost his job. . . . I get the whole lose your job thing. But a lot of these people jumped in without enough income. Most of these people were pushing prices up. It had to stop. They're the reason my hundred-thousand-dollar condo is now worth eighty thousand."

Black curtains form a backdrop at the front of the room. Black cloth covers the tables. All the men from the auction company are dressed in black—suits or tuxedos. One stands out: he is Jeffrey James (J. J.) Johnston, thirty-five, a bald man with intense eyes. He's been called a "ringman," but his official title is "bidder's assistant." He and two other bidder's assistants, all three in tuxedos, will work amid the audience while the auctioneer barks; their jobs are to signal when someone is bidding. Their role is not just to stand and point; they will be loud, theatrical.

J. J. stretches, touches his toes, as if preparing for a workout. He runs three to five miles a day to be in shape for this job, he tells me.

REDC vice president Trent Ferris takes the microphone to announce that the auction will soon begin.

"It's a sad and tragic thing that these homes have been foreclosed on, but that business is done." It's time to move on, Ferris says. He talks about blighted neighborhoods and the risk of decay in America. "This is the opportunity to put these houses back into homes and to get them back into the tax base." Ferris tells the crowd that yesterday REDC sold a condominium on Nag's Head for some $300,000—two years previous, it sold for $1.2 million. "There are some great opportunities out there."

The crew goes through a mock auction to show the crowd how things work. They pretend to "sell" the California home owned by one of the crew. It goes for just over $1 million.

"Oh, I didn't tell you that it's a mobile home," announces an auction official. On the big screen appears an image of a Great Depression–era wooden shack perched on the bed of a rickety truck.

Laughter—but it is muted.

The real auction begins with house number 1112. A picture of it appears on the screen. The bidding comes and goes so fast that it is hard to follow the action. Bam. Another house comes up. Auctioneer Michael Carr's trilling of "bbbbdddd-bbbbbbddddaaaaaa" between the numbers is at the same time both hypnotic and jarring. The next house—

"—Ten cents on the dollar!" Carr shouts. "Seventy-five hundred . . . bbbbdd-bbbddbaaabbbbddaa . . . seventy-five hundred . . . bbbbdddbbbaaa . . . You can't rent a storage locker for a year for that much! . . . Going once for six thousand, going twice, sold! Sold it for six thousand, believe it or not!"

House number 1142 is located in a rural town far south of Louisville. It has over 1,700 square feet on a half acre, valued at $129,000. The opening bid is $1,000. It goes up, but the price stalls at $20,000. Carr works it hard:

"—Twenty-two five hundred . . . bbbbbbddddddbbbbddddaaaaaaa . . . twenty-seven five hundred . . . bbbbddddddbdddbbbaaa . . . Do I hear thirty? . . . bdddd-bbbdddbbbaa . . . now thirty-two five hundred . . . bdddbbbdddddbbbba, going once . . . bbbdddbbddddaaa, going twice . . . Sold for thirty thousand! What a great time to be alive!"

And so it goes. House after house at ridiculously low prices. A 2,500-square-foot house on a half acre in the outer suburbs that had previously sold for $260,000 goes for $77,500; other homes go for $16,000, $5,000, on and on.

Each bidder's assistant has his own style. A thin-mustached man prefers to yowl when someone in his section of the audience makes a bid; he translates this to Carr by extending his hand and opening his mouth to emit a long and raspy "Aargggggghhhhhhh!" that, in an apt mixed metaphor, is something between the cry of a raven and the scream of a bobcat.

J. J.'s style is different. When bidding is low on a home, J. J. takes out a handkerchief and, with great burlesque, twists it in his ear as if he can't believe what he's hearing. Instead of crying out to let Carr know there's been a bid, he'll do high kicks toward Carr, then twirls, then a rooster walk. Later, when Michael is looking at the images on his Nikon digital camera, the succession of shots makes it look like J. J. is doing ballet.

J. J.'s moves are the dance of America—capitalism at work. One might characterize the buyers as bottom feeders, but what they're doing is markedly less obscene than what happened in the early 2000s, when greed caused "flippers" to buy a house and then sell it a month or two later for profits of tens of thousands of dollars. Greed made many of us believe that house prices would never fall. The argument that sustained this belief posited that America's population was ever-growing and that people required places to live. Supply was scarce, and thus homes were worth more than gold. Left out of this logic was falling income. A nation working for Wal-Mart wages could not sustain these escalating prices. It can be pointed out that Calcutta has an ever-growing population, too—but many of its residents sleep on the streets and will never be able to rent, much less purchase, a home. How can one feel sorry that many flippers were eaten by sharks?

At the end of the auction, as successful bidders fill out paperwork at tables in a nearby room, J. J. tells us that he was born in Madison, Missouri. "Dad was an auctioneer." J. J. ran his first auction at age eight, when he sold pies and quilts for a church fundraiser. He likes performing. On the side, he is a percussionist and a standup comic.

"I like to make it exciting. You get a little showmanship so it's not so boring. I'm goofing around with the auctioneer. You can see a blank wall coming over them. Sometimes a joke or a high kick will make them laugh. You see a pressure release. I wish no one was kicked out of their house. But I can't tell you how many times people stand up and cheer. I've had people hug me. We're helping people get into a house."

He's been with REDC five years. "This is the big league of auctioneering. This is a big wheel to keep running." The company rents halls and pays for moving the sound system and flying the crew everywhere. Being on the road for twenty-five days each month is a brutal schedule. Today was easy—it was a small auction. Ten- and twelve-hour marathon auctions in big cities are more the norm, with hundreds of homes being sold. They start at 9:30 A.M. and end at 10 at night. "And we do them back to back. I sometimes get sick. My immune system gets worn down. I'm slamming Red Bulls all the time."

Tomorrow, he'll work an auction in Springfield. The day after, Kansas City.

J. J. is happy for the early quitting time. He turns to leave, then pivots and points his index finger back at us as he bids farewell.

"Now a cheeseburger and a white Russian! Dude!"

EDGE MEN: NASHVILLE

The towering billboard on the bank of the Cumberland River, north of the Y formed by the juncture of interstates 24 and 40 in Nashville, is owned by McIntyre Outdoor Advertising. In mid-July 2006, the company rented the 15-by-60-foot surface to Harrah's casino in Metropolis, Illinois, on the Mississippi River, to announce a show featuring singer Kenny Rogers and comedian Ron White. Rogers's bearded, smiling face was in the center; White, smoking a trademark cigar, appeared to one side.

Ed watched as workers came at the end of the billboard's run to remove the thick plastic sheets that made up the advertisement, which were slated to be discarded. Ed asked if he could have them.

He built a wooden frame at the base of the billboard, 16 by 38 feet and 8 feet tall, and stretched the plastic over it to keep off the rain. He assembled two queen-size beds, a clothes dresser, tables, a car battery, and a 750-watt inverter to create house current to run a small television and a fan in the summer. On a dresser, he placed a picture of his daughter, Keisha, in a frame. Ed had a home.

Now he awakens looking directly up at the smiling face of Kenny Rogers on his ceiling. White's mug makes up most of the west wall. White's cigar, long as a human torso, looks like it could drip ashes on Ed's head. Being inside his home at noon is like being behind a translucent movie screen with the faces of these stars frozen in a scene.

Ed's home is part of a sprawling tent city on the bank of the Cumberland, which closely resembles a Latin American shantytown. Tents and shacks run into the woods along the bank. Each shanty has a wood-burning stove made from a 55-gallon steel barrel, thanks to Ed, who was a welder till he lost his job some eight years back. Ed welded flu pipes and doors into the barrels, and now each shack has winter heat.

Early one afternoon three years after Ed built his house, he and his nearest neighbor, Clem, are in the courtyard of sorts between their shanties, cooking slices of Spam in a pan set on a propane stove. The men sit on log rounds. Spam sizzles. A few other men come, and Ed makes Spam sandwiches for them. Ed and Clem tell their stories of how they arrived on this shore. Both had worked long years, as had others in the tent city. Ed, fifty-three, suffers from diabetes. But that's not all—he and the others suffer from something else. I'm not yet sure what.

The village of tents and huts is borderline fetid. There are a few portable toilets some distance away, so there isn't the usual smell of shit one finds in a squat or a wino hangout. But it's not a clean place—junk is piled high, litter is everywhere. I look for signs of acute alcohol or drug abuse, but no one is obviously addicted. At the moment, the men are certainly sober. One man, twenty-five, says he is camping here, "waiting things out" till the economy gets better. For men in their fifties, there is no such talk. They merely exist.

Back in the 1980s, Michael and I never found camps like this. In those days, there were basically two categories: new timers (the newly homeless) and the old-style winos who were the "zombie homeless." The world of Ed and his neighbors is a "'tween" situation. These men are not zombies. Yet they don't leap from their beds each morning to scan the help wanted ads or go fill out job applications. A cynic could dismiss them as wastrels.

We talk about them as we drive away toward the rolling hills of north central Tennessee. What is different?

I think of a passage Louis Adamic wrote in *My America,* a diary entry dated December 15, 1931, when he found himself depressed by the sight of men in a soup line:

> A good many American "proletarians" have been living from hand to mouth in so-called "good times." Now that they have lost their jobs millions of them are completely down—and I think that is where, alas! many or even most of them are going to stay. . . . I have a definite feeling that millions of them, now that they are unemployed, are licked as men. . . . They are licked by the chaos of America, by the machine, by industrialism, by . . . their futile, frustrated individualist psychology on the other. It is horrible to say this, but it is true—millions now unemployed are mainly or completely paralyzed, impotent, "washed up," doomed never again to be part of the vital, constructive economic processes of the country.

Conditions today are different, for sure, but in some ways worse. Adamic was writing about people who had come through the roaring '20s, yet were economically on the bottom. And he saw that their attitudes were in the cellar less than two years into the Great Depression.

The men in Ed's camp have endured thirty years of their own Great Depression, of stagnant or falling wages and rising prices amid allegedly good times. These men have spent a lot more time in the shadows than those Adamic wrote about in 1931. If I try to put myself inside their heads, I can understand their position, utterly. One can exist in survival mode for many years, working for five or six bucks an hour and yet have nothing to eat after the rent is paid. Why not come to live for free on the bank of a river? In making this choice, these men have flung themselves to the far edge, the extreme outer orbit, of society. It certainly simplifies one's life to go to this edge.

Of course, it's not members of the solid middle or upper-middle class who succumb to this cold reality, at least at first. It's the men and women, mostly men, on the lowest rung of the working class, men like those in the Nashville shantytown. They are Edge Men, in self-exile from "normal" America. Edge Man Ed is one of many thousands like him. The families aren't out yet in numbers, according to social workers and shelter operators, who warn that they will be coming along if things don't change.

PRETTY BOY FLOYD ARMED WITH A PLASTIC CARD: TENNESSEE

State Route 52 across the top of central Tennessee passes through towns of lost jobs: Oshkosh B'Gosh closed plants in the 1990s in Hermitage Springs, Red Boiling Springs, and Celina. In Livingston, 250 jobs were cut back at a furniture factory in 2007. There are others. It's a road flanked by despair.

In 2000, we spent time in Celina, near Dale Hollow Lake. Oshkosh had opened a plant here in 1953 that at its peak employed twelve hundred workers. It closed in 1996, the jobs shipped to Honduras because of the North American Free Trade Agreement. I interviewed women who made $14 an hour at the plant; after it closed, they made $5.35 in retail. They were the lucky ones. As much as a third of Clay County was jobless, a local charity official said, far higher than the federal estimate.

Nine years later, we're again driving along Route 52. We round a bend near Red Boiling Springs. A cherry red pickup truck is parked on the north side of the road, in a turnout cut into white limestone bedrock. A store-bought sign announces: GARAGE SALE. Items include a wheelchair, a line of shirts blowing in the wind, an axe, a scythe, and ephemera on a metal folding table. A man wearing a camouflage ball cap, with hair nearly as gray as his sweatshirt flying from the edges, stands with eyes on the gravel. He doesn't look up as we pull over. Two signs, red crayon on cardboard, are attached like flags to wooden sticks thrust on both rear bumpers of the 1983 Silverado with 243,000 miles on it.

B. T. says he's from a town to the west. He's an auto mechanic, in his fifties. He was laid off from a garage a year and a half ago. "There wasn't enough work," he says. "I can't get a job now. When you lose that job, you lose everything."

B. T. takes long pauses between sentences. When he speaks, it is to the earth. He clearly doesn't want to sell most of the items—he needs them. "I'm taking a donation for food, gas, and lights." He's vague when asked about his housing situation. He tells us the electricity is still on, but later admits that he lives in a small RV, a camper. "But it's nice," he says of the trailer. Did he have a house recently? It seems so, but he doesn't answer.

"I'm ashamed. I'm the kind of guy who works. I always worked. But you can't give up. You sit back and give up—a man can do something to pick up a buck. If there's a way to do it myself, I'll do it. I haven't gone to the church yet, because I'm a little embarrassed." He's been here since very early morning.

"Do people stop?"

"No. It's been hours. I got ten dollars this morning. That will help. The ten dollars so far is for gas. . . . The next money I get will be for food."

There is another long and uncomfortable silence. Then he continues.

"You get a man in debt, you can't get out. The people who've got the money, they aren't spending it."

Pointing to the line of shirts, strung between the sticks holding up his cardboard signs, B. T. says, "They are my shirts. I used to wear those shirts. They're good shirts. I cleaned them first."

B. T. says there's bad circulation in his legs. He sits in the wheelchair that has a $10 price tag on it.

A vehicle pulls up and parks behind ours.

"That's my brother."

"How you doing?" Danny, the brother, asks B. T. as he saunters up.

"Still hanging on."

Danny is well dressed. He's with his son, Dalton, sixteen. A woman stops to look at B. T.'s goods. While B. T. stands silent as the woman slowly eyes knickknacks on the folding table, I fall back to talk with Danny and Dalton.

Danny is an electrician who wires houses. He's been laid off for one year. There had once been a lot of construction work in Nashville and other places in the area. But that dried up. He had started doing farm work, but now everyone is after those jobs, and they're difficult to get. Danny and his son are spending the day driving around seeking spot work, from grass cutting to construction. "I'm the jack of all trades," Danny says. "You do whatever you have to do to stay above water."

The woman walks away from the folding table, saying nothing, and gets in her car. B. T. looks stricken. Michael talks with Danny and his son. I go back to B. T. Stung by the failure to make a sale, out of earshot of Danny, B. T. confesses, "I haven't been making it."

Danny and Dalton bid farewell.

"You take care," Danny says to his brother. "You look real good."

B. T. looks down, doesn't respond. There's an awkward moment. Both men know it's a lie. The brother walks off. The doors of Danny's truck slam shut.

"That boy better watch it," B. T. says as Danny works through the gears and heads west on Route 52.

"What do you mean?"

"He spends money. You can't spend it now." He pauses. "You got to have help from the Lord. He gives you added strength. He is the way to the truth and the light."

There's a growing tightness in the pit of my stomach. Our job is to get the story and tell it to the wider world. But it's not easy for us, or B. T. We're playing our assigned roles as documentarians; B. T. is playing his as subject. My role dictates that I ask more questions: Why don't you get food stamps, even though it's embarrassing? Or why not go to a food bank? And so on. But I don't ask them. I can no longer play my role.

I do something unusual. In thirty years of documenting workers and the homeless, I've given money to people only a handful of times. Now here is a man filled with pride who isn't going to eat tonight. You don't want to appear to be paying for a story. But we're done, saying goodbyes, and B. T. doesn't expect this—

I pull a twenty-dollar bill. B. T.'s eyes widen. He sputters. It may as well be hundreds of bucks. B. T. clutches our hands, trembling, puts us in a prayer circle. The prayer he recites is for us to be safe in our journey.

His head hangs. We walk to our car. Michael uses a big lens to take a few pictures of the downcast man at the side of the road (one appears in this book, at the end of the first section of photos). Michael lowers the camera. "It's like the FSA pictures in the Depression," he soberly comments, referring to the Farm Security Administration's photography unit. "People on the sides of roads, trying to sell stuff to survive."

B. T.'s head still droops. We drive off, quiet for a long while.

A bit farther down Route 52, in the town of Moss, we come to Porky Shake, a Dairy Queen–kind of joint. Like many signs on businesses these days, Porky Shake's is hand-made; owners often can't spend money on professionally made signs. As hand-painted signs go, this one is great: the smiling pig is cut out of plywood, painted white and green, and fixed to the roof. The pig wears a chef's hat and a bow tie and clutches a spoon. My eyes fall to the screened order window, with a FOR SALE sign to its right.

As the counterwoman gets our sodas, I ask what is up.

"There's no work around here," she says. Business is bad. Far fewer tourists are coming. She says most of the boats on Dale Hollow Lake, the huge and beautiful Tennessee Valley Authority reservoir near Celina, are locals who don't spend money.

Continuing east on Route 52, we come to Celina and park next to the Clay County Courthouse. Michael takes a picture of a building in foreclosure across the street. A man comes up to us. I'll call him Johnny. We become the ears for the story he wants to tell, because I bet no one around here wants to hear it.

Johnny's details: He worked for many years at Oshkosh. "All my people, they bought their homes off of Oshkosh," he tells us. When it closed down, he got a job at another company, making sun visors for Corvette and Peterbilt, "every kind of car and truck." But that company also closed. He's not working now, save for part-time jobs—"pickup work." He's forty-seven, a strong-looking man, jovial, friendly, yet at the same time sad. He has a pal who works at a concession on Dale Hollow Lake. "He said there has been a twenty-five percent drop in boat rentals."

"This is a ghost town," Johnny says. "This is the poorest town in Tennessee."

"Where do people work?"

"They draw nut checks," Johnny asserts, his term for federal Supplementary Security Income for disabled people, just over $600 monthly. "Or they're retired. Schoolteachers. They work for the county. And buddy, if you don't got one of those jobs, you don't got a chance here. I'm going for my nut check.

"Most people here with a little bit of money, they take care of their kids. The kids live at home. They're hurting. They aren't paying to get anything done, like grass mowing. Nothing. People argue, is h'it a recession or a depression? I say, 'Buddy, I've been in one all my life.' Buddy, I paint. Trim trees. Weed-eat and mow. Right now, most people aren't hiring. I never seen anything like h'it. You can't hardly get hold of a dollar now." A county official emerges from the courthouse.

"It's Brokeville, all right," the county worker says. "Tell Washington, D.C., to send help. We're about to shut down."

The official unemployment rate is 15 percent, but it's certainly higher because it doesn't count people like Johnny, who have given up. In 2000, when we were last here, 2,300 people in Clay County, out of a population of 8,000, had jobs; 629 of those people worked in the county, and the rest commuted far away. Now the most recent statistics show that only a little over 2,000 people in the county have jobs—some 250 fewer people employed.

Deputy Clerk Rhonda Bailey comes out. Rhonda worked at Oshkosh, in research and development. "I knew it was coming. I left before it closed," she says. She knew because she was in charge of readying the machinery to be shipped to Honduras.

"NAFTA, how do you feel about it?" I ask.

Rhonda rolls her eyes. "That was the start of a slow strangulation."

All manner of restaurants have closed, she tells us. "The hardware store closed because of Wal-Mart."

We leave the courthouse and go say hello to Elizabeth, sixty-two, a woman we met in 2000 after she lost her job at Oshkosh who is now working at a drugstore. Her son is twenty-one. "There's just no work for him around here. In that age bracket, if you don't go to college, you're just screwed," Elizabeth says.

One of our goals in coming to Celina is to interview another woman who had worked at Oshkosh B'Gosh. She had been a loyal worker: in fourteen years of sixty-hour weeks, she'd been late only once, because of a snowstorm. When I'd met with her nine years previous, after the factory closed, she and her husband had already racked up $40,000 in credit card debt. Their notion was to use the cards to maintain a middle-class lifestyle while they got their two daughters through school. (It was not difficult: banks had stuffed their mailbox with credit card offers.) The woman said she'd either declare bankruptcy or work till she died to pay off that debt, the latter not a likely prospect given that her salary at a drugstore was $5.50 an hour, one-third of what she'd earned at Oshkosh. Most likely, it seemed back then, she'd go bankrupt, essentially one big flip-off to the system—banks, Democrats, Republicans, the whole rotten lot that had sold out her family. Revenge.

Some may find this reprehensible, but I see dark beauty in her act. She is a Dillinger or Pretty Boy Floyd using plastic cards, not a tommy gun, to take at least $40,000, probably a lot more by 2009, from the Big Boys who run the Ponzi scheme otherwise known as the U.S. economy. Songs could be sung about this woman who is so much smarter than the bank robbers of the 1930s Depression. Her daughters were by now up and out in the world. I wanted to learn the end result and have a beer with her.

I'd arranged for us to meet, so I call her a few more times during our visit. But she never responds. She stands us up.

Back near the courthouse, while Michael is shooting a town scene, a man emerges from a car—Judge Jimmy White, someone else we met nine years earlier. We simultaneously recognize each other. White says business at his private practice is way down. An attorney friend who does bankruptcy cases, however, is very busy.

"He gets more work than he can handle, and I get some of that. I'm getting by. It's been an interesting time." He says the economic downturn has hit everyone, high and low. "We're usually a bit behind everyone else," he remarks, noting that Celina tends to feel the effects of recessions later than other places. "I'm sure the worst is yet to come."

Johnny sits in front of the laundromat, where he had been waiting on a wash cycle to finish when he first came up to us. Hours have passed. The laundry is surely long since done. He's just killing time.

We wave goodbye and drive east on Route 52.

Near Livingston, at dusk, a woman sells stuff at the road's edge. She tells us several nearby factories have closed. We're too numbed by the day's tales of woe to pay much attention to the details. I don't give her any money.

We drive on through the night on our way back to the East Coast. We don't talk much.

I wonder about all that we weren't able to witness in the city neighborhoods and farm communities that raced past our windows as we drove through the night from this spot to that place in the land of 80–90 the previous five days. It's difficult not to come away with an uneasy feeling about America.

PART 1 **AMERICA BEGINS A THIRTY-YEAR JOURNEY TO NOWHERE** THE 1980s

In the present crisis, government is not the solution to our problem; government is the problem.

—Ronald Reagan, inaugural address, January 20, 1981

Greed is all right, I want you to know that I think greed is healthy. You can be greedy and still feel good about yourself.

—Investor Ivan Boesky, later convicted of insider trading violations, 1986 commencement address at the University of California, Berkeley, business school

There is simply no way in the world [Reagan] can fire 13,000 or more of us.

—David Evans, president of Los Angeles Local 502 of the Professional Air Traffic Controllers Organization, August 3, 1981

Nothing so serves public tranquility than a few screams of anguish from the very rich.

—John Kenneth Galbraith, lunch conversation with the author, Harvard University, 1987

It's morning in America.

—Ronald Reagan campaign slogan, 1984

1979	Wal-Mart employed 21,000 workers in the United States.
1979	General Motors employed 618,000 workers in the United States, an all-time high.
1982	In its September issue, *Forbes* magazine debuted its Forbes 400 list of the richest Americans. It took $91 million to make the list.
1978	The average CEO in the United States was paid 35.2 times what an average worker was paid, according to the Economic Policy Institute.
1981	President Reagan fired all striking air traffic controllers. Their union was crushed. This set the stage for a wave of strike breaking and violations of workers' rights to organize and bargain collectively.

The official unemployment rate in 1982 was 10.8 percent, which meant 12 million jobless Americans. The unofficial unemployment rate was much higher: many men and women had given up the search for work and were not counted. They were invisible. A large number of them were on the road.

1 ON BECOMING A HOBO

Clickity clack. Clickity clack.
Lookin' back. Lookin' back.
Where ya' goin'? Where ya' goin'?
Where ya' been? Where ya' been?
Clickity clack. Clickity clack.
Don't come back. Don't come back.
—An old hobo chant

The Burlington Northern freight train was going some 70 miles an hour. It was just after 2:00 A.M., April 27, 1982. We were north of Mount Shasta, at the top of California. The snow pack was deep. The temperature was in the high 20s. The wind chill factor was stunning: I'd been in actual air temperature of minus 20 degrees, and that's what it felt like. The other notable sensory torment was the clatter. This was no cushioned Amtrak ride. An empty boxcar pulled by a speeding train makes a lot of noise, as it violently rocks not just up and down but sideways, slamming you and throwing you around. I've been accused of overstatement when describing it as having a metal garbage can placed over your head and then having someone repeatedly strike it with a baseball bat, but that's precisely what the sound was like.

Yet I could hear Michael's teeth chattering. He lay against the front wall in a cotton sleeping bag designed to be a child's comforter for summer beach camping. He wore a sweater, denim jeans, and white tennis shoes. I paced in front of the boxcar door because I'd given up on my equally useless sleeping bag. I wore long underwear, thick pants, a heavy coat, hiking boots, and wool socks, and yet was beyond misery. I looked at the couple we were traveling with. They huddled beneath a thick sleeping bag, their two dogs piled on top of them.

His name was Wayne. He was twenty-four. She went by Lisa, never told us her real name. But she showed us her tits while we waited thirty-six hours in Sacramento for a freight train to catch out on. It was a hot Central Valley afternoon, and we were sitting in the shade of an old icehouse in the Western Pacific yard. She suddenly pulled off her shirt and bared her breasts. Wayne was legally blind, and perhaps she felt that he couldn't visually appreciate her womanhood as she thought we might. It was hardly a turn-on; she was still a child. She said she was nineteen, but no way was she much over sixteen.

Traveling with Wayne and the girl hadn't been our plan. We were here to write about and photograph a different kind of homeless people, who happened to be hobos. We—

The train slowed, jarringly. Wayne and Lisa stirred. The dogs jumped up. I peered out the door. Lights of a town: "K-Falls," Klamath Falls, Oregon. Far ahead, someone was shining a jacklight on the train. No Thumbs, the old hobo we'd really wanted to ride with, had warned me that the K-Falls yard was hot and that the bull, the railroad cop, would light the train to catch riders. No Thumbs had been teaching me how to be a hobo, and he was going to be our guide of sorts for what we were really after. But No Thumbs, damn, he caught out early.

We entered the yard. I hid by running to the front of the boxcar. As we passed the bull's truck, one of the dogs walked into the jacklight that was blasting on the door. Maybe we could run off. I tried to hurry the others but confess I was equally slow; I was severely hypothermic. By the time we gathered our gear, the bull had driven the gravel road parallel with the stopped train. His left hand held a flashlight beaming on our eyes. His right hand was hard on a sidearm. He demanded identification; one of his sidekicks took the ID. The girl didn't have any. The bull ignored that.

"If the jail wasn't full, I'd be takin' you in," a voice behind the glare snapped. "I see you again, you're goin' to jail for five days."

The bull drove off. He wasn't so bad. No Thumbs had told me the bull in Dunsmuir, on the Southern Pacific line on the other side of Mount Shasta, routinely cracked heads.

We went into a meadow, spread sleeping bags, and lay shivering on the ground, cold and hard as frozen rib meat. For Michael and me, our world of a newspaper office was two days and a lifetime behind us. That morning, the girl had pointed to a passing Amtrak and called it the "people train." What she meant was that we weren't people.

We were hobos.

It was a transformation that had begun not long after I met Michael at the *Sacramento Bee* newspaper, where I was the new day police reporter. I hated cops but was happy to be working. I'd been living out of my Datsun truck for three months after driving out from Cleveland to seek newspaper work, sleeping in national forest campgrounds or at the side of roads. In August, the city editor, Bob Forsyth, said that he wanted to hire me. But there were no openings. Bob asked me to phone once each week. On the last day of October, he told me to call the following Wednesday, the day after the national election.

"I've got good news and bad news," Bob said when I rang.

"What's the bad news?"

"Reagan is president."

It was a fairly big newsroom, and I didn't meet everyone right away. One afternoon there was a fire in a trailer park: a Christmas tree had burst into flame. An editor barked that I should meet the photographer in the photo car lot. I raced out the door. The sound of feet came from behind. Abruptly, on my left, there appeared a photographer I had not yet spoken with.

"You a runner, too?" Michael asked.

I knew exactly what he meant. The newsroom was full of plodding staffers. There are two kinds of journalists. Runners. And walkers.

"Yeah."

Michael passed me. I ran faster.

No one died in the fire. There was time before we had to file. Michael drove us to a Wendy's on Freeport Boulevard and parked in back. Hobos sat on the other side of a chain-link fence in the Western Pacific rail yard. This prompted Michael to talk about a photographic essay that he wanted to do on winos.

As we ate burgers, Michael told his story, which explained his interest in the wino project. His mother, Valerie, was a barmaid who had had five children by four different husbands. Here is what Michael learned about his birth from family members growing up. While Valerie was pregnant with Michael, she was living with Jimmy Williamson. Jimmy went on tour with the U.S. Navy and came home on leave from Japan to discover that Valerie was pregnant. He'd been gone longer than nine months. Jimmy could do math. He threw Valerie down a flight of stairs. Valerie went into premature labor, and Michael was born before term. The man thought to be Michael's biological father was killed shortly after his birth.

Each of Valerie's children spent time in orphanages and foster homes. Michael had episodically lived with his mother, accompanying her to work in bars. Through this, he'd come to know a lot of drunkards. He hated what alcohol did but grew to become extraordinarily sympathetic toward alcoholics.

When Michael was eleven, Valerie got him out of a foster home, gathered all her kids under one roof in Los Angeles, and tried to fix her life. That Christmas Eve of 1968, the Los Angeles County Coroner's office telephoned with bad news. Their mother had been driving on the Pacific Coast Highway when an ambulance blew through a red light at 77 miles an hour, broadsiding her. She died at the scene. Michael was back in foster homes.

Twelve years had passed since his mother's death. At our age, that seemed like a long time. To some degree, Michael was still the orphan who feared becoming homeless.

As for me, I had a working-class background. One grandfather worked at Otis Steel in The Flats of Cleveland; the other was employed by the B&O Railroad, which brought coal for coking the mill's furnaces. My father made industrial metal cutting tools for one of the largest manufacturers in the world, Cleveland Twist Drill. He put in an eight-hour shift at the plant, grinding steel tools to razor sharpness. These tools, the most common of them called "end mills," work not only vertically like a drill but also horizontally. They can be reused many times. Dad's day job was responsible for his other job, a side business in our basement, where there was a collection of massive machines. He came home and ground steel, resharpening this same kind of worn tooling for small manufacturers.

At the age of twelve, I began grinding steel on those machines. Dad paid me 10 cents per tool. I grew up with steel dust in my lungs. I later operated a lathe in a plastics fabrication factory while continuing to work for my father. I dropped out of college after some three years, never graduated. I began freelance writing for the Cleveland newspapers while still working with steel and eventually wrote my way out of the factories. Still, I feared failing. When I left Cleveland that summer of 1980, the flames of the steel mills were licking at my ass. They wanted me back. At my new job at the *Bee,* I didn't see that much distance between me and the hobos on the other side of the fence behind the Wendy's.

Michael and I made a pact that day at the Wendy's to document stories ignored by most others in the media—about the poor, workers, outcasts. I'd write and he'd shoot. Michael was twenty-three; I was twenty-four. We started with the wino story, which ran with a lot of photos. It began as shown here.

JAN 17 1981

Detox Center Is Home To Winos

JAN 17 1981

By Dale Maharidge
Bee Staff Writer

Also F

Burl stumbled through the fog, his broken hand flapping at the end of his rigid arm, blood streaming down his face. He'd been beaten up for the "fun" of it.

That had happened to him before, and it probably will again. No one cares about a wino.

We teamed up on similar stories in the ensuing year. When 1982 rolled around, there was a new city editor, Bill Moore. He often drank at the Old Tavern on 19th Street, the "O.T.," next to the Western Pacific main line. The O.T. was a hangout for hobos when they got a little dough. One afternoon that April, Bill sought me out. The previous night at the O.T., old hobos had complained to him about all the job-seeking new timers crowding them out of boxcars. Bill told me to find out what was going on.

The next day, I went into the Western Pacific yard behind the Wendy's. I ended up in the "bone yard," some fifteen tracks wide with long rows of rusting boxcars put out of service. I heard voices in an abandoned boxcar and saw wisps of cookfire smoke coming out the door. A young man stuck his head out and offered a friendly hello.

Inside were four people. No Thumbs stood out. He had a big snowy beard and a deeply lined face. I joined them, sitting on the steel boxcar floor littered with empty white port wine bottles with 99-cent price tags, opened tins of Vienna sausage, yellowed newspapers. It was hot. Flies buzzed. I told No Thumbs about the story I wanted to write. He offered to help—it was part of the hobo code, he said, for elders to teach greenhorns.

He shook from advanced Parkinson's disease, and he was missing both thumbs. He'd lost them in 1945 to a license-plate stamping machine, at the federal reformatory in Chillicothe, Ohio, where he served a brief sentence after a conviction for interstate auto theft. I later learned that he was sixty-five. He looked a lot older. No Thumbs was jovial—he often smiled, revealing bare gums; his mouth was nearly toothless. When he laughed, which was often, it came out as a wheeze. His real name was Thomas Jefferson Glenn, but no one called him that. Up and down the line, he was known as No Thumbs, Tom Thumb, or Alabama Tom.

I spent that day and the next two with No Thumbs. He showed me how to jump on moving trains and talk with engineers using hand signals. He also explained how to keep yourself safe by doing things such as jamming an old railcar brake shoe in the track of a boxcar door—this way, the door couldn't close and lock you in when the train got underway, and you wouldn't die of exposure if the train was "sided," left for days in a remote location.

The third afternoon, No Thumbs and I were seated in the shade of the icehouse. He showed me what I call the "hobo microwave." He got an empty wine bottle and filled it with water.

"The water's gotta be right to the brim," he said.

He set the bottle on the gravel, tore up cardboard, piled sheaves around the bottle, and lit a match. In minutes, as the cardboard burned down, the water was boiling. He made coffee with it.

"You got it full, the bottle won't crack."

No Thumbs picked up a scrap of the cardboard. He borrowed a pen and scrawled a word game on it, which I pocketed.

"See, the words line up; spell the same words across and down," he said.

Several hobos joined us. One was a Vietnam veteran, who said that after each war, men hit the rails and never went back to regular life. The vet told me that the hobos who began riding after World War II and Korea had helped him. No Thumbs said that he'd been taught by hobos from the Great Depression. I imagined how that generation of hobos might have been broken in by men after World War I, how those guys must have learned from veterans of the Spanish-American War, or even the 1894 Depression, when Coxey's hobo army rode to Washington to protest unemployment. I knew that from reading about Jack London, who had been a misfit member of that army. And those guys must have been trained by Civil War veterans . . .

I marveled at this hobo history, but there was, frankly, nothing romantic about it. I was scared of the trains. I also wondered about the hobo jungles. No Thumbs reassured me with one rule he repeated several times over the days I spent with him: if you never cross anyone, you will be safe.

"I can walk into any jungle, and I don't have to worry," No Thumbs said.

In the next breath, he confessed that he wanted to stop tramping. He increasingly feared a vicious breed of hobo he'd been seeing since the economy turned bad, the "crazies," those with nothing left to lose.

The next afternoon, I went back to the yard. A hobo, a stranger, was the only one present. He informed me that No Thumbs had caught north that morning instead of waiting until the next day, when we were supposed to go with him. That's how we ended up with Wayne and Lisa.

On that first trip, we met new timers in K-Falls, then headed back south at night on the Southern Pacific. The only available ride was on the open back ledge of a grain car. Because of the mean bull in Dunsmuir, Michael and I climbed on top of the grainer and clung to its roof before entering that yard. The picture of me sleeping, more or less, the next morning (which appears in the second section of Michael's photographs) was taken on this grainer as the train wailed us south through the heart of the Central Valley.

Just outside the big Roseville yard, east of Sacramento, our train sided for a northbound. As that northbound slowly lumbered past, No Thumbs appeared in the door of an open boxcar.

"Dale!" he cried. "Dale! How ya' doing? I missed ya!"

We whooped and hollered back.

No Thumbs' train moved at the speed of a walking man.

"Let's go catch it and ride with him!" Michael pleaded. (He hadn't met No

Thumbs in the Western Pacific yard because his boss hadn't given him time off to join me.) I protested: we had only a few days left, and I wanted to see what was going on down in Fresno.

"We'll catch up with him down the line," I said.

As No Thumbs' train picked up speed, he hung from the door edge by his right arm and waved with his left. He continued waving till he became a speck.

We did other stories that summer about the new homeless. Amid this, we queried *Life* magazine and got an assignment to ride the rails. When I talked with the editor by phone, he suggested that he wanted to focus on a couple with a baby. Those who knew how the magazine worked told us that this was not a suggestion, but an order.

As we negotiated the *Life* deal, my *Bee* colleague Paul Avery came up to my desk in the newsroom. (Paul would later be played by actor Robert Downey Jr. in the movie *Zodiac,* about the serial killer who terrorized the San Francisco Bay Area in the 1970s. When he was with the *San Francisco Chronicle,* Paul owned that story, and he'd been threatened with death by the Zodiac.) That afternoon at my desk, Paul looked grim. He wanted to interview me because he was doing a story about the murder of three hobos in Oroville—among the dead was No Thumbs.

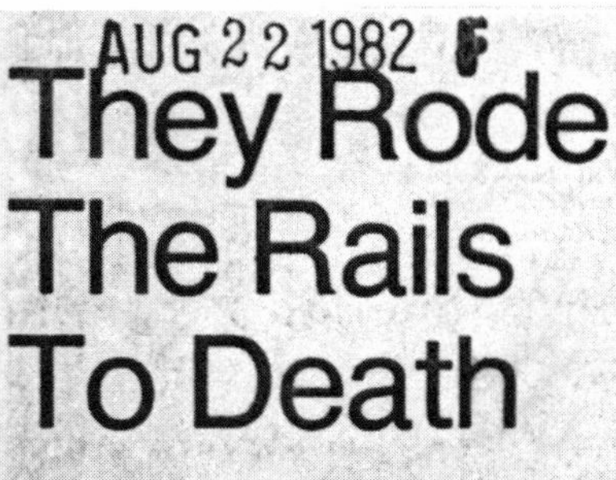
AUG 22 1982 F

They Rode The Rails To Death

By Paul Avery
Bee Staff Writer

OROVILLE — For Wade Southern, Bernard Moseley and Thomas Jefferson Glenn, riding the rails was a way of life. It also led to their deaths.

Southern, 46, Moseley, 51, and Glenn, 65, were found slain Aug. 8 at a hobo camp in the Western Pacific

Thomas Jefferson Glenn was a legend among railroad hobos.

The facts: No Thumbs had been at a campfire in a hobo jungle with the other two victims, Wade Southern and Bernard Moseley, on the night of August 8, 1982. Someone shot Southern and Moseley. All three men had been repeatedly stabbed, each of their throats cut. There was no sign of struggle. No Thumbs' body was nearest the fire, some 15 feet away. Southern and Moseley were found by a Western Pacific worker about 50 feet distant. The men had not been robbed. Police suspected a transient who would "kill for the sake of killing."

On August 28, a check for expenses from *Life* magazine arrived. Days later, Michael and I caught a freight to Oroville. There, the freight was broken apart, and we had to wait for a new train. We went to the camp where No Thumbs had been slain. The ashes of the dead men's fire were between two feral walnut trees in a field of sun-baked star thistle. What appeared to be blood still blackened the stones.

We rode for three weeks: Salt Lake City, Denver, Portland, Los Angeles. Everywhere we heard that we had just missed hobo families by days—in one case, hours. We joked that it must be the same family, riding just ahead of us.

In that late summer of 1982, it was mostly men on the streets. We never did find that couple with a baby. When we'd first talked to *Life,* the magazine was running a cover of actress Brooke Shields in a swimsuit, titled "Brooke Brings Back the Bikini." In the end, our story wasn't deemed worthy—the magazine killed the piece. It didn't matter. We were on to something bigger.

The human impact of what was going on in the country needed telling in a form longer than an article. We set out to land a book contract, sans agent. I simply sent a letter of a few pages with our clips to ten big publishing houses in New York City on a Thursday. The following Tuesday, January 11, 1983, editor James Fitzgerald telephoned from Dial Press and said he wanted to publish our book.

How to do that book?

Many new hobos were from back East, where they'd lost jobs in manufacturing plants. But a person didn't just suddenly become a hobo. It was a process, and we had to show it. This meant going to one of the dying steel towns and documenting why its residents were leaving. Our model was *The Grapes of Wrath:* Steinbeck had to show Dust Bowl Oklahoma in order for readers to understand the Joads in California.

We picked Youngstown, Ohio, described as a "necropolis" in a *Wall Street Journal* story. The city had been especially hard hit by the closing of steel mills. Here it was not merely a "recession"; something bigger was going on. There had been a de facto decision by political leaders and moneyed elites, both left and right, to shun industrial policy. These neoliberals and conservatives told us we didn't need to make hard goods. Those who argued that all wealth comes from the soil or the sea, as it has throughout history, were dismissed. The Wall Street/Beltway types told us it was a new paradigm: we could import steel from other nations and let our steel industry perish, and all would be well.

It didn't make sense to me. I'd grown up seeing how my father's work, grinding steel—which came from coal, ore, and limestone—made our lives possible. Things extracted from the earth literally put food on our table.

A few weeks later, Michael and I flew one way to Cleveland. We bought a $600 1973 Olds Delta 88 from an unemployed guy. The car's body was lime green and rusted. The rear floor had a hole rotted through—you could see the ground. The tires were bald. But the car had a tight front end, good brakes, a sweet-sounding eight-cylinder engine.

"It's a real tuna boat," Michael said.

We named the car Das Boot, after the Wolfgang Petersen film about a German World War II submarine. We flipped a coin to see who would sleep in the front seat. I lost. (We had no money for hotels.) In the coming months, when we weren't riding trains, traveling by Greyhound, or hitchhiking, my knees had to deal with the steering wheel at night.

Even though we'd ridden trains the previous year, we were scared. That first experience had merely been a warm-up exercise compared with the enormity of what lay on the road ahead. We feared violence because of No Thumbs' murder and other incidents from the previous summer. Someone had pulled a gun on us in the Oroville rail yard that day we rode in and saw where No Thumbs had been slain—two men commandeered our boxcar as a train was leaving for Salt Lake City. In Denver, when I was alone, guarding our gear while Michael went to photograph a hobo named Ken who was looking for work (pictured in the second section of photographs, sleeping on the piggyback car in Glenwood Canyon, in Colorado), a man who had been sniffing glue came at me with a wire in his hands, intent on strangling me. I had to fight him off.

Thinking about the story itself also caused us some fear. Could we pull it off? Who the hell were we to tell it? Some rejections we'd gotten from publishers had mocked the very attempt. And, on a larger scale, forces were arrayed against the message we wanted to deliver. Charles Murray was at the conservative Manhattan Institute with copious amounts of funding, wrapping up his book *Losing Ground: American Social Policy, 1950–1980,* which would come out in 1984. He had already begun speaking and writing articles blaming welfare for the problems of the poor, and he called for ending welfare programs. The biggest problem, however, was not welfare, which reached only about 5 percent of Americans. Another 10 to 25 percent, depending on how you counted, were being ignored—tens of millions of working-class people who were suffering. Yet welfare dominated political discourse, framed by what Reagan called "welfare queens." It almost seemed like a deliberate attempt to ignore the plight of workers by throwing out a red herring to divert people's attention.

So, in the Reagan era, our job was to document the working poor and newly homeless and hope that the broad public would take notice. Could we succeed?

On top of everything, there were financial and personal worries. We'd taken unpaid leave from the *Sacramento Bee*. Purchasing the car and airline tickets had taken nearly a quarter of our $7,500 book advance. What remained wouldn't even cover our mortgages. We barely had any money saved. Michael, newly married, had a young and unhappy wife back home.

We drove out of Cleveland in a snowstorm, at night, toward Youngstown. Snow came at the windshield, blinding us, emphasizing the void we were heading into. There was no false bravado in the car that night. We'd talked about myriad worries on the airplane flight to Cleveland, but not now. It was too real to bring up. We were silent.

2 NECROPOLIS

On April 28, 1982, a contractor hired by the U.S. Steel Corporation dynamited four blast furnaces at the Ohio Works in Youngstown. Each furnace fell in clouds of dust. This clip was often played on television news to illustrate America's declining heavy industry. We could import cheap steel rather than making it here, we were told. Free trade would boom. Everyone would be better off in the world that was evolving: wealth would trickle down. New jobs were coming, and the old simply had to be allowed to die.

Eleven months later, Joe Marshall Sr. stood at the edge of what was left of the Ohio Works—acres of twisted steel, heaps of bricks, overturned office desks. Rubble was still being hauled away. A mile-long meadow was being created on the banks of the Mahoning River.

The first mill to "go down" in Youngstown had been the Campbell Works—it went cold on Black Monday, September 19, 1977. In the next few years, other mills shut, leading to the loss of some fifty thousand jobs, directly or indirectly tied to steel, in the Mahoning Valley. At one time, twenty-eight blast furnaces had churned out molten iron, and more steel was made in Youngstown than in any other city in the nation. The mills lined the banks of the Mahoning River, head to tail, for over 20 miles.

The ruins of the Ohio Works were less than a mile from Joe's house, but he and his son, Joe Jr., hadn't been here in nearly three years. It was just too painful. We'd met the Marshalls a few times before gingerly asking if they would give us a tour. I now wondered about the morality of our request.

Joe sighed. He placed an arm around his son. The two men ventured into the wasteland where they and thirty-five hundred others once worked. Michael and I, mute, followed a dozen steps behind.

Steel had been Joe's life since he'd arrived in America from Czechoslovakia at the age of thirteen, in the late 1930s. At age fifteen, after his father had a stroke, Joe got a job at Republic Steel. By 1942, he was at U.S. Steel's Ohio Works, but he left to fight in Europe. He was wounded when he landed on Utah Beach in Normandy. Out of his battalion of 867, he was one of only four survivors.

Joe came home and returned to his job at the Ohio Works. He became a stationary engineer, tending steam engines that pumped air into the blast furnaces. He married and had a son and a daughter. When Joe Jr. graduated from high school, he too became a stationary engineer at the Ohio Works. They were part of a cycle of sons following fathers into the mills.

Then came April 6, 1980, when their part of the mill closed.

"This is incredible," Joe Jr. muttered. "I don't want to look at this place." He stooped and clutched a piece of coke with his large hand. He fondled the charred lump and kept muttering, "Incredible."

The men continued down what had been a pathway into the plant. The sidewalk was now flanked by chaotically heaped bricks and blocks of concrete.

"For thirty-seven and a half years, I walked this sidewalk," Joe Sr. said in a gravelly voice. "Back there were the open hearths. Over there, six blast furnaces. Over there, a ten-million-gallon pump. There's where the Bessemer blow room was. I worked there most of my life. This was a good place to work. A good place to live. We weren't obsolete! We were the best!"

It had been a rough three years for young Joe. Each day, he filled out applications, often standing in job lines with hundreds of other people. It's difficult to find employment when you're twenty-nine and have been trained to operate a steam-powered machine that was obsolete in 1910. "We had pumps from 1891 and 1892 that were still working," Joe Jr. said. Finally, he had had to move back home. His $19,000 savings had been reduced to a few hundred bucks.

Joe Sr. shook his head. "How could they shut it down? It was so big. You could hear the noise from this place at my house." He wasn't speaking to Michael or me, or to his son. He talked to the March wind. "It's quiet now."

The wind punctuated his words.

"What Hitler couldn't do, they did it for him."

"I guess we're down," said Ken Platt, seated at his kitchen table. It was midday, when he'd normally be working. He rested his red-bearded head on his arm, which was huge from a life of working with 6-foot-long wrenches. The fingers of his free hand nervously tapped the Formica tabletop. This father of five- and eight-year-old kids had worked only a few weeks in the past year at his job as a millwright at Republic Steel's rolling mill, one of the few operations still running in the valley.

"I've always worked. We worked seven days a week. We just about lived there. Now we're nobody. We don't matter. My wife's brother was a good worker. Now he questions his self-worth. He drinks. I don't think he could work anymore. It's like something rotting away."

Ken hated the thought of America's waning industrial might. He suddenly slammed the table hard.

"We're supposed to be the best country in the world! Why can't we have better? We're going to wind up like England. The companies want to pay less. When you make minimum wage, you invest in bread and bologna. How can the economy survive like that? I can't afford a new car. I'm scared to spend one hundred dollars. I used to say people on welfare were cheating. Now I know better."

Politicians talked about a $10 million plan to build a high-tech school in Youngstown, with an offer of free land.

I telephoned Atari, which had just moved jobs out of California—to Hong Kong and Taiwan. Would they ever move jobs to Youngstown? The spokesperson laughed. And then laughed some more. I called Karen Gervais at Hewlett-Packard. She was more diplomatic: "At this point, the Midwest area does not offer the quality of life we are seeking. It doesn't have the spark that lights the fires of high tech."

"How are they going to teach someone like me about something like that?" asked Ken. "What do I know about computers? A twenty-pound sledgehammer is what I know. I know gears. I don't even know how to play Atari. And maybe twenty percent of the people I worked with in the mill couldn't read or write."

In the five years since the mills began shutting, only one new major business expressed interest in Youngstown: a blimp factory that promised seventy-five hundred jobs.

Blimps. High tech. People laughed. It was the sad laughter of people desperate for hope but refusing to be teased by such bizarre promises.

"Do you retrain these people?" asked Dr. John Russo, a labor studies professor at Youngstown State University. "Retrain for what? For high tech? That's just another humiliation. People are rolling the dice in terms of their lives."

Numbers told some of the story of misery.

Official figures showed a peak of 21 percent unemployment. It was probably closer to 30 percent because so many had given up and were no longer counted, said Russo. Child abuse cases had risen by 35 percent since 1979. One mental health clinic reported four thousand calls for help in one month. Suicide attempts climbed by 70 percent in two years. Personal bankruptcies reached two thousand in one year. The wages lost from the plant closings, according to Russo, totaled $1 billion. Each week, up to fifteen hundred people visited one Salvation Army soup line, a local Salvation Army official told me. Burglaries, robberies, and assaults doubled, even though the population declined, the FBI reported. The population of the city of Youngstown proper was 140,000 in 1970, according to the U.S. Census Bureau; in 1980, it had dwindled to 115,000; and by 1983, some speculated it was below 100,000. A number of small cities clustered around Youngstown, places like Girard, Campbell, Struthers, also saw an exodus.

Empty homes were quickly vandalized, windows smashed. Fires were common. We rushed to the scene of one house fire. As the flames crackled, the firefighters stood back and watched the abandoned home burn. It was official policy: not putting it out saved money. "Arson," was the verdict of one firefighter. "At least one house a day burns in this neighborhood."

Decay, rust, and death pervaded all aspects of life in the city. The psyche of Youngstown was something of a cross between living in a war zone and the spooky feeling one gets reading Juan Rulfo's *Pedro Páramo,* a dreamlike novel in which the dead speak and walk the streets of a ghost town.

Michael and I entered the Brier Hill Works. Towering over us was the Jeanette blast furnace.

We came to a long twilit corridor. Our footsteps on metal floors created echoes that reverberated. We descended into the ore pits. Water from snowmelt now rushed where once there had been a million tons of taconite ore, coke, and limestone. Secret passages led off into darkness. Icicles hung from the ceiling like daggers.

The blast furnace once produced 700 tons of metal a day. The floor around its base was littered with tools dropped there on the last day of work, six years earlier. Iron ladles, 12 feet long; wrenches, some weighing 50 pounds. Over there, a pair of goggles; here, a pair of shoes. Slag, frozen where it cooled, dripped like tears at the base of the furnace, now forever cold.

We kept going back to the abandoned mills during our time in Youngstown. We didn't need any more observations or photos, but something intangible drew us, over and over, to commune with the dead. A lot of workers had committed suicide.

We needed to hear their stories.

And perhaps it was the trauma of listening to a daily litany of people telling us about their ruined lives. Odd as it may sound, the rotting mills provided solace. It was easier to deal with ghosts than with the misery of the living. In the funereal quiet, we spoke in whispers, if we spoke at all. The only sounds were the rush of springmelt waters, the banging of loose folds of metal in the wind, mysterious creaks and thumps.

Often, Michael and I would split up and spend an hour or two alone. We went to the dead mills as some go to the wilderness to commune with God, deities, or nature.

The days in Youngstown passed. We kept meeting people who wanted to head south and west to look for work. Get out. Move on. Go where it's better. We wanted to leave with one of them.

But they weren't yet at that critical point of desperation. We'd learned from the previous year's hoboing that most of the new homeless didn't rationally plan for hitting the road. They'd get into a fight with a family member and be thrown out; they would stare at overdue bills and panic; they'd get drunk and wake up with a hangover and an epiphany, load the old car, and bail with not much money in their wallets; or—

Well, the ways were many. Once they left, events tended to follow an all-too-common pattern: The car broke down, and they had no money to fix it. Or their money ran out, and they couldn't put gas in the car.

They hitchhiked and found that difficult.

Someone told them about riding in boxcars.

The trains were like free buses. The new timers weren't interested in the traditional hobo way of life. They simply wanted to get from Point A, where there was no work, to Point B, where they heard there might be jobs.

After getting a cheap retread for Das Boot when a balding tire blew, we hit the road. We didn't have anyone to travel with. We'd find people broken down along the way, we reasoned. We were silent as we drove down Interstate 77. We had no idea where we were headed, other than vaguely west.

3 NEW TIMER

The night we left Youngstown, we traveled through Kentucky in a sheeting rain. We could barely see to drive. Tired, we simply pulled over to the edge of the road at 3:00 A.M. Michael bedded down in the back seat beneath a purple sleeping bag purchased with *Life* magazine expense money. It was our first overnight in Das Boot. A leak in the right corner of the passenger window dripped on my shoulder.

Maybe an hour after we more or less fell asleep, a cop shined a light on us.

We presented quite a sight to the officer. We'd been eating a lot of bananas and had been attaching Chiquita and other stickers to the passenger dash; we called the seat the "Banana Republic." A yellow fiberglass hardhat with the name "Frazier" scratched into the paint on the back and the number 073 on the front, curated from the Brier Hill Works (the hardhat pictured in the second section of Michael's photographs), was on the rear window ledge, next to a Youngstown State University decal on the glass. The hardhat and decal were in part to honor Youngstown on our journey, in part to serve as bait. We'd heard that the cops in Houston, an eventual destination of ours, hassled job seekers from the north. Appearing to be unemployed steelworkers might dictate how we'd be treated.

The cop asked for ID. No warrants were out against us, and the car had valid plates. Vagrancy laws had long since been ruled unconstitutional. There wasn't much he could do, save for telling us to move on. And so, without sleep, we rolled on.

Rain fell, cold rain, almost snow. It was a frigid April. Rain pocked the surface of the Mississippi River as we crossed into St. Louis. We went to the Salvation Army mission on Washington Street, where the major in charge told us that ten to fifteen new timers showed up some nights. St. Louis was still the gateway city, as it had been since pioneer times and the days of Route 66. Westward-migrating people from the industrial heartland were funneling through. We asked the major if we could come back that evening to see who showed up.

We arrived early and sat across from the intake door, watching a steady stream of homeguards, the local homeless, check in. Then a man carrying a racquetball racquet and an Adidas bag entered. He was young, fit, clean-shaven, wore a fresh flannel shirt beneath a coat. His eyes were darkened from sleep deprivation, but there was life in them. He zeroed in on us.

Sam came right up to us, he said, because we didn't look like anyone else in the mission. We told him we were journalists. He didn't seem to care. He was scared and simply wanted to talk to someone he could relate to.

His story tumbled out. He was twenty-eight, had a wife and three children. He had lost his business in the downturn. The previous night, he'd slept on the floor of the bus station until the police evicted him. This was his second night on the street.

Here was a man we'd wanted to meet—a man at the precise moment of descent, about to spend his first night in a rescue mission. Now that we'd found him, I had a knot in the pit of my stomach.

I asked the major if it would be okay for us to take Sam out to dinner. The major agreed but warned that we had to be back by lights out, 8:00 P.M. We went to the closest diner. As we walked, Sam pulled a rag from his pocket and squeezed it, over and over. He compressed and kneaded it so hard that if it had been wet, every drop of water would have been wrung from it.

Sam confessed that he had 58 cents in his pocket. We of course said we'd buy. Sam ordered a tiny burger. We didn't ask questions; we just listened. Sam explained that he had owned a cleaning service that contracted with a major grocery chain. When the economy turned south, the chain canceled the contract, and he had to file for bankruptcy. He lost the family's house.

His wife was angry that Sam wouldn't get welfare, but he was too proud. I'll find work, he kept telling her. He asked the chain for a job. "It was humiliating to ask to be a bagger. And I couldn't get it." Marital problems ensued. His wife and children moved home with her mother. Sam went back to his parents' farm. The previous week, he'd hit that critical point of desperation: he bought a one-way Amtrak ticket to St. Louis, got a cheap hotel room, and began looking for work. His money had run out the previous day.

"I feel like I've stepped into Bangladesh. I grew up having everything. We grew up in the fifties and sixties. We had all the good things. I thought 'poor' meant you didn't want a job.

"I feel like I'm suffocating more each day. You get a feeling from relatives . . . like, when are you going to get a job? They don't say that, but you feel it. You feel like an idiot. Every meal you get for free from them, that feeling builds. I'd stand in line for five hours to apply for a minimum-wage job. When I'd get home, everyone would ask how I did in the interview. People at home said I was a great guy and had lots of experience and that I should get the job. They didn't understand—I was one of dozens. I spent maybe two minutes with the interviewer. Each time they're saying, 'We'll let you know,' it's like another nail in the coffin.

"That weighed me down. I tried to kill myself, by taking pills, but they saved me. When I came to, I regretted that. When I took the pills, I felt relieved. I had no emotion. It didn't matter anymore. The next day, I read in the paper that the recession is over. That was great. Everyone else is making it, and I'm not. It's like a knife gouging through your gut—

"I tried to sell my blood today. I'd never done that before. They told me my blood pressure was too high and they couldn't take me. It was because I was scared. I never had high blood pressure before in my life. They would have paid me seven dollars. It's unbelievable what seven dollars can mean. It sounded like gold to me.

"I thought of stealing food. That scared me. The only thing I ever stole before was a piece of candy when I was a kid. You can sit in a university like I did and talk about the poor. You can speculate what you'd do. But hunger reduces all variables. Hunger will make you do anything.

"I carry my racquetball racquet because it makes me invisible. It deflects people.

People think I'm a college student, that I belong, that I'm part of society. I used to love to play. The day I quit racquetball is the day I knew I hit bottom. Today, I put my head down in the library and they said, 'You can't sleep here.' I rode around on the bus all day. It takes up a lot of time. When I got off the bus, I cried. It was the only thing that was familiar to me. The bus became human. It was the only friend I had. And it left me."

Tears rolled down Sam's cheeks. We put a hand on his shoulder as we walked him back to the Sally. Sam pulled the rag from his pocket. I couldn't take my eyes off his hand clenching the rag so hard that his veins showed in the light of streetlamps.

We were a little late, but the night man was cool with it because Sam's leaving had been okayed by the major. The Sally was full up. We hadn't thought about signing in ourselves earlier that day, so we drove off into the rain, heading out of town. Finding a safe place to sleep in the car was a major undertaking each night. In Das Boot, we felt like a target for every wannabe Zodiac killer.

Sam's situation was troubling on a human level, and troubling journalistically. "How am I going to take his picture?" Michael asked. We were freaked out. We'd never experienced anything like this in our role as journalists. This was a man who might kill himself. He was closer to this brink than anyone we'd ever documented. The people we had met in Youngstown had not yet reached this low point. Alone, homeless, broke, new to the street in a strange city—this was a terrifying combination. We weren't formally trained as journalists; Michael had even less college than I did. We'd both just started working at newspapers, learning on the fly, but no matter. There was no training for this kind of journalism.

This was human. This was real. This was life.

We drove southwest of the city. After miles of travel, we pulled off the freeway. Chain-link fences surrounded businesses and empty homes on overgrown lots. It was perfect. We pulled behind a vacant store. Michael crawled into the back seat. I went to the trunk and got a portable manual typewriter that I'd bought for twenty-five dollars in Cleveland. To save the car battery and to lessen the glow of Das Boot to cops and ne'er-do-wells, I lit a candle lantern and hooked it to the rearview mirror with a chain so that it hung low, below the bottom line of the windows. I set my notebook beneath the lantern's light and transcribed the interview with Sam. After the candle burned down and wax had dripped out of the lantern and onto my notebook, I lay in the front seat with rain dripping on me from the leaking window—I'd unsuccessfully tried caulking it. I went to sleep, wondering about the enormity of what we were doing.

We awakened in the morning to a knock from a friendly cop, who told us that we were in Times Beach, its 2,240 residents then in the process of being evacuated and their village permanently demolished because of dioxin contamination. The levels of dioxin detected in the town were two thousand times higher than the dioxin content of Agent Orange, the herbicide sprayed as a defoliant in Vietnam during the war.

At eleven o'clock sharp, Sam was waiting on the south steps of the city library. He announced he was again going to try to sell his blood plasma.

He was more cheerful today. On the way to the plasma center, he said, "A guy tried to talk me into hopping a train to Tampa this morning, but I'm thinking of Denver. I keep hearing there's lots of jobs there. 'Come with me,' he said."

Sam asked the man about hitchhiking. "He said, 'No one will pick you up. They know you're desperate. They know you're hungry. They're afraid of that.' "

Sam declined going to Florida, still wanting Denver. He wondered about hoboing. We told him we had some experience jumping on trains.

Sam entered the plasma center. When he didn't come out, we figured his blood pressure had dropped and they'd taken him. We mulled over the situation. We could just drive Sam to Denver. But that would be altering the story. A journalist is merely supposed to observe. On the other hand, the previous night's conversation was fresh on our minds. What was the line between being a human being and a journalist? Of course, by joining Sam, in a car or on a train, we would alter what would happen to him by our presence—that is, if he would allow us to come along. Even if we were to walk away now and do nothing, we faced a moral choice. Sam seemed too fragile to be left alone. No matter what we did, there were consequences.

Sam emerged, clutching seven dollars. He asked us more questions about trains. We walked to the Missouri Pacific rail yard, the "MoPac." It was a big yard, and it wouldn't be easy to catch out from there. We knew from our hobo travels that trains went from here to Kansas City, then on to Pueblo, south of Denver. We sought hobos to help us learn the tricks of this yard, but found no one.

Michael had the idea that we could use the sixty-three-story Gateway Arch, erected to commemorate the city as a path to the West, for reconnaissance. We went up in the arch and had an airplane view of the rail yard. We watched where trains were being built, in areas called "hump yards," where the cars were assembled for their intended destinations, and we figured the best spot to catch out. Sam was excited by the idea of jumping on a train.

Michael began taking pictures. Sam didn't seem to mind. Michael told Sam that when he made it back from being homeless, the pictures would be great to show his kids. If he felt they shouldn't be used, he could tell us after we got to Denver. We joked about how someday years hence we'd reunite and laugh about our coming trip.

The day burned past. We signed in at the Sally. We were ushered into the overheated chapel to be "earbanged," subjected to a mandatory sermon, before we could eat. A haggard woman played a piano badly. The preacher wore a cheap suit. Another person, with Coke-bottle-thick glasses, clapped and yowled. The preacher called the men sinners and alcoholics. He didn't account for the presence of people such as Sam.

Sam buried his head in his thin hands. He pulled the rag and squeezed it. The preacher was talking about the evils of money. I wrote in my notebook, "I'll take the money!" and showed it to Sam. He smiled.

After the sermon, we showered. As we dried off, the mission stiff on duty hurried us. "You got beds, find them!" he ordered.

Sam took the top of a sagging double-deck steel bunk bed. I went below, Michael nearby. The mission stiff was in a glass booth. We talked from our beds.

"I want to ask that preacher, 'What happened to the Parthians in the second century, sucker?' They [religious people] act so much better than you. They treat you like a dog. I had eight thousand dollars in the bank. That's bubble gum when it starts going. By the time I went down, my neighbors were out of work too. One guy got down and left his family. The other died. And this was suburbia! It's scary to look at that guy," Sam whispered, pointing to a shriveled wino two beds away, "and feel you're going that way. It's a panic thing. If I can get one little job, it will bring me back."

Sam tossed. I never really went to sleep. Man smells and farts were intensified by the overheated air. Every move prompted loud squeaks from the springs of the rusting army surplus bunks. Men gasped, hacked, and snored.

Five A.M. came. The mission stiff clicked on the lights. "All right, gentlemen, time to run!" he said with a laugh. We were thrown into the darkness.

Sam never asked about our driving him west. So we decided to jump a train with him. He seemed to be emboldened by our presence, and we felt grave responsibility for his well-being. We bought him a five-dollar sleeping bag at a secondhand store.

Our immediate task was to ditch the car. We drove it to a safe location, and I stayed with Sam as Michael parked Das Boot. Once he stashed the car, Michael excitedly ran back to us. He'd called his wife collect from a pay phone and learned that he'd won second place in a competition sponsored by Nikon cameras, for his pictures of hobos taken for the newspaper and *Life*. The prize paid $500. Brenda would wire the money to us. It would keep us going.

Dusk. The MoPac train rumbled past. I threw my gear on an empty automobile carrier and clambered aboard. The others followed. We passed a switchman.

"Watch the main yard in K.C.!" he shouted. "It's hot! The bull's been throwing everyone in jail!"

I yelled, "Thanks!"

The train picked up speed. We went to the roof of the car carrier by climbing an outside ladder. The Gateway Arch dominated the skyline.

"Goodbye, St. Louis!" Sam hollered. He jumped up and down, shaking a fist. "Good riddance! No regrets! I can starve here or in Denver!"

A misting rain fell. We climbed back to the shelter of the first level. Sam tried to pee out the back of the car. Wind doused him with his piss. Sam laughed till his sides hurt. He said it was the first time he'd laughed in weeks. When he rubbed his eyes with filthy hands, they turned into two white spots surrounded by blackened rings.

"Believe it or not, this is a lot better than the mission," Sam yelled as he crawled into the secondhand sleeping bag. It was freezing. Our train was a hotshot. We sped on, a rough ride through the Ozark Mountain night.

We made the Kansas City MoPac yard at 3:30 A.M. The train creaked to a stop. A switchman told us our train was being broken into pieces, adding that the bull had thrown two hobos in jail yesterday.

We jungled up in a ditch, freezing, not sleeping. At dawn, we walked through a cattail swamp south of the yard, toward an abandoned grain elevator. We wanted a safe place to hide while plotting our next move. All the doors and windows of the grain elevator were sealed, but someone had chiseled a torso-size entrance hole in the concrete at ground level. We squirmed through and climbed an interior ladder to a tiny room halfway up the six- or seven-story structure. I used a braided wire cable in the room to lift our packs, as Sam guided them, through an open window. We swept away rotting grain and bat droppings, collected wood and built a fire on the concrete floor, and had our first sleep in two days. We were low on food. A reconnaissance mission to find a market proved fruitless.

Sam perched himself in the window overlooking the MoPac yard. He showed us pictures of his children, ages two, three, and five. "I'd work in the bottom of a salt mine to get them back." He pointed to rows of freight cars in the yard. "If I can ride one of those suckers across the country, I can do anything. Eighty percent of the people I know couldn't imagine me here. They think I'm a soft guy. But I'm a competitor. I've played sports all my life, and I know when I'm behind in the game. I'm behind now. But I'm starting to feel I'm going to score. Since I hopped that train, things have changed. I've got a feeling about Denver."

The sun vanished. We ate the last Spam and crackers as well as cans of soup Sam had bought with blood plasma money. A few packets of instant oatmeal and one jar of peanut butter remained.

Everything for sale. Times Square, New York City, 1990.

(overleaf) Nightfall. Big Springs, Nebraska, 2007.

(above) Malta, Montana, 2008.

School that closed in March 1953. Gascoyne, North Dakota, 2008.

(overleaf) Ghost stacks. Youngstown, 2009.

(above) Helena, Arkansas, 2009.

Ruins of an African American grocery store. Machipongo, Virginia, 2000.

Magazine page welded to the floor by rain, in an abandoned trucker motel on U.S. Route 1. College Park, Maryland, 2001.

Nothing for sale. Brownsville, Pennsylvania, 2002.

Former supply company, now a church. York, Alabama, 2007.

Wheaton, Maryland, 2009.

Ruins of the Avanti automobile plant. Youngstown, 2009.

Lower Ninth Ward, New Orleans, 2005.

Women returning for the first time after Hurricane Katrina, searching for pieces of their missing house.
Lower Ninth Ward, New Orleans, 2005.

Hair salon. New Orleans, 2006.

Beauty parlor. New Orleans, 2006.

Ballroom of the Lee Plaza Hotel. Detroit, 2009.

Michigan Central Train Station. Detroit, 2009.

Rotting doll in the ruins. Detroit, 2009.

Girl who had been searching for diamonds with her parents, whose business had fallen on hard times.
Crater of Diamonds State Park, Arkansas, 2009.

Edge Man Ed at home. Nashville shantytown, 2009.

(facing page, top) Sally, who once lived in "the house on the hill," in a food bank line. Michigan, 2009.

(facing page, bottom) The "Dancer," Jeffrey James (J.J.) Johnston, signaling a bid at an auction of foreclosed homes. Louisville, 2009.

B.T. selling his shirts and other items for food and gas. Red Boiling Springs, Tennessee, 2009.

Sam reminisced. He missed reading. He said he had some two thousand books stored at his parents' house.

Talk soon faded. We crawled into our sleeping bags.

"What a blessing! A floor that's not moving," Sam said.

Railcars banged in the hump yard as workers built new trains, perhaps the one that would take us west. Frogs croaked in the swamp. These sounds quickly lulled us to sleep.

Come morning, we explained to Sam that it would be difficult to catch out. We might end up in jail. But if we played it right, we could beat the bull. This appealed to Sam's competitive edge. He hadn't pulled the rag from his pocket since we'd gotten off the train in K.C. We ate the last of the oatmeal and went to the edge of the yard, in a wooded area.

We waited. And waited. Sam was learning that hobos often spend a whole lot more time waiting for trains than actually riding them.

Finally, a train began building. There were no empty boxcars, and an open grain car ledge was out of the question because of the bull and the threat of snow. The only ride was on a car carrier loaded with small pickup trucks. We ran across the open area and took it.

The cabs of the trucks were locked, and we couldn't find the hidden keys. We piled our gear into one truck bed and sat quietly in a second bed for an hour. The crew had not yet hooked up the units. The car carrier was a risky choice: bulls were especially watchful of them because of people breaking into vehicles. So when we heard approaching footsteps in the gravel, we plastered ourselves against the bed. Sam's eyes were wide. We heard the person jump on the car carrier in front of ours; feet on gravel. Metal clanged as the person jumped up into our carrier.

Silence. Whoever it was stood 30 feet from us. The feet landed back on the stones and walked past to the next carrier car. Was it the bull? We'd never know.

The train barreled across Kansas through a late season snowstorm. Snow swirled inside the carrier. We were cold to the marrow of our bones and wolf hungry. Michael announced it was time for the peanut butter, our last food. He went to his pack, his hands shaking violently from the cold. The jar fell and shattered. We stared at the blob of peanut butter peppered with glass shards—there was no eating it. Michael was nearly weeping. We consoled him. It wasn't his fault.

The train sided often to make way for eastbounds. The night was long.

Dawn brought a magic view: the snow-capped Rocky Mountains.

Nineteen hours after leaving K.C., we entered the Pueblo yard. A glow to the east drew us: a McDonald's at an interchange off Interstate 25. We ordered nine big breakfasts, and each ate three of them.

We went to a ramp to hitchhike. The sun was warm. We lay down for a minute. We didn't fall asleep—we passed out. We awakened hours later. I was confused. Why the hell was I on the shoulder of a freeway entrance ramp?

Sam rubbed his eyes and pointed to Pike's Peak. He again pulled out pictures of his children. "I'd like to show them that sometime," he said of the mountain.

We put out our thumbs and caught rides to Denver.

"Just get in?" Ben, an unemployed machinist from Lima, Ohio, asked Sam. "So did we. If we don't find anything here, we're heading for California." Others in his group called out a litany of hometowns from Florida to Michigan.

Men with backpacks were everywhere downtown. There were more people seeking work here than in St. Louis. Sam grasped his head, muttering that he might never work again. We slept that night in the hobo jungle on the bank of the South Platte River. Sam was again squeezing the rag.

The next day, I went with Sam as he looked for work, watched him fill out applications. Michael and I went off to the side to talk. What could we do?

We could do this: we took Sam to a fleabag hotel and used half of Michael's prize award to get Sam a room for one month. We couldn't leave him on the street. With a room and a real address, he had a much better chance of landing a job.

The three of us went to the Greyhound station. It was April 11, 1983. I bought the $144 tickets for two with my credit card, creeping close to my limit. Sam stood on the sidewalk watching as our bus pulled away. We waved. The next day, in St. Louis, I paid $18 for parking and $25 for 23.8 gallons of gas with the card. Our ability to keep working was threatened as our credit ran low. But we had to get Sam that room.

As we drove on to Texas, I kept thinking of the hundreds of other Sams walking around Denver.

4 HOME SWEET TENT

For six blocks, the cop car was on my tail. I'd turn and he'd follow. "He's going to tag us," I said.

"We haven't done anything," Michael pointed out.

The cop flashed his rooftop lights. I hit record on my tape machine and slid it beneath the seat as the cop walked toward us. He paused at our rear bumper, eyed the Ohio plates, Mr. Frazier's hardhat on the rear window ledge, the Youngstown State sticker. The bait worked. The cop came forward with a hand on his sidearm.

"How long you been here?"

"Two days."

"We know. We saw this car when you come in. Whatcha doing here?"

We waffled, never really answering his question.

"Well, how long you staying?"

"About another week, then we're heading to California," I said.

"Okay. If we see this car here past one more week, I'm going to throw you in jail!"

In unison, we asked, "What for?"

The cop put his hand on his chin and squinted. He examined Das Boot for an excuse and then pointed to our balding retreads. "Tires!"

We'd heard worse. People in Youngstown who'd come to Texas seeking work told tales of harassment and jail. One man said police escorted him to the freeway and told him never to return to this city of 2 million. Our greeting was not an isolated incident, admitted Houston police spokeswoman Phymeon Jackson when I phoned.

"Yes, there have been complaints," Jackson said. "Especially from Michigan people. There's an anti-northern bias."

In the stunning heat of an afternoon, north of Houston.

Wind coming off the swamp was hot. We stood next to Das Boot and studied three canvas tents across the campground, which were clustered around a wooden platform. There were two cars: one with Ohio plates, the other from Michigan. The latter made the owners "blacks," in the parlance of Houstoners, who used this pejorative because of the hue of the Michigan tags, not the owners' skin color, though the sentiment was the same.

A mother, father, and two children were sitting in chairs on the platform.

"It's your turn," I said to Michael.

"No, it's yours!" Michael insisted. We argued as we walked the circular lane that linked all the camp sites.

We were worn out from a constant stream of stories of despair—we'd already heard quite a few since arriving in Houston. How many could we listen to?

After walking the circle five or six times, I gave in and suddenly marched right up to the family. A big part of me wanted them to tell me to go to hell. Then we could drive away and have an excuse. But the woman was smiling.

"We were sitting here talking about you," she told me. "I said, 'They want to talk to us.' We were wondering when you'd walk up."

Sheepishly, I explained what we were doing, and they invited us to sit. That began the good part of a week in which we lived next to Bonnie and James Alexander and their two children—Jennifer, twelve, and Matthew, eleven—and their neighbors, Cindi and John.

Jim had built the platform from scrap lumber after the time the swamp rose and flooded the three tents, which they called "bedrooms." Water lapped at the edge of Matthew's bedroom. Bonnie had just finished cleaning Jennifer's bedroom. The platform in front of the big tent—Jim and Bonnie's bedroom—was called the "living room." On it sat a kitchen table, cupboards, a stove built on a plywood box. On the front of this box was the word "LOVE," carved in wood, as if handwritten. Four dogs were present: Bear, Boo, and two puppies. Zinnias were planted around the perimeter of the living room.

Bonnie gave us a tour. "We now have a three-bedroom house again," she said. "We had a three-bedroom ranch in Michigan. Typical America."

Bonnie explained that they had just bought the big tent so they could have their own bedroom. They sold their washer and clothes dryer to pay for it.

A copy of the *Houston Post* lay on a table in the big tent, folded to the help wanted section. The tent also contained a television with a hand-size screen on a stand, a double bed, a lamp. Bonnie apologized for the unkempt appearance; the previous day a windstorm had wreaked havoc.

Jim sat on a rusting glider couch that was covered with sun-bleached cushions, rocking back and forth. His eyes were on the swamp. Sweat beaded off his forehead and glistened from his mustache. His mouth was downturned. He'd quit a job in disgust today and now wondered if he'd done the right thing.

Bonnie had a mouth that looked like she laughed a lot. Although things had not been going well lately for the Alexander family, Jennifer's and Matthew's latest grade-school report cards were salted with As. Above all else, what counted was that the kids were doing well, Bonnie said.

The couple had been married for twelve and a half years. Jim had worked in a salt mine in Port Huron, Michigan. After he was laid off, they lost their home to foreclosure. That was four years ago.

"I got into pipe welding and came down here," Jim said. He'd been a welder in the Texas oil fields.

"The economy was fantastic," Jim recalled. "But the layoffs started coming . . . now these good old boys are taking care of their own."

They could no longer afford their apartment rent of $500 a month. "We tried to survive on the minimum wage," Bonnie said. "We couldn't." They'd moved into the campground last month.

"I was opposed to the idea," Jim added. But there was no choice.

Bonnie worked part time in the front office, which paid the expensive camping fees. Just enough remained for a little food, but not enough.

The air was moist with a superheated haze. The sun vanished before it hit true horizon. Frogs bellowed from the swamp. Mosquitoes emerged in force. Dogs barked. Bonnie prepared dinner for the kids. When she reached into a cooler, I noticed that it was nearly empty. Supper was sandwiches.

We were introduced to Cindi and John, who lived on the adjoining site. The couple was from Cincinnati, Ohio. They, too, had landed at the campground because they couldn't afford to keep an apartment. We talked into the night. A fire blazed in a pit in the center of the platform. The glow flickered on faces. Jim smoked Marlboros.

"This is great," Cindi said. "I never want to live in a house again. Look, we got fresh air. No hassles. I'm sorry we didn't start living like this years ago."

John nodded. So did Jim and Bonnie.

"I've learned to cook on the grill," Bonnie said. "I thought I'd never do that. We're reverting to what we used to be." Bonnie talked about how the experience had made them a stronger family.

The four adults went on about how happy they were. Later that night, as we bedded down in Das Boot at a nearby site, Michael and I talked about how their voices rang hollow.

Several days passed. We left the campground each morning to interview people in and around Houston. Jim spent his days seeking work.

The campground had a small recreation hall with a billiard table. Jim mentioned that he liked playing pool. One evening, we bought a case of Lone Star beer and invited Jim out for a few games.

I racked. Jim broke. He stuck out his tongue and took aim down the stick. The cue ball careened off the triangle of balls and scratched in a corner pocket.

"Well, it's been a long time," said Jim.

Michael and I cracked open Lone Stars, and we offered Jim one. "No, thanks," he replied. He had given up alcohol two years ago; now he just drank coffee.

"It makes me feel my Wheaties," Jim said of booze. It got him in too many fights. Bonnie didn't like him coming home drunk.

Jim won the first game. Oh, what the hell, he said, it's hot. Just one beer. Another game. Well, just one more. Another game, another beer. And so on into the night. And, to my surprise, Michael, who typically didn't drink, kept pace with me and Jim.

Jim had been wild years ago, he told us. "'Specially after I come home from 'Nam." He had been a U.S. Marine and had gone through the Tet offensive. He was proud of his service. He came home, settled down, and married Bonnie, and the couple bought that three-bedroom home in Port Huron. One day, he said, he walked into what he thought was a meeting of the National Rifle Association but was instead a gathering of the American Independent Party. He turned to leave. They invited him to stay. One hour later, he walked out, a candidate for the Michigan state assembly. He lost but was happy he could run.

Jim sank the eight ball. He whooped. We were all drunk. The three of us laughed and shouted when we made shots, groaned when we weren't so good. We pitched empty Lone Stars at the trash.

Jim put quarters in the slots and discovered the locked panel to the coins was broken and easily popped open. He took out some quarters to use.

"What the hell . . . they make enough money off it. You gotta get a break once in a while," Jim said.

We played free from then on. Jim racked the balls. Without prodding, he began talking about his family's descent into economic trouble. He hadn't wanted them to live in a tent.

"I lived in tents in Vietnam. I went through a typhoon in one."

He viewed the tents as failure. But what could he do? They'd been kicked out of the apartment.

"I've given up on the idea of owning a home. If I don't have one, I can't lose one."

Jim fell quiet for a moment. He told us that the windstorm of the other day brought back thoughts of Vietnam. It was an experience he was still sorting out.

"I joined the marines when I was seventeen. I'd go on patrol, walking through the jungle. Once, I was standing in a clump of trees, and a 'gook' walked by me, about eight feet away." The man turned out to be part of a large Vietnamese patrol unit. Jim was with only a few other Americans, badly outnumbered, so they hoped to remain unseen and thus survive. "You want to know what scared is? I froze. I was afraid he could hear the sweat dripping off my nose. I really thought he could hear it. Things like that mess you up."

And there were the things that every person who goes through active combat on the front lines sees and does—the experiences ate at him.

"I came out thinking I was tough. I was a marine! I'd walk into bars and open my big mouth and get into fights. I don't think I ever won any. I'd pick the biggest guys. I was just feelin' my Wheaties."

He suddenly began to lose badly at pool. Michael and I weren't playing much better—we were a trio of scratches and blown shots.

Jim told us about his last job, in a welding shop—the one he had just quit the day we met. He had been there only a few weeks. It paid the federal minimum, $3.35 an hour, enough for food and gas but not much else. He kept being ridiculed by co-workers who hated northerners. He was glad he walked out, he said, but there was uncertainty in his voice. The family was low on food and had little money left.

"I earned in one week what I used to earn in one day at that job. Talk about exploitation. I kept getting called a 'dumb Yank' and made fun of. You're not accepted. I couldn't take it anymore. The good ol' boys let the dummies from the North do all the work. The nonunion shops are really bad.

"I've been in a foreign country where the signs say 'Yankee, go home.' And you get called a Yankee down here! It's a culture shock. For the first time in my life, I know what it's like to be on the receiving end of prejudice. I tell these Texans they should go to a foreign country and feel what it's like to be called a Yankee. I feel like an invader from the North. I feel like a foreigner in my own country. If the opportunities don't exist where you're from, where do you play ball? They're still fighting the Civil War. They have pride. What do they have to be proud of? Proud of the Civil War? Hell, we won the Civil War. They're proud they're bigger. Yeah, bigger. Bigger roaches. Bigger snakes. The windstorms are big.

"I'll tell you what happened to us. I rolled through a few stop signs near Galena Park. I went to jail for twenty-four hours because of it. The cops wouldn't even let me make a call. Bonnie was worried sick. I didn't get smart with them, because I'd heard the stories."

He spent the night in a cell. When they let him go, he had to pay a fine that exactly matched all the paper money he had in his wallet. He was left with 83 cents. And he had to pay to get the car out of impound.

"If you're a Yankee, don't go to jail down here. They're meaner than cat shit."

The hour was extreme.

Jim replaced a respectable number of quarters in the slot, and we drunkenly staggered across the campground in the early morning darkness. The air was thick with the sound of night bugs and frogs. We felt alive. We hollered. A dog barked. Jim told a few stories about wonderful women he had known years ago.

As we neared the tents, he sobered up enough to worry that Bonnie might be angry that he had broken his vow of abstaining from booze. I suddenly felt bad that we had bought the beer. Jim shushed Bear and Boo and slipped in through the door, hoping not to awaken Bonnie. Muffled whispers told us that he hadn't been quiet enough. We could not discern the conversation. But Bonnie's words sounded kind.

Our last night with the family came. We had one more thing to do before we left Houston and then we were headed to west Texas, Mexico, on to Arizona, and a wrap in California. The family had no food left. I offered to make dinner. We bought veggies and fixings for a dish my mom cooked—slumgullion stew, which consists of ground meat, onions, noodles, stewed tomatoes, topped with cheese. It's cheap, tasty, and feeds a crowd. Jennifer ran over and peered in the pan as I fried the ground meat and onions on the Coleman stove. On the other burner, I boiled water for noodles.

"We don't have to eat bologna sandwiches tonight!" Jennifer announced.

The huge pot of slumgullion was soon reduced to bottom scrapings. Matthew and Jennifer had three helpings. Jim wrestled with Matthew, and then the kids ran off to play, arguing as only siblings can. Jim put his arm around Bonnie, smoked a Marlboro. He stoked the fire in the pit to ward off the dampness of evening. Tonight, he drank coffee.

Hot wind blew across the swamp. Night birds sang. In the distance, a Southern Pacific freight rumbled, its diesel horns blaring out of the darkness. It seemed that, everywhere, the unemployed wound up near the tracks, even if they didn't ride the rails.

Bonnie chased the kids to bed. As they dressed in pajamas, the tents glowed like blue and orange Chinese lanterns. Jim seemed eager to continue the conversation that had begun at the billiard table. He leaned forward and talked in a whisper so the kids wouldn't hear. His face reflected the fireglow.

"Material possessions are meaning less and less to me. The way the whole economy is going, it's a good time to be highly mobile. There's an undercurrent in this country. An undercurrent people in power are not aware of. They don't realize the bitterness and anger they are stirring up. There's a bitterness and seething that will erupt. There's going to be rioting in the streets."

Jim chucked a cigarette butt into the fire. He clamped another Marlboro in his lips, flicking his lighter with an anger that made the flame leap wildly.

"I'm not a philosopher. But when the middle class erupts, they're going to be sorry. Uncle Sugar hasn't learned that better-educated people will be out to change something that is their right to change. I never thought this would happen to me. I never thought this could happen in America. I've gone from the land of plenty to nothing. And we're living in the lap of luxury compared to a lot of people."

Jim went into the master tent. He produced a .357 Magnum revolver and a 9 mm semiautomatic pistol. He brought the revolver out to the living room. It shone in the firelight. His long arm made a sweeping arc, motioning to the swamp and the empty fields on the other side of the campground. It was all privately owned.

"They won't let you use that land to survive. I could go out there and grow a lot of food. If you try that, they'll arrest you and put you in jail. This is America! There was a time when all we had to eat was one potato between all four of us."

"Boy, I sliced it real thin," Bonnie added.

"The kids went to bed hungry that night," Jim said. The word "hungry" came out sounding like someone had jabbed a fist in his gut. He clutched the gun in a shaking hand. "I'm *never* going to let that happen again. I'm trying my damnedest as an upright citizen. First, I'll go hunting for food. If that doesn't work, I hit a 7-Eleven. I'll hold up a store. I won't take money. But I'll take food. My kids won't starve."

5 TRUE BOTTOM

Our first day in Houston, before we met the Alexanders, we had gone to skid row.

At the Star Hope Rescue Mission on La Branch Street, we saw hundreds of men sitting on street curbs. A police cruiser approached, and the cops glared at us. We breathed a sigh of relief when they moved on. Down the street, they stopped and questioned two men. Suddenly, the cops began beating them bloody with nightsticks and threw them in the back of the cruiser. No one but us seemed to notice.

The mission opened its doors, and men mobbed the entrance. Two hundred was the limit. The rest were turned away and would spend the night on the street.

As we walked back to Das Boot, we spotted a curious-looking van parked near the mission, with a sign on its side: BOOZE CRUISER. When we asked about this van, homeless men erupted with stories.

"Don't go," one man said. "They rip you off."

"It's a cult," another said. "You sign your life away."

The foundation that operated the van ran a work camp in a distant city. We were told by the homeless on skid row that you would be pressured to sign a form essentially committing yourself as a ward of the organization for thirty days. The men we spoke to claimed that the city where the work camp was located didn't want the foundation importing the homeless and allowed the camp to operate only on the condition that, when wards left, they had to be driven at least 20 miles beyond the city limits. This meant that if you attempted to flee, you were in violation of this agreement, and the police were called in. (Or this may have been a line the foundation used to deter its wards from leaving early.) After your thirty days, if you chose to end your commitment, the foundation would drive you back to Houston.

But this was easier said than done. We heard that in order to get out of the camp, you had to ask permission, after which the camp held group "therapy" sessions, as is common in some cults, where others would cajole you into staying. If that didn't work, and you tried to escape, cops reportedly chased you down and returned you to the camp. Many who went to the camp were addicted to drugs or booze; the foundation wanted these individuals because they were easier to coerce.

In Youngstown, we'd heard about these kinds of camps; Texas was dotted with them, people said, with state authorities looking the other way. The purpose of the camps was to contract out workers and make a profit. They're one of the peculiar mysteries of the Texas way of doing things, in which some situations are allowed to exist that would not be tolerated elsewhere.

After saying farewell to the Alexander family, we had that one last thing to do in Houston: investigate the foundation. We returned to skid row, parked Das Boot in a long-term lot near the Greyhound bus station, and loaded up our packs. I'd argued with Michael about the wisdom of taking a camera. Homeless men had told us that the work camp would lock up all your gear. But Michael wasn't going anywhere without a camera. He wrapped it tight in clothes and placed it in the bottom of the pack.

As we walked up, the Booze Cruiser was parked on the street. I chose to be an alcoholic. Michael wasn't sure he could pull that off. He never drank, even socially—or at least he hadn't before we became hobos and before we spent that night playing pool with Jim Alexander—so he decided to be ambiguous. One foundation worker, a heavy-set man, sat in the open sliding door of the van. The other was in the passenger seat.

"What's this van? Where does it go?" Michael asked.

The Big Man went into an awkward pitch. "We take in lots of people who want to get off the streets," he said. He told stories about how the Houston police were mean and would arrest Yankees like us. This part of the pitch certainly rang true.

"The cops will get you. Come try it."

I acted like I had a serious hangover. The Big Man asked if we wanted to change our lives.

"Yeah," I said. "Can we get some food?"

"Two hots and a cot. Hop in."

We pretended to hesitate. We looked at each other, mumbled that we had no better option.

"Sure," I said.

We jumped in. The door slammed, and we sped off. There were no seats, so we had to lie on the metal floor. The van had a bad muffler, and exhaust fumes leaked inside. The van broke down twice, and the driver and his partner tinkered with the engine. Darkness fell. It was late by the time we entered a compound in the distant city. The fumes had given us headaches. I heard crickets and felt the heat. The door to the van was opened by a camp guard, who watched the exits.

We were ushered into the office. Michael waited in an outer room while I was interviewed. The Big Man told us that the camp owner normally did intake, but that he was out of town. As the Big Man dug around for all the forms I had to sign,

I read a sheet with the camp rules, among them that all gear had to be placed in the main office, kept in lockers in an adjoining room.

"You a drug addict or an alkie?" the Big Man asked.

"I drink, yeah," I said. "But I don't know if I'm an alcoholic—"

"Denial? Doesn't matter," he quickly answered for me. "We take in a lot of people with life problems." I inquired about what he meant.

"There are a lot more of them because of the economy. A lot of them are from out of state. We get most of those from Michigan and Ohio."

I signed some dozen forms with fine print that he didn't give me time to read. Before reciting the rules, he prefaced the list by saying, "This place is fucked." He smiled. I wasn't sure whether he was bitter, making fun of me for having just signed away my rights, or attempting humor.

"No phone calls. No getting money from outside. No TV. No nothing. You have to shave your beard. For thirty days, you will be a weasel—"

"Weasel?"

"New guys are called that. One pack of cigs a day is your pay." If I did okay, I would "graduate" out of being a weasel and move up in status. "After ninety days, you get paid WAM, if the foundation can afford it."

"WAM?"

"Walking around money."

When he was done with me, I sat in the outer room as the Big Man interviewed Michael, who answered with incomplete sentences as he stammered about some vague addiction. Michael was overacting, and I felt he might blow our cover.

"Son, you need some help?"

"Umm, umm—"

"This is the place to get help, but, son, I really need to know what the nature of your problem is."

"Prob-lem?" Michael said languidly. He drew out words, paused briefly at the syllables. "I do-o-on't know if I have a prob-lem."

"Well, son, do you have some kind of abuse problem—either drugs or alcohol?"

"Guess so."

"Son, are you retarded?"

I managed to hold in laughter.

"I do-o-on't think so," Michael said.

"We'll write, 'learning disabled.'"

I again barely squelched laughter, but turned sober when Michael and the Big Man emerged. The Big Man made us shave and then led us to a bunkhouse. He never asked for our packs. We held them low against our bodies as we walked across the compound. Multiple snores came from the darkness beyond the door. The Big Man told us to find empty beds.

We were lucky. Had the owner been there, he surely would have taken our gear, we later learned from camp mates. The bunkhouse smelled like someone had just thrown up. We stashed the packs in a closet on a top shelf, behind stacks of sheets. We lay down at 1:00 A.M. and fitfully slept. At 4:00 A.M., there was a racket in the center of the compound—a worker striking a metal triangle, the kind you see in old-time cowboy western films.

Twenty-five of us piled out of bed and were taken to a mess hall, where we ate. Bacon, nearly raw, was served with sticky grits, overcooked scrambled eggs, and stale muffins. We stood in a line to get our daily ration of one pack of cigarettes. We then gathered in the center of the compound, where the weasels, most of the group, including us, were ordered to sweep the gravel driveway with brooms as dawn's light broke.

Trucks lined up. We were assigned to crews. I was put in the bed of a pickup truck driven by a man in his late twenties with a face like a fox. Jay was put in the truck bed with me. Jay was young, maybe thirty, tops, and he wore dark shades. Thin and tanned, he seemed too cool to be here. What was up with him?

We were taken to a suburban home owned by a dentist. Foxface led Jay and me to the backyard, where we were to build a retaining wall with old railroad ties. For the next ten hours, we hauled ties, fit them in place, backfilled them with dirt and rocks. Foxface sat in a chair and gave orders. Jay worked hard and so did I, though I often excused myself to pee. I was really writing notes in the bathroom. When Foxface was back at the truck or chatting with the dentist, Jay and I got to talk freely.

"I look at any job as if I put my name on it," Jay said. It was his thirtieth day at the foundation. He now could leave but had not. I was puzzled.

Jay was a bricklayer and stone mason by trade. He'd had a good life in Tulsa, Oklahoma, where he'd earned $12.50 an hour. He was married and had a house. Then construction work fell to nothing, and he lost the house. Marital problems ensued, and he split with his wife. A year ago, he had ended up in Houston, so broke that he hocked his work tools and started sleeping in his car. Eventually he had to sell the car. He began drinking and sleeping under bridges. He sobered up for a few months and found day-haul work, but it wasn't enough to pay for a room. His tale of falling out of the middle class and into the depths of economic despair was typical of what we'd heard dozens of times—except for his description of that afternoon thirty days earlier.

"I woke up that morning and said, 'This is it?' I was sober, had been sober. I had no wife, no job. I asked myself, 'Is this all there is?'"

He got drunk. Real drunk. So drunk that he was puking and sick.

"That's when they picked me up," he said, referring to the Booze Cruiser. In another sixty days, he'd get WAM, he told me. "I'll stay for that."

I was incredulous, asking why he would work like a slave. WAM was just a few bucks a day.

"They keep you working so hard, there's no money, so it's impossible to leave. So you stay sober." He disliked the foundation but believed that it was the only thing he had going.

"You got to know when you have no other options," he said.

At lunch, the dentist and his wife fed us peanut butter and jelly sandwiches, chips, and Kool-Aid. For someone who was a ward of the foundation, I pushed my luck, asking a lot of questions. (I acted curious.) The dentist told me he bartered with the foundation, fixing teeth in exchange for cheap labor. (The foundation, which claimed that it was helping rehabilitate men through hard work and counseling, charged clients $6 per hour per worker.) I told the dentist that I was brand new and was surprised they weren't paying me for such hard labor. "But they get three squares and a roof over their heads," he replied, speaking to me in the third person as if I were not one of the guys doing slave labor on his wall. "It helps them."

When the dentist went back into his house, Jay and I sat and ate lunch in the shade of an oak. Jay looked at the swimming pool.

"It must be nice to have something like this. Lounge around the pool all day. This is real nice."

Jay daydreamed more about the dentist's life. Then we resumed building. We labored into the afternoon, getting most of the wall completed. Foxface drove us away at five o'clock. Jay and I sat in the open truck bed, wind in our hair. I liked Jay and almost told him that we were journalists, but thought better of it. I did confess that Michael and I would soon leave.

"You better not be talking like that around here. They'll call a game on you," Jay said. A "game" was an evening ritual, a session in which the group picked on one man. "One of the things you signed says they can call a game. They try to talk you out of leaving, and they humiliate you. They get very abusive. They ridicule the hell out of you."

He warned us that if we tried to escape, we'd regret it.

Back at the compound, Foxface ordered the weasels to the center of the yard, where we had to wash all the trucks. Foxface stood with his arms crossed, talking with the guard, watching us from a distance.

"After being a weasel, you get to the point where you can be an asshole with power," Jay whispered about Foxface, who had stayed long enough to become second in command of the camp. "A lot of guys try for it. They want power."

Michael's truck came in. He told me he'd worked digging a ditch all day for a U.S. Air Force guy named Ed, who had gotten a flier on his windshield advertising the foundation. He was shocked when Michael told him that the workers were not paid.

Jay looked at the watch on Michael's wrist. He commented that if Michael had pawned it, "it would have brought you one more day of freedom."

It was near sunset when we finished washing the trucks. The non-weasels were in the mess hall eating dinner. Foxface said us weasels had yet more work to do before we could eat. After dinner, he announced, there would be a game—it was unclear which man was being targeted, and that caused worry. Was it one of us, the newcomers?

As we wondered what was up, Foxface drove a dump truck, its bed filled with tons of concrete aggregate, tree trunks, and other debris, into the center of the yard. He pulled the lever that raised the bed and allowed the load to tumble out in a cloud of dust. The bed lowered.

"Okay, weasels," Foxface announced, "now fill it back up."

We set to work reloading the truck by hand, forming teams that passed debris.

"I hate this shit," Jay said.

It was a contradiction I couldn't understand. Jay felt enmity, but he was terrified of what he called "the outside."

"But don't you feel they are ripping you off?" I asked.

Jay scratched at the hard ground with a foot, scraping at the dust. When he looked back up, he said, "No-o-o." He paused. "No."

I shut up.

I realized what I was seeing: this was a man who had given up, utterly. Sam and the Alexanders still had fight in them. But the fight was blown out of Jay.

He had arrived here a destroyed man, beaten by life and the vagaries of the economy. Now he seemed brainwashed, like the cult members I'd written about for the newspaper. Like a cult, the foundation was exploiting his weakened state of mind in order to manipulate him. The work camp practiced classic sleep deprivation: it worked men hard and then roused them after just a few hours' sleep to do it all over again, seven days a week. Jay said this was how it had been for the previous thirty days.

One must be defeated to be controlled.

Michael and I whispered to each other that we'd witnessed enough. Because the owner was returning the next day, we thought it best to make a break for it that night. The owner was smart and a real bastard, the men had told us; he might figure something was odd about us.

We were still reloading the dump truck. When Foxface went into the office for a few minutes, I entered the truck cab to see his photocopied log sheets. The records showed that the foundation had grossed nearly $1,000 the previous day; the previous week, it had grossed $6,900. I shoved records down my pants. I feared the papers would crinkle and I'd be busted, so I claimed a need to hit the restroom. I ran to the bunkhouse and stashed the paperwork from the truck under the sheets in the closet, with the papers I'd gotten from the front office the previous night.

When the truck was refilled, we were told to go to the mess hall. Everyone was hungry and tired. No one noticed when Michael and I fell back and ducked into the bunkhouse. I looked out the window. The guard and Foxface went in to eat. For the first time, the compound was empty of people. It was our chance. We grabbed our packs from the closet and rushed out the door.

"Shit, I don't even have one picture," Michael said.

"Fuck it! Let's go!" I urged.

We ran to the south entrance and out to the street.

"We made it!" Michael exclaimed.

A block away, I had the horrible realization that I'd forgotten the paperwork stuffed under the sheets.

"You asshole!" Michael said.

I insisted on going back for the papers.

"You asshole!"

"Hang here!" I barked. Michael secreted himself in some bushes while I ran back to the entrance. The compound was quiet. I rushed into the bunkhouse and grabbed the papers. At the door, I peeked out: the coast was clear. I broke for the exit.

"HEY YOU! GET BACK HERE!"

Foxface! He'd emerged from the mess hall. I ran harder.

"Runner! Runner!" Foxface screamed. "We got a runner!"

I heard trucks firing up as I neared Michael in the bushes. I shouted, "We're fucked!"

He was already at my side by the time I made the bushes.

It was a poor part of town. People sitting on a porch laughed hysterically in a manner that revealed this was not the first time they'd witnessed runners. We ducked down an alley and headed toward the main road and its entry ramps to the interstate.

Luck held, and the foundation's trucks didn't head down the alley. We were behind a White Castle hamburger joint and figured that we could hide inside its dumpster. Incredibly, a taxi was in line at the drive-through lane. We ran up and jumped in either side, both doors slamming shut at the same moment, unable to believe our luck. We crouched low.

"I'm not on duty," the cabbie said.

"Twenty bucks, we'll give you twenty bucks, just take us five minutes away," I pleaded.

"Well, let me get my dinner."

The car smelled of whiskey. The cabbie was drunk out of his mind, prattling in booze talk about nothing. We nodded and laughed at his empty words to humor him. As we pulled out into traffic after the cabbie got his burgers, the two-way radio crackled.

"Car 38! You call us now! You're in trouble! We're calling the police! We're reporting your car stolen!"

I asked who the dispatcher was talking about.

"Me," said the driver. He launched into a tale about how he hated his bosses, telling us that he'd checked out the cab that morning, started drinking, and hadn't answered the dispatcher all day.

We implored him to take us to the Greyhound station. He agreed but couldn't quite find it. At one point, we ended up out in the country, way beyond the suburbs. He occasionally swigged from a bottle of whiskey. Two hours after we jumped in the cab, he finally got us to the bus station. In the end, he took only $15. We caught a midnight Grey-dog back to Houston.

We reclaimed Das Boot and drove toward the foundation the next day. We had a long sleep in an interstate rest area.

Michael wanted a picture.

We stopped a few miles from the foundation to prepare. Michael got in the back seat with his camera, driver's side window rolled down. I put on mirror sunglasses. The plan was to drive through the center of the compound when the trucks came back for the evening, where Michael would shoot as many pictures as he could before I sped us out the exit.

"When I say go, I mean GO!" Michael said. We drove to the entrance. The compound was filled with men and trucks. It was make-work time for the weasels.

I drove down the center lane, then stopped. Foxface was talking to a man I recognized as the camp owner, based on pictures in the office. Michael's Nikon motor drive whirred behind me.

Foxface looked at us, his eyes indicating a slow realization. The camp owner started toward the car.

"Can I help you!" he said, not as a question but as a demand. "Can I help you! Can I FUCKING help you!"

The camp owner, a big man, shirtless, was at a full-tilt run. He lunged through the air at Michael's face. I'd already hit the gas, as Michael screamed, *"GO! GO!*

GO!" The owner's hands scraped along the fender, which was greasy with tuna fish oil from cans we'd opened and drained to eat for dinners while driving. Gravel sprayed as I raced to the exit. I stopped, briefly, couldn't resist—I flipped the bird. Then I burned out, got us on the interstate. We headed west.

POSTSCRIPT

The stories of Youngstown, Sam, and the Alexanders appeared, in a different form, in our book Journey to Nowhere. *But the story of Jay and the Texas work camp has never before been told. I was a young writer at the time and didn't know what I had; when space grew tight in that early book, the chapter was omitted. Now, with the perspective gained after nearly three decades, I believe that this experience may have been the craziest we had in all those years, and the most revealing about what losing a job and a home, falling out of the middle class, can do to a human being. Sam had surely sunk into despair the night we first met him. And the Alexander family had hit a low. But neither Sam nor the Alexanders represent true bottom. Jay does.*

In the late 1990s, I was in Texas on an assignment for Mother Jones *magazine, in the same city as the foundation. I wondered what the group had been up to lately. I already knew that the Booze Cruiser was no longer working to pick up guys in Houston.*

One afternoon, I drove the interstate and got off at the exit. The White Castle, where the drunken cabbie had reluctantly allowed us to become his passengers, was now some other business.

I turned the corner. My anger grew. I had an intense flashback memory. I neared the compound, intending to go into the office to confront the owner. Who the hell did he think he was to treat men that way? This would be one more way to bring some kind of resolution to my 1980s.

The compound was abandoned. The buildings were boarded up.

Back at my hotel, I looked in the phone book and discovered a number for the foundation. There was no address. I rang. A man picked up and answered, using the name of the organization.

"I'd like to donate something to the foundation," I said. I asked for their address so I could stop by.

Click. The man hung up without saying anything.

PART 2 **THE JOURNEY CONTINUES** THE 1990s

Glass-Steagall is no longer appropriate for the economy in which we live. It worked pretty well for the industrial economy . . . and today what we are doing is modernizing the financial services industry, tearing down these antiquated laws and granting banks significant new authority.

—Bill Clinton, November 12, 1999, at the signing ceremony for a bill abolishing the Glass-Steagall Act of 1933, which had helped prevent speculation in part by making it illegal for bank holding companies to own other financial companies

In the 1930s, at the trough of the Depression, when Glass-Steagall became law, it was believed that government was the answer. It was believed that stability and growth came from government overriding the functioning of free markets. We are here today to repeal Glass-Steagall because we have learned that government is not the answer. We have learned that freedom and competition are the answers.

—Republican senator Phil Gramm of Texas, the sponsor of the bill, to applause, November 12, 1999

With this bill, the American financial system takes a major step forward towards the 21st century, one that will benefit American consumers, business, and the national economy for many years to come.

—Treasury secretary Lawrence H. Summers, November 12, 1999

. . . Well my daddy come on the Ohio works
When he come home from World War Two
Now the yard's just scrap and rubble
He said "Them big boys did what Hitler couldn't do."
The mills they built the tanks and bombs
That won this country's wars
We sent our sons to Korea and Vietnam
Now we're wondering what they were dyin' for.
Here in Youngstown
Here in Youngstown
My sweet Jenny, I'm sinking down
Here darlin' in Youngstown . . .
When I die I don't want no part of heaven
I would not do heaven's work well
I pray the devil comes and takes me
To stand in the fiery furnaces of hell.

—Bruce Springsteen, 1995, partial lyrics of "Youngstown," a song that channels Joe Marshall Sr., inspired by *Journey to Nowhere*

1992 Wal-Mart employed 380,000 workers in the United States.

1992 General Motors employed 362,000 workers in the United States.

1990 It took $260 million to make the Forbes 400 list of the richest Americans; in 1995, it took $340 million.

1989 The average CEO in the United States was paid 70.5 times what the average worker earned, according to the Economic Policy Institute.

Michael and I entered the onetime Western Pacific rail yard in Sacramento. It was October 20, 1995, thirteen years after we had first jumped on a train here. We walked the tracks, climbed atop railcars, sat in the shadow of the icehouse. It was a reunion: we had not seen each other or talked by phone very much for a few years. We'd grown a bit estranged because our 1980s had been so fierce—each of us was a reminder to the other of troubled times. In the 1980s, we'd covered the war in El Salvador, where we'd had some bad experiences, and the revolution in the Philippines, among a slew of other intense projects. We had also produced two more books on American poverty. After *Journey to Nowhere,* we had spent three years commuting to Alabama to discover the fate, a half century later, of the sharecroppers profiled during the Great Depression in *Let Us Now Praise Famous Men,* by James Agee and Walker Evans. That work resulted in the publication of *And Their Children After Them.* Our final book from that decade was *The Last Great American Hobo,* about a Great Depression–era hobo named Montana Blackie, the men of his camp, and our reflections on poverty after being immersed in the subject for so many years.

Michael was now at the *Washington Post;* he'd come to Sacramento for a conference. I was teaching at Stanford University, hiding from the world on the quiet campus.

We ended the day in the hobo jungle on the Sacramento River, where Blackie once had his shack. At sunset, we drank beer and unloaded about *Journey to Nowhere,* the hardest part of our 1980s. Out tumbled a flurry of words about the killing of No Thumbs; speculation about what had since happened to Sam, the Alexander family, the others; amazement that we hadn't died riding trains.

"We fucking survived," I said.

Michael had learned that day that his wife was pregnant with their first child. Before he headed back east, he was going to take a week off to photograph landmarks from his damaged youth, including the place where his mother died in Los Angeles, to create a photo/word journal of his life for Sophia, the unborn child.

A glimpse into our state of mind comes from a response I'd mailed just weeks before, on September 6, 1995, to an editor at Gale Research Inc., the publishers of *Contemporary Authors.* The editor had asked for comment about how we had covered American poverty and the working class in our trilogy of books. I concluded, in part, by writing these words:

> . . . As reviewer Katherine Dieckmann of the *Village Voice* said so aptly of our *And Their Children After Them,* any attempt to understand poverty by a member of the

> upper class is in essence a "Sullivanesque" experience. She was referring to Preston Sturges's classic 1941 film *Sullivan's Travels,* about a rich man who sets out to learn about poverty, which turned into a fool's mission. . . . Perhaps one can never understand. All I know is that each book took a chunk out of our lives. One sets out to educate Americans about poverty in the hope that in some small way conditions will be changed. Then comes the realization that Americans don't seem to care. This, along with the horror of the lives one documents, takes a toll. I can't speak for Michael, but I plan to never again write a non-fiction book about poverty.

We were in retreat from our 1980s, trying to move on with our lives. Both of us reject the psychobabble word "closure." We certainly didn't have it in the hobo jungle that evening. But our conversation was cathartic.

I drove the two hours back to Stanford. When I awoke at 10:00 A.M. the next morning, there was a message on my answering machine. I hit play and heard the voice of a woman who said she worked for Bruce Springsteen: he wanted to meet with us in one week, when he performed at Neil Young's Bridge School Benefit Concert. Surely Michael was pulling a joke.

I called the number. It was no prank. The woman explained that Springsteen had been inspired by *Journey to Nowhere* to write some songs—exactly how many, I was not told at that point—for his forthcoming release, *The Ghost of Tom Joad.*

I phoned Michael at his Sacramento hotel. When I finally got him to believe me, he rearranged his schedule. On October 28, we went to the Shoreline Amphitheater in Mountain View, not far from where I lived.

In Cleveland during the mid-1970s, WMMS-FM played "Born to Run" at 6:00 each Friday afternoon. The station, as I recall, had a "leaked" preofficial release copy. The deejays extolled Springsteen as the blue-collar troubadour. I listened to "Born to Run" at high volume, usually on my way to getting drunk after finishing my sixty-hour week operating a lathe at Plastic Fabrication Inc. I resented the station's pandering to what it thought a blue-collar guy like me wanted to hear. I didn't want to be reminded that I was blue collar. I was a regular at the Agora nightclub downtown, but I had never made the effort to drive my motorcycle there when Springsteen played for a $4.50 cover charge.

My outlook changed after moving to California. Some of Springsteen's songs, such as "Seeds," were exactly what I was writing about. No one else "commercial" sang about these people. I was now a fan. I wrangled an assignment from the newspaper to cover the "Born in the USA" tour when Springsteen and the E Street Band played the Oakland Coliseum on September 18, 1985.

I had no special access for that tour and didn't want it. I'm uncomfortable around anything related to celebrity. I drove hours early to Oakland and spent time with tailgating fans in the Coliseum parking lot. I continued reporting in the nosebleed seats with those fans when the concert began. Springsteen was a pin dot on stage.

At the Shoreline Amphitheater, we met Springsteen's managers, Barbara Carr and Jon Landau. We had dinner with Wavy Gravy, who was the emcee for the night; he had emceed the 1969 Woodstock festival. Michael had long before spent a night in a jail cell with Wavy, when Michael, photographing a protest at the Diablo Canyon nuclear power plant, got caught up in the crowd as cops arrested Wavy and other activists. But Wavy didn't remember that.

Jon and Barbara sent us out into the audience to hear Springsteen perform. After the concert, we hurried backstage. Neil Young was slapping Springsteen on the back. Bruce saw us, shouted our names. A door opened behind me. A woman flew out and nearly knocked me over. It was Chrissie Hynde of the Pretenders, who was next up on stage.

Bruce invited us into his dressing room. The door closed.

"So how the fuck did you hear about our book?" I asked, in the first words out of my mouth.

"I bought it when it came out," Bruce said. I didn't think to ask exactly which songs had come from our book. (Weeks later, we learned that two tracks on *The Ghost of Tom Joad* had been inspired by the book: "Youngstown," in part about the Marshall family; and "The New Timer," in part about No Thumbs and his murder. No Thumbs is "Frank" in the latter song.)

Bruce offered whiskey. He wondered aloud about the fact that *Journey to Nowhere* was long out of print. I asked him if he'd be willing to write an introduction so that we might try to get the book re-released.

"Sure," he said.

We spent another half hour with Bruce and then talked with Terry Magovern, his assistant.

Michael and I drove home to my rented condo on the Stanford campus and started talking. We couldn't simply reissue the book, we agreed—we had to update it. Who would we see? Just a week earlier in the hobo jungle, we had shuddered about the thought of again meeting Sam—would it feel like visiting a graveyard ghost, akin to Dickens's Marley seeking out the chain-rattling specter rather than the other way around? You just don't voluntarily go to that place.

We decided against trying to find Sam, just a dozen years after we had ridden the trains with him. I did try to find the Alexanders but hit dead-ends. I was secretly relieved by this failure; the pain we had encountered and shared in those days was still fresh.

We flew to Cleveland on November 17, 1995, and began a trip that was fast and furious because of our work schedules. Despite what I'd written for *Contemporary Authors,* Bruce got us back on the story.

7 WAITING FOR AN EXPLOSION

Here are a few scenes of the America that we found in late 1995, on that eleven-day, one-way road trip between Youngstown, Ohio, and California. For many, the shock of the 1982 recession had now become a permanent state of being. Millions lived in the shadows. The working homeless had become common: we found them everywhere.

The Chicago school of economic theory dominated political and economic discourse. This libertarian ideology, which rejects many of the lessons learned from dealing with the fiscal crisis that followed the 1929 crash, was shaped by Professor Milton Friedman at the University of Chicago. Friedman attacked John Maynard Keynes, the preeminent economic theorist of the 1930s, who maintained that government had to intervene to help the economy. Friedman and his libertarian disciples—the "freshwater" economists, as opposed to the liberal "saltwater" economists on the coasts—believed that the markets were best left to take care of themselves. If jobs were shipped overseas, no matter. The markets were wiser than any government intervention. President Ronald Reagan embraced these free-market ideas, and Friedman's influence continued into Bill Clinton's terms in office.

RAGE

Youngstown was even more devastated than we had found it in the early 1980s. Mile-long meadows, studded with 20-foot trees, stretched where the dead hulks of steel mills once stood. Whole city blocks were fields and forest.

WCI Steel Inc., in Warren, north of Youngstown, was the last full-service ore-to-finished-steel mill in the Mahoning Valley. There had been a labor dispute not long before we arrived. Dr. John Russo at Youngstown State University said workers feared that the company was going to be sold in a corporate maneuver, risking their union jobs and pensions. They wanted a succession agreement, which would have maintained the United Steelworkers as their bargaining agent in the event of a sale, and they also wanted an improved pension plan. John explained that this would have made the company less desirable because a buyer would not have been able to hire a lower-paid, nonunion workforce and would have been liable for the pension plan.

To the workers, it was a lockout. The company called it a strike and hired professional strikebreakers. The workers called them "goons."

Many of the seventeen hundred union members were refugees from the closed Youngstown mills. All had friends who had been victimized by the shutdowns.

Gerald Hartshorn, who'd been at Youngstown Sheet and Tube, said one guy put a .357 in his mouth and pulled the trigger. Another, Timmy, lost his mind. "He hasn't worked a day since 1977," said Gerald, referring to the year when that mill shut. "He said fuck it. I met him in a bar not long ago. He has a big bushy beard, and he wears these headphones that play loud music. There isn't a thing he says you can understand. He was talking about computers and God and life after death."

The line between Timmy and the locked-out workers was very thin. They were determined to fight. Workers shot out lights. Dozens of car windows were smashed with rocks and clubs when goons crossed the picket line. A worker was run over by a goon. A goon was shot. Homemade bombs were thrown. Local merchants backed the steelworkers. Many cops looked the other way when the cars of the outside replacements were stoned. The town was collectively saying to hell with the Wall Street Big Boys who had ruined so many lives elsewhere.

We met with workers and heard what they had cried out, what had been shouted during the action: *Fuck you! You will not take our jobs! We will kill you! Someone is going to die tonight!*

After fifty-four days, the company caved. John believed that the union members would have dynamited the blast furnace, destroying the heart of the mill, had they lost. "Blowing it up would be better than going through that again," said one worker of the previous plant closings.

It was a stunning action in an era when labor, by and large, didn't fight. Yet the national media gave the lockout only cursory coverage. My colleagues in the press, their collars so white, ignored the story of these workers.

John predicted that white-collar workers would eventually learn what the steelworkers in Youngstown already knew.

Anger, deep and bitter, remained. Could it be channeled into politics? John looked at history and saw a dire lesson.

"There's a lot of anger in working people," he said. "It's not unlike the anger in prewar Germany and prewar Italy." But in America's Great Depression, Franklin Roosevelt and the New Deal came along. John pointed out that U.S. capitalists allowed themselves to be saved by FDR, because communism was then seen as a credible threat. "There had been the Bolshevik revolution fifteen years earlier,"

John noted. Today, however, there was no threat from the left. Capitalism had nothing to worry about.

John feared that the anger would turn toward right-wing hate. "There is the old famous line by the CP: the worse it gets, the better it gets," John said, mentioning the Communist Party's belief that bad times recruited members. "Now the reality is that the worse it gets, the worse it gets."

Perhaps a special politician could tap this wrath, a latter-day Roosevelt. Would he or she come along?

During our visit to the town of Warren, someone slipped us a pipe bomb made by one of the steelworkers. It was painted black and felt cold to the touch.

We placed the bomb in the trunk of our car and drove west.

THANKSGIVING DAY

A babbling man with missing teeth sat in a village of shacks in sight of the skyscrapers of Houston.

Every other sentence was nonsense. Amid gibberish, he said he once was a trucker who hauled steel in Youngstown. His grandfather had worked for Youngstown Sheet and Tube. I showed him a copy of *Journey to Nowhere,* and he suddenly became lucid when he saw the pictures of the dead mills. He'd left after the collapse and worked in a Galveston shipyard. When that job ended, he went downhill.

"I've been fooling with this bullshit eight, ten years," he said about his life on the street. He then went off on some incomprehensible tangent, finishing with a cackle. He was, to paraphrase Maxim Gorky, a creature that once was a man.

If we'd met this man years ago, he would have been an example of the newly homeless, recently arrived on the street. Now he was among the wasted old guard homeless, someone we would have ignored back in 1983, when we were seeking out the homeless who were more sympathetic. We went out of our way in those days to avoid writing about people like that man, in large part because of public enmity toward the homeless. I saw this animosity when I wrote stories about them for the newspaper and watched the hate letters fill my mail slot; I also had one editor who derisively called me the "bum writer." We were young and didn't know how to deal with the complex story.

I knew so much more now. What separated this man from the workers of the Warren steel mill? Not much—just a dozen years. The cackling man revealed to me the arc of descent a human being can travel. I couldn't stop thinking about him as we drove on, heading west. His downfall aptly fit the title of our first book: he truly had gone on a journey to nowhere.

THE VOLUNTARY HOMELESS

On the Nevada side of the Colorado River, in the gambling city of Laughlin, was the Colorado Belle, a mock riverboat. A few players emerged from dark game rooms to stand on deck, blinking at the early morning sun and staring at a jungle of tamarisk, an invasive shrub, on the Arizona shore. Hidden in the brush, 600 feet distant, were Frances, forty-six, and Frank, forty-four. The couple had just finished a late-night shift, spent serving those gamblers. Frances and Frank lived in a homemade hut.

Frank was greeted by three barking pets—John Dog, Trapper, and Springer—as he arrived home from work. He pulled off his uniform. The shack had a calendar, a mural, a bed.

"We've been two years in coming here," said Frank. Frances makes just over five bucks an hour, and he earns just over six. When they lived in an apartment, they could pay for rent and groceries but nothing else, and the struggle seemed futile. So two months ago, the couple became homeless voluntarily.

For the first time in years, they saved money and now had $580 in the bank. Their dream was to save enough to buy a used $1,400 trailer. A trailer space rented for $250 a month, half the cost of an apartment.

"Only you can make the sacrifice if you want to get something," said Frank. "I'm going to have something. I'm not going to give it to rent. There's no middle class. Either you're rich or you're going to be poor."

Frances said they sleep all day, awakening at dark to go to work. When they come home in the morning, they fall into bed. They have allowed themselves one luxury: occasionally they spring for a $14 room in a gambling hotel, to take a break from life in the shack.

"Eventually, when our dream comes true," said Frances, patting the wall of the shack, "we'll leave this for somebody else. People can survive, no matter."

THE EXPLOSION

A section of Route 66, in California's Mojave Desert.

The pavement was cracked, flanked by occasional burned-out gas stations and abandoned motels. We ignored a ROAD CLOSED sign at a washed-out bridge, driving into a dry gulch to circumvent it. The road beyond was utterly empty.

Creosote bushes raced past. Our eyes were on the faded center stripe that vanished into the silver ribbon reaching to the horizon. Far down this line there materialized a lone man at the road's edge. As he grew larger, we saw he was on crutches.

The West is full of men wandering desolate roads 100 miles from anywhere. But we'd never seen anything like this. We stopped.

Crutches clicked against the pavement, followed by the sound of his dragging right foot, which was a prosthesis. He advanced about 18 inches with each click and drag. Over his shoulder was a bindle made of an army blanket, with the handle of a shovel erupting from an opening. His head was nearly a globe, and his frame was frightfully gaunt.

I offered grape juice and a box of granola bars.

"It is much appreciated," George said. "I haven't eaten in four days. You are very kind."

I gave him all the rest of our food and a twenty-dollar bill. "Buy food when you get to Needles," I said. Days earlier, George told us, he had dived into a dumpster for scraps back near the interstate. "I really hate doing that, but I was hungry." The owner of the restaurant ran him off.

George was cheerful. He didn't get to talk with many people. I asked if he was hitchhiking. He shrugged at so foolish a question.

"No one stops. I don't even try."

He said he set out on the road in 1982. I didn't care to ask why. I guess this was because I was thinking in that moment as a human being, not as a journalist. The questions didn't seem important in the face of his hunger. He was here in the desert, and that was what mattered now. He volunteered that he had once hopped freights, but in 1989, while he was on a train in the mountains of Montana, a load of steel on the flatcar shifted, and his leg was pinned. He was taken by helicopter to a Salt Lake City hospital. "They did a good job. Took it off below the knee."

He gave up being a hobo. Now he walks. George had been prospecting for gold on California's Feather River. He'd heard there was better placer mining near Flagstaff, Arizona, and so he left on one foot and crutches in September. It was almost December. Two days earlier, he'd slept near Amboy, California, 11 miles behind. The next arguable patch of civilization was in Needles, nine walking days ahead at his rate of progress. It would take him one month to reach Flagstaff.

He knew how to survive. When camped on the Feather River, he ate wild onions and other flora. He never stayed at rescue missions. George had flung himself beyond the outer orbit of being an Edge Man. He wanted nothing to do with society: he lived not on the margins but utterly apart from this country that we call the United States of America.

He was headed east. We were driving west, so there was no giving him a lift. We bid him farewell. George crutched off into the creosote to set up a camp.

We turned the car down a dirt track. At the end were discarded appliances. We took the steelworker's bomb out of the trunk and placed it inside a water heater. We weren't sure of the fuse, so, to be safe, we lit a cigarette and poked it over the wick. It would take the cigarette at least five minutes to burn down. We ran over the crest of a hill and waited. We waited a long time. Just as we thought it might be a dud, there was a satisfying *BLAM!*

We ran to the hilltop in time to see a cloud of smoke wafting toward Route 66, Steinbeck's "Mother Road." The smoke quickly dissipated. There was silence, brittle and absolute and troubling. We wished for another bomb, another explosion.

8 WHEN BRUCE MET JENNY

As the reissue of *Journey to Nowhere* neared, Michael talked with Bruce Springsteen by phone and asked if the *Ghost of Tom Joad* tour would include Youngstown. Soon after, we heard that Bruce was booked there for a performance on January 12, 1996.

At the same time, a *CBS Morning News* producer had phoned me about doing a story on the book and had suggested that we meet in Youngstown. Bruce's publicity people had turned her down for an interview, yet she wanted us in Youngstown anyway. I was teaching the day of the concert, but I caught a red-eye to meet up with the CBS crew and Michael, arriving the day after Bruce was scheduled to leave.

A huge snowfall hit. It was a miracle that my plane landed on time in Cleveland. I drove to Youngstown and met the CBS crew at the city's steel museum, where I was surprised to run into Terry Magovern. Bruce had stayed on an extra day, Terry said, because he wanted to go inside the ruins of the Jeanette blast furnace, the "Jenny" in the song "Youngstown."

Bruce came up to us. I told him that the company that owned the site had been arresting trespassers. We'd have to sneak in, and it would be risky.

"Bruce, they especially would want to arrest you," I said. "They'll want to make a point."

"Let's go," Bruce said.

Professor John Russo had a plan. After loaning Bruce some heavy boots, he drove Bruce, Michael, and me down a back road where the guards would have less chance of seeing us. Then he sped off.

The Jenny, across a half mile of meadow knee-deep in snow, was a rusting black hulk, in sharp contrast to the world of white. A few days before Bruce's show, someone had climbed the rotting stairs to Jenny's top, at great risk of bodily injury, to place an American flag, which flew in the frigid air. It was bitterly cold. Bruce wore a porkpie hat like the one in a picture accompanying the liner notes to the three-album *Live/1975–1985: Bruce Springsteen and the E Street Band.* We waded into the snow, angling down a steep hill to an abandoned building so that we'd remain unseen. I went first, testing the way. I fell and made a face plant in the snow.

"Watch out for that rock, Dale," Michael said, mocking my fall.

"I was just testing to see if it was there."

A second later, Michael began falling. Before he went all the way, Bruce grabbed him and pulled him up. (Michael said later he was "strong as an ox.")

The going was rough. We ended up back on the railroad tracks, where I didn't want us to be. We were exposed to the guard shack for a few minutes.

"If we get arrested, I'll just say you two guys said it was okay," Bruce replied as a joke, after I expressed worry.

Bruce and Michael tried walking the rail.

"Slippery as shit!" Bruce exclaimed.

We struggled along, finally reaching the slag pit near the dead blast furnace. We fell silent, slowly approaching its base. This is the furnace that stands behind Ken Platt and his son on the cover of this book. I stared dumbly, my head filled with troubling memories of the time this place of the dead had been our refuge from the woes of the living.

There was a low-pitched squeaking sound. My eyes rose at the same time as the others' did: 20 feet over our heads was a massive "mobile." From a steel cross member hung a ghost steelworker—a life-size "man" made of tightly wound rusted wire, complete with arms and legs, cloaked in a silver asbestos hot-metal suit. He held a giant wrench. I'd heard guerilla artists were sneaking in and creating works like this out of materials found amid the ruins. The sculpture spun in the 10-degree air; the wire that suspended it made the sound.

We spoke in hushed tones, and not just because we feared the guards—it would have been sacrilege to talk normally. We went deeper into the ruins. Just as Michael and I had done years earlier, we all split up, each lost in our own personal wilderness. I wondered what was on Bruce's mind. The previous night, he'd met the Marshall family. It's difficult for me to talk with someone I've written about, and I can only imagine what Bruce felt. Do we really get the story right? I know that the Marshalls thought he did. It was surreal that we were back in these ruins, with or without Bruce. I trembled from memory.

We eventually reconvened in a room behind the blast furnace heaters. Now it was just three guys having fun. We were like boys sneaking around and getting away with something. We talked for an hour about the state of America, politics, our feelings. We'd never talked like this in the times we'd met since Neil Young's Bridge Benefit Concert.

I brought up *The Grapes of Wrath,* the scene of the house being knocked off kilter by the tractor, and the anger that Steinbeck captured in that part of the novel. Looking around at the dead mill, I asked: "Where does this anger go today? Who do you blame?" I wondered why no politician was coming forward to take control of the debate and lead America.

Bruce asked whether people really believed the Republicans. If they do, he said, it's scary.

"The Republicans have been setting the tone for the debate," Bruce said. "It's 'Those people are doing this, doing that.'" He wondered why the Democrats weren't explaining how the Republicans were hurting America by fostering this attitude, which leads to polarization.

"Why don't people know?" Bruce asked. "I have to admit it, I was twenty-eight before I read a history book."

Now he reads a lot, Bruce told us, some of the same authors I had recently been reading—William Greider, Haynes Johnson, and others.

Bruce talked about how isolated Americans are from each other. All three of us grew excited as we spoke. Michael saw us becoming a "niche" nation: he recalled how American mass culture once had been more universal, invoking as one example Ed Sullivan's TV show with its Lithuanian plate juggler, black singers, and the rest. Now we have BET, the Oxygen network, and so on—segmented, compartmentalized. I mentioned the book *The Geography of Nowhere,* by James Howard Kunstler, who shows how we are kept separate from each other by the design of modern America. I told Michael and Bruce about my research for my latest book, *The Coming White Minority,* in part about the walling in of rich Californians and how we are becoming more and more separated by class differences.

Bruce said this "niching" has gone on in all parts of society: housing, movies, music.

"That's the problem: we're getting more and more isolated, and we have more ways to be isolated," Bruce said, as a train carrying steel pipe rumbled past.

"Almost no commercial stations play your new music anymore," I noted. His music was relegated to "oldies" stations.

"Yeah," Bruce agreed, adding that in New York City there were no commercial stations that played his new material. He grinned: "I'm not in the mainstream anymore.

"There are a lot of twenty-some-year-olds at the shows," he added, "so they're getting it somehow."

Bruce worried about Asbury Park, New Jersey. "It's gone down," he said. I expressed similar concern about my native Cleveland. We lamented what was happening to the cities and to working people. People were hurting worse than ever, and it was supposed to be good times. What was wrong? Why didn't Americans of means care about their fellow citizens?

Bruce looked at us gravely and said we had to do something.

What could we do? It was the question Michael and I had always asked each other.

Bruce mulled this over for a bit and then wisely pointed out that all we had was our art—music, writing, taking pictures. What we did was the best thing we could do. We just had to keep putting it out there.

Up to that point at the Jenny furnace, I had never truly felt at ease around Bruce because of my discomfort with celebrity. But that day he was not a big rock star. He was just a guy standing in a dead steel mill wondering and worrying about the future of the United States of America, a guy creating art to help make us understand and ask questions about what that future might be like.

We left the mill and trudged back through the snow as fast as possible, scarcely able to believe our luck at not being busted. John Russo met us at an appointed hour with two cups of steaming hot coffee for Michael and me, tea with honey for Bruce.

Back at the steel museum, Bruce explained the chord structure of the title track on *Ghost* to Michael and then asked about the CBS camera crew outside. Michael told Bruce that they were doing a story on *Journey to Nowhere;* Bruce wasn't aware that his publicity people had rejected an interview request.

"It's for the book?" Bruce asked.

He went out to talk on camera. The story aired long for an American television piece.

I realized then, and even more so now as I write these words years later, that Bruce was right about putting things out there. When we first sold *Journey to Nowhere* in early 1983, it was a miracle that we convinced a major publisher to buy the book—the book business was already becoming much more corporate. We'd never be able to sell it to a big publishing house today. At the time, I was naïve and foolishly thought the book might make money. Yet despite all odds, it more or less broke even.

The book had its run, got remaindered, and had long been out of print. It had started to feel like bones buried in the earth. Just a few weeks before Bruce contacted us, I had told my students at Stanford University that you never know who reads your work and what impact it has. Suddenly, because of Bruce, *Journey to Nowhere* came back to life, like Jason in those *Friday the Thirteenth* movies. It punched off the coffin lid and dug out through the dirt.

When Bruce later did the rock version of "Youngstown" with the E Street Band, recorded on the *Live in New York City* release, it appealed to a much wider audience. The song had moved beyond what I'd written in *Journey;* most listeners certainly don't know the genesis of the material. Some friends thought this would bother me, that our work had been subsumed into Bruce's, but quite the contrary.

I'm reminded of the song "Bridges," by the late hobo folk singer Utah Phillips, whom I once interviewed in Nevada City, California, where he lived. In the song, Utah sings, in part,

> Time is an enormous long river
> And I'm standing in it
> Just as you're standing in it
> My elders were the tributaries
> And everything they thought and every struggle they went through
> And everything they gave their lives to
> And every song they created
> And every poem that they laid down
> Flows down to me . . .
>
> And I can reach down into that river and take out what I need
> To get through this world
> Bridges
> From my time to your time
>
> As my elders from their time to my time
> And we'll put into the river
> And we let it go
> And it flows away from us, and away from us
> 'Til it no longer has our name, our identity
> It has its own utility, its own use
> And people will take what they need to make it part of their lives

A piece of our first book, via the song "Youngstown," is now part of the river. Because of Bruce, our message in the original *Journey* has reached millions of people it otherwise wouldn't have touched. Steinbeck's *Grapes of Wrath,* as well as works by other authors and photographers, have shaped our approach. In turn, someone might listen to "Youngstown" and be inspired, raising the collective consciousness.

That's what Bruce was talking about that frigid day in the ruins. You do "art" and then let it go into the river. If you are doing it for the right reason and are very, very lucky, the work gets picked up downstream. It becomes a continuation of a story that must be told, a voice speaking over the decades and centuries.

PART 3 **A NATION GROWS HUNGRIER** 2000

Market history . . . rests on the side of long-term investors. Recently, in my book *Dow 40,000: Strategies for Profiting from the Greatest Bull Market in History,* I based my predictions for the year 2016 on an annual growth of nine percent, conservative considering that the Dow's average annual growth for the past 75 years has been 11 percent. Others have written that the Dow will reach 100,000 by 2020, or even that the Dow currently should be at 36,000 based on an innovative method of valuing stocks. No matter the method, the message remains the same—all signs point to a continually rising market.

—David Elias, March 1, 2000, president and chief investment officer of Elias Asset Management and a regular guest on CNN's *Moneyline* and *Business Day, CNNfn,* CNBC, and PBS's *Nightly Business Report*

Labor unions are nothing but blood-sucking parasites living off the productive labor of people who work for a living.

—John Tate, a former Wal-Mart executive vice president and board member, at a 2004 meeting of Wal-Mart managers, shaking his fist as he spoke of his life's work—keeping unions out of the company—while hundreds of managers clapped and roared with approval

For years, it was considered shameful to take out a second mortgage: it meant you were in financial trouble. In the 1980s, Charles Humm, a marketing guru at Merrill Lynch Credit Corporation, set out to encourage these loans after the government changed the banking regulations to make it easier for big banks to engage in such lending. By 1999, the idea had

gone viral. Fallon Worldwide, an advertising agency, sold Citicorp (Citigroup) executives on an ad campaign titled "Live Richly," on which the bank spent $1 billion between 2001 and 2006. The *New York Times* quoted a former Citi executive who said that by rebranding second mortgages as "equity access," it made them sound "more innocent." Some ad slogans from Citi's "Live Richly" campaign:

"There's Got to Be at Least $25,000 Hidden in Your House—We Can Help You Find It"
"Play as You Go"
"Open a Cravings Account"

In the early 1980s, the value of outstanding second mortgages in the United States was $1 billion. By 2008, it would reach $1 trillion. In the 1980s, Americans owned 70 percent of their homes. By 2008, Americans would own less than 50 percent of their homes.

In 2004, the average hourly wage of a Wal-Mart worker was $9.70, compared with an average wage of $14.01 for all large retail, according to a study by the University of California's Center for Labor Research and Education.

In 2004, five family members of the late Sam Walton, Wal-Mart's founder—his widow, Helen, and their four children—tied for fourth place on the Forbes 400 list of richest Americans. Their combined worth: $90 billion.

2000 Wal-Mart employed 885,000 workers in the United States.

2000 General Motors employed 195,374 workers in the United States.

2000 It took $725 million to make the Forbes 400 list of the richest Americans.

2000 The average CEO in the United States was paid 298.8 times what the average worker earned, according to the Economic Policy Institute.

9 HUNGER IN THE HOMES

It was a boom time. Dot-com start-ups were the darlings of Wall Street. The federal budget was balanced. The illusion of wealth was pervasive. Early in 2000, the bubble in high tech was going strong, and many people were living beyond their means off second mortgages and credit cards. When I was a kid, my mother and father had a term for people who spent money they didn't have: "fifty-cent millionaires."

It was a curious time to get a call from Frank Lalli, who had taken over as editor of *George* magazine after the death of John Kennedy Jr. Michael and I had a reputation for covering the working class, he said, and he wanted a story that would show the falsity of America's illusion of wealth.

"I want to run twenty-four open pages on child poverty in the backyards of George Bush and Al Gore," Frank told me. Twenty-four pages meant some twelve thousand words and a lot of pictures, an unheard-of amount of space in a major American magazine at the millennium, especially for such an important and yet dark topic. (It turned out that we were one of the last stories to appear in the magazine: its corporate owner cut back, and Frank was able to run only thirteen pages of our work, still an amazing amount of space, a few months before the magazine was killed.)

The piece would be published before the 2000 presidential election. Our job was to humanize some stunning numbers in an election year that followed nearly a decade of unparalleled economic expansion. America had never been richer—on paper.

But the reality was that 13.5 million American children were living in poverty, according to the Children's Defense Fund. That was one out of every five kids. And 74 percent of their parents worked—they didn't take welfare. Many held down two or even three jobs, but the wages weren't enough to bring their children out of poverty or protect them from hunger.

Wages were stagnant or falling. The federal minimum wage was $5.15 an hour, and studies showed it should have been closer to $10 an hour in order to keep pace with inflation.

Even twice the minimum wage wasn't sufficient to pay rent in many places. Perversely, the booming dot-com economy had actually hurt America's invisible children, causing rents to skyrocket even in areas far away from high-tech jobs. (We found lofty rents for shacks and rotting trailers in Appalachia.) Some parents forked out what they made at one job entirely on rent. A study by the U.S. Department of Housing and Urban Development found that a record 5.4 million households paid half or more of their income for rent or lived in "severely distressed housing." In Austin, Texas, a 1,000-square-foot apartment went for $950, almost double the $500 it had cost in 1990—without a commensurate rise in wages. One research firm located just seven two-bedroom apartments under $650 in the entire city. The National Low Income Housing Coalition reported that renters needed to earn $12.04 an hour to afford a two-bedroom unit in Nashville. They needed to earn $13.44 in Austin and $22.44 in San Francisco (the nation's highest cost).

Often, there was little left for food after the rent was paid. Working families went hungry at the end of the month, despite heroic food distribution efforts by America's Second Harvest, the leading food bank network (which later changed its name to Feeding America). In 1990, this network gave out 476 million pounds of food. In 1999, the quantity more than doubled, to 1 billion pounds. Yet this charity by the ton wasn't enough. Because of increased demand, many working families received only a single bag of food each month, enough for a few days.

Child poverty in 2000 did not mean distended bellies. But it meant children still went hungry—and they hurt. Hunger was not always in shacks and trailers. In fact, we found it in suburban and rural houses whose trim appearance disguised the despair inside. A majority of the parents we documented for the magazine worked in the service economy.

In the political arena, the focus on welfare defined the poverty debate, but this obscured bigger problems. The majority of poor people in America have always worked. Bear in mind that at their peak welfare programs served 5.5 percent of Americans. Four years after the 1996 reform that limited the time a family could receive aid, the rate was down to 2.3 percent and falling. Welfare was now essentially over. Now what? I thought. This was one question that I really wanted to answer in the story.

I began flying around the country. Later, Michael and I drove thousands of miles for the final reporting. We found working people as desperate as the job-searching homeless we'd seen in the 1980s. There were startling similarities between those 1980s hobos and the housed working poor in 2000. Powerlessness. Desolation. Sometimes hunger.

If children are the future, one-fifth of that future had a hungry face.

I met with Frank when he was visiting in San Francisco not long after our first telephone conversation. I expressed easy confidence that we'd find hungry people directly tied to both Bush and Gore.

In truth, I wasn't so certain. A lot of phone and Internet research hadn't turned up anything in the way of leads. So Michael and I simply drove to Carthage, Tennessee, where Al Gore lived in a brick house on 88 acres at the pinnacle of a hill outside town. On a hunch and winging it, we went to a nearby 1968-vintage public housing project. It was a warm spring day. I spotted a woman sitting on a porch in the thirty-eight-unit complex of duplexes, set amid trees. I asked, utterly vamping, "I hear there's some guy around here who used to work on the Gore farm." The woman pointed to a house across the lawn.

"He lives over there."

We walked across the grass. George sat on his porch, where he spent his days staring at the gum trees dotting the complex. He lived in the unit with his wife, Lou, and eleven-year-old son, Michael. The son, who stood in the doorway looking through the screen at his father, watched with the gray eyes of a life-worn adult as George, fifty-seven, told us that he was waiting to die any day now of a stroke. He'd had a few strokes already and could no longer work.

"I'm sitting here waiting for an aneurism," George said. "They said if they operate, it will kill me. And if they don't operate, it will kill me. In these two buildings, there have been three deaths in the last few months. I feel like I'm on death row."

George was one of the 44 million Americans who lacked health insurance in 2000. He was uninsured when he had a heart attack in the early 1990s and later when he had the series of strokes. He had to lose everything before he could qualify for TennCare, the state medical insurance program. He sold off many of his tools, worth thousands of dollars, for a fraction of their value to pay medical bills and make ends meet. If there had been national health care, George and his wife and son wouldn't have sunk under the weight of his health problems.

George had labored hard at many jobs. One of his last was on the Gore family farm, in 1989.

"They only paid five dollars an hour," he said, "and I needed to make five hundred a week. I said I'd go to work if I could put in enough hours to make that."

He did carpentry and odd jobs. George didn't feel he was underpaid, though there were no benefits, and he always worked more than eighty hours a week, sometimes hitting his goal of a hundred hours. The elder Mrs. Gore was not happy with what he earned. "My, she complained about it every week. But he [Al Sr.] had plenty for me to do."

Now, George and his family were getting by on a little over $9,000 a year, mostly George's federal disability benefits. George really wished he could work again. "I can't go out and make a dollar. I hope you never have to be broke. I have the same ten-dollar bill in my wallet I had last week."

Did his family ever go hungry?

He answered by talking about God.

"I'm a born-again Christian," George asserted. "God promises you that if you serve him, you will not go hungry. I've got nothing but fun stories to tell. I'm not going to put anyone down. God says I'd be sinning if I did."

Almost a month later when we returned, Lou opened the refrigerator to offer us iced tea. She barely cracked it, shielding the mostly empty chamber. The family was having cabbage and bread for dinner.

What we discovered at George's home was not uncommon. In our visit to dozens of working poor families in Tennessee and Texas, we frequently saw nearly empty refrigerators. All were people who worked hard, professed a strong belief in God, and didn't take any public subsidies.

In Austin, the Capital Area Food Bank was located in a 51,000-square-foot facility, where an army of volunteers and staffers gave out 8 million pounds of food in 1999 and projected distributing 10.5 million pounds in 2000. The warehouse was cavernous, with rows upon rows of stacked food.

Officials from the Austin food bank were very helpful, and I kept returning to town to hang out at their distribution lines around the city in the hope of meeting the right person. One day, I flew into Austin and went to a mobile unit that was giving away food in the Montopolis area. Two hundred people in line watched as workers unloaded bread and dozens of boxes of tomatoes and other vegetables from a truck. This wasn't your homeless I-see-Jesus-in-a-mud-puddle crowd. Nearly everyone I talked with was employed. Many had children in tow.

At the end of the line, I found Maggie Segura, twenty-four, on lunch break from her full-time job for the Texas Department of Protective and Regulatory Services. George W. Bush, then the governor of Texas, was her ultimate boss.

It was her first visit ever to a food line.

10 THE WORKING POOR: MAGGIE AND OTHERS IN AUSTIN

Maggie Segura was struggling. Her two-year-old daughter, Mary Frances, had been born with congenital problems—a bladder inside her bladder, malformed kidneys, and other conditions.

"I almost lost her twice, at a month and again at six months," Maggie said of the operations to repair her girl's organs. The child was still at risk because of ongoing treatment. Maggie had to leave work without pay for over a month during her daughter's last hospital stay.

"I'm paying for it now," she said as she put tomatoes in her box that day at the food bank line. "This month, my daughter has been sick. I've had to take off from work. I didn't even get half my paycheck this month. I have all of my bills paid, except there was no money left over for groceries. Food is like the last thing I buy. The prescription money comes out of grocery money."

Maggie and her daughter lived in a $40,000 house that Maggie helped build through Habitat for Humanity, the program that pools construction labor among those in need of homes, sometimes supplemented by volunteer laborers. It was one of twenty-four Habitat homes on an Austin cul-de-sac. Maggie told us that seventeen of these roughly 1,000-square-foot tin-roofed homes were owned by single mothers.

To get the house, Maggie went to a church meeting, where she put her name on a list with three hundred others. Six were picked, including Maggie. There was one lot left on this cul-de-sac, which was walking distance to her mother's house, where Maggie had grown up. She wanted to be in that neighborhood. She took time off from work and labored long days to put in the two hundred hours of "sweat equity" work required by the Habitat program. Only then could she call dibs on the lot.

I was impressed by the cul-de-sac. The homes reminded me of demonstration projects built by the U.S. government in the 1930s that were documented in Farm Security Administration photographs—not drab public housing, but fine-looking homes that were made to last and be a community.

Inside Maggie's home, her furniture was sparse—two beds, a kitchen table, two couches. A friend owned a furniture store and had given her a deal.

The walls were mostly bare, though on Maggie's living room wall hung a picture of the builders, signed by forty workers—all women. Also in the living room was a shelf studded with religious icons—a depiction of the Last Supper in the center, an angel statue from her godmother, a figure of Christ on the cross. A magnet on her refrigerator proclaimed, BLESS OUR HOME.

"Just me and her," Maggie said as she held Mary Frances. Maggie was proud. Hers has been a family of strong women, from her grandmother to her mother.

"I was raised by a single mother," she said, along with her brother. "You can do for yourself."

She recalled a boy at school she had always felt sorry for when she was young; she had given him food.

"I thought he was the poorest boy in the school," Maggie said. But her mother recently told her, "'That boy was better off than you were.' I told my mom I didn't know we were poor until I was an adult."

George W. Bush didn't know Maggie. But his wife, Laura, was aware of her. I learned this story on my third visit to Maggie's house. In 1999, Laura Bush was invited to join a group of governors' wives in "First Ladies Build," a Habitat for Humanity project to spotlight women who help other women construct homes. The Habitat plan was to have the governors' wives go to one house in each state. Laura Bush was invited to come to Maggie's home to hammer a few nails for a photo op.

Maggie hoped to talk to Laura as they hammered. She imagined telling her about the hard times state employees were having. Employee websites were rife with stories of workers struggling. One employee survey in 1998 found that 240 secretaries, janitors, and food service workers at the University of Texas in Austin were getting food stamps.

But, after lending her support in words, Laura Bush never showed up. Nationwide, only two of the governors' wives did not appear. The other was Alice Foster of Louisiana, said Fiona Eastwood, with Habitat's national staff.

"She didn't want to commit to it," Maggie said. "I'm one of his employees," she added about Laura's husband. Maggie said an aide told her Laura would visit her sometime. She was still waiting.

Maggie earned $10 an hour. I jotted down this fact and mentioned it in an e-mail to Frank Lalli, my editor. He shot back a message commenting that $10 sounded like a good wage, on the surface—readers might say, "So what?" He wisely advised me to break down just what that meant. I went back to Maggie and asked if she could share her monthly budget. This is what she told me:

Mortgage	$312
Car payment	298
Pampers	150
Furniture payment	100
Car insurance	80
Food	80
Health insurance (daughter's, the half not paid by state benefits)	70
Food for grandmother (provides day care)	70
Gasoline, car	60
Electric	50
Book club (for reading to her daughter)	30
Phone	20
Natural gas	20
Coloring book, one per month	10
EXPENSES	1,350
TAKE-HOME PAY	1,240
	−110

"I don't go out. I don't do anything," Maggie said. "My mortgage payment is really low. If I had to pay rent, all of my check would go to rent."

Her list didn't include incidentals, such as toilet paper, soap, and toothpaste. Missing as well were cleaning supplies and car repair costs. Nor did it cover medical copayments. When her allergies flared up the previous month, she spent $20 in copayments for prescriptions, plus another $36 for one not covered. Worse, her copayments would double for some drugs in 2001.

"We don't buy new clothes," she added. "I go to the thrift store." Her great good fortune is the Habitat house, with its abnormally low mortgage.

"Without Habitat, I'd have to live with my mother," she said. Another bit of good fortune was her grandmother, who provided day care.

One month after first meeting her, we saw Maggie back in the food line, even though she'd taken a second job, working nights as a waitress, pushing her into more than a fifty-hour workweek.

This assignment was a tough story to write, and even tougher for Michael to photograph. It was much more difficult to visually convey what was happening to the American working poor in the year 2000 than it was to picture the homeless of the early 1980s.

A photo of a dirty child standing before a tent captures that child's horror. But a picture of a poor child in front of a suburban house like Maggie's—well, the child looks middle class. How do you photograph hunger, or even translate it into words?

I found an answer in Hector. I had first met the boy in the months before our road trip. I'd been coming regularly to Austin, visiting the River City Youth Foundation, an after-school program for impoverished six- to ten-year-old kids in the Dove Springs area. It tutors, feeds, and mentors them.

By day, the neighborhood looks like most any suburb. Behind the walls, however, some apartments house three families in a single unit. Many parents are janitors, laborers, cooks.

"We did a study of low-income housing," executive director Mona Gonzalez said, "and of the four hundred units in this immediate area, ninety percent are headed by single females. Last summer, I had kids coming to my door begging for food. It's a different kind of hunger. But it is hunger. There's a pain in your belly. You can't think about anything else."

It wasn't that kids were dying. As was true in so many other aspects of their parents' lives, they had too little, as if they were batteries charged to only 70 percent capacity: they functioned, but weakly. Pointing to a group of kids across the room, Mona added that they often dealt with their hunger by eating candy bars.

I explored this neighborhood. One day, I visited the nearby Hermelinda Rodriguez Elementary School, where 89 percent of the children were fed free by the government's school lunch program. Everywhere we traveled, we saw how this program helped kids.

For some, "this is their main food for the day," said principal Suzie Cunningham. "They eat like they're starved to death."

We walked across the campus. An eight-year-old boy ran ahead to hold the door. Suzie thanked him. As he ran off, she said that he had recently been busted for shoplifting a candy bar. "He was hungry."

Back at the River City Youth Foundation one day, I saw a picture drawn on a computer by Donovan, age six.

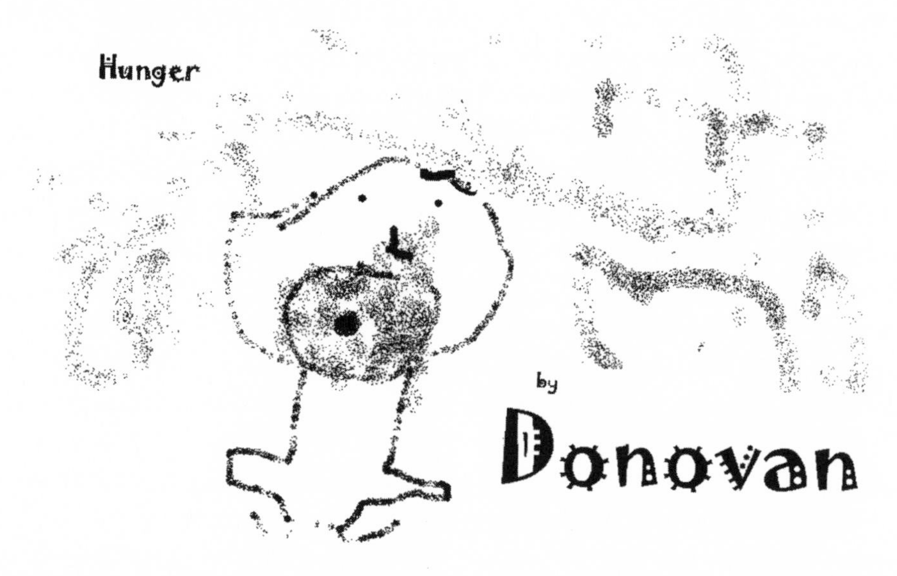

The children were antsy, their attention spans short. Hector, whom I'd been getting to know, was often frustrated, angry. His house was crowded. I met Hector's mother. She loved her boy—she wanted the best for him—but like so many immigrants, her wages were low, and she had to work ceaseless hours to earn a living. She was caught in a defeating loop. I spent a lot of time around Hector. Like all the others, he had huge eyes that bespoke an emotional need. Like the other kids, he was extremely quiet. I would talk, encouraging him, and he would listen as he did his artwork and other projects at the foundation, but he did not say much in return. Despite Hector's shyness, I felt a bond with him after several long visits to the foundation over the months.

One Saturday, I watched Sue Cole teach the children on the computers at the foundation. At lunchtime, the kids were eager to eat.

Donovan ran to Sue. "Can I help?" he asked. He set out plates on an outdoor picnic table while the other children played. James, a small boy, watched eagerly as Mary, the cook, set out the food. "I'm hungry," he told her. James repeated this. He eyed the *sopa*—rice with turkey—and a pot of corn, plates of watermelon slices, Gatorade.

The kids crowded in, arguing who was first. "Everyone will get to eat," Sue told them. Donovan quickly cleaned his plate, proudly showing off the bare dish. I went inside and chatted with Mona, the director. Hector approached, shyly.

"Are you a mentor?" Hector asked. He had big eyes and was nervous. "Could you be my mentor?"

Mona told Hector that I lived very far away. Later when I walked to my car, I felt hollow.

That night in my hotel room, which had been arranged for me by *George* magazine at a cost of $159 a night, I could not sleep. I walked the streets around the nearby Capitol building, followed by the eyes of Texas state troopers. I came back to the fine hotel, and the eyes of the clerk bore down suspiciously. I swam laps in the hotel pool in the morning, but water could not wash off what I felt on me.

It was the knowledge of kids such as Hector. It's easier when you don't get to know the invisible children. Low wages and long work hours for their parents mean that these kids can grow up lacking not only enough proper food but also deeper nourishment. Even though Hector lived in what appeared to be a suburb, he was growing up in gnawing solitude, in some ways more bereft of emotional wealth than many Third World children.

Hector did not have a distended belly caused by his poverty. His hard-working mother, the federal lunch program, and the help of the River City Youth Foundation saw that he had this minimal support. But he had an emotionally distended soul.

11 MR. MURRAY ON MAGGIE

Back in the 1980s, I'd read *Losing Ground: American Social Policy, 1950–1980,* by Charles Murray, who was later dubbed America's "most dangerous conservative" by the *New York Times Magazine.* His 1984 book argued that the government social service network, which he deemed a failure, had to be abolished in order to save the poor. The book was embraced by the Reagan administration and congressional Republicans. And when President Bill Clinton signed welfare reform into law in 1996, co-opting the issue, he was in fact embracing Murray's argument. On Murray's web page at the American Enterprise Institute, *Losing Ground* is called the "intellectual foundation" for that legislation. Murray got just about everything he dreamed of in that book.

All through our journey for the *George* magazine assignment, I wondered what Murray thought of the working poor. By 2000, welfare was no longer the issue. What about hard-working people who were falling behind—losing ground—in a "booming" economy?

I rang him up and asked about a solution for working impoverished families.

"I don't have one," Murray said. "After seven or eight years of economic boom, what help do families need? If you are married with one child or two, sticking in the labor force, the general trajectory is up and away. You can make a decent living without the government helping you. And if you have five kids, a high school education, you will probably be below the poverty line."

I began speaking about what we'd seen in broad terms—

"Give me an example," Murray said. I started telling him about Maggie Segura. He again interrupted.

"Is she a single mother?"

"Yes."

Murray shot back that her child was "illegitimate" and that she shouldn't have made the mistake of marrying the wrong man.

"The point of welfare reform is not to get women off welfare, but to drive down the illegitimacy factor. Give me another example."

Murray wanted me to describe a specific intact family. I was befuddled by his sharp dismissal of Maggie. It threw me. I thought about pushing him more on his coldness, but I did not. Instead, I told him about Linda and Obie, a working family I'd also documented in Austin. Obie was a janitor and made $10 an hour, and Linda worked part time. The family needed the support of the food bank. Obie had scoffed when I asked if his three daughters went hungry. When his paycheck wasn't enough and the food bank ration ran out, he sold blood plasma for $18. "For my family, I bleed," Obie said.

"What is the appropriate success for working families?" Murray asked. "The guy is making ten bucks an hour, the wife is working part time. They've got three kids. Should we feel bad?"

Murray did some quick math, slightly overstating the family's income, which was really less than $500 a week. I didn't correct him. "If I had to, I could figure out ways to live on $550 a week with three kids. I probably wouldn't live in Austin. I'd go someplace else, where it was a lot cheaper. I'd make choices."

I noted that even in Appalachia, we found that rents for rotting trailers and shacks were exactly what Obie and Linda paid in Austin. The couple was lucky—their rent was just under $500.

"I'm not saying $550 a week is an easy living," Murray continued. He explained that if the government spent money to help this family, it would come from other working people with children, thus hurting other families.

"What is the obligation of the rest of us to augment their income? When we have income transfers, a lot is not coming from the rich. That's a tricky moral equation."

PART 4 **UPDATING PEOPLE AND PLACES** THE LATE 2000s

You've heard of mental depression. This is a mental recession. We may have a recession; we haven't had one yet. We have sort of become a nation of whiners. You just hear this constant whining, complaining about a loss of competitiveness, America in decline.

—Phil Gramm, advisor to John McCain's presidential campaign, July 2008

I got a request here from a major American print publication. "Dear Rush: For the Obama [Immaculate] Inauguration we are asking a handful of very prominent politicians, statesmen, scholars, businessmen, commentators, and economists to write four hundred words on their hope for the Obama presidency." . . . So I'm thinking of replying to the guy, "Okay, I'll send you a response, but I don't need four hundred words, I need four: I hope he fails."

—Rush Limbaugh, January 16, 2009 (bracketed word was inserted by Limbaugh)

And the banks—hard to believe in a time we're facing a banking crisis that many of the banks created—are still the most powerful lobby on Capitol Hill. And they frankly own the place.

—Senator Dick Durban (D-Ill.) on Chicago's WJJG 1530 radio, talking to host Ray Hanania, April 27, 2009

In 2008, Sanford Weill, former CEO and chairman of Citigroup, barely made the Forbes 400 list of the richest Americans. His net worth was listed as $1.3 billion.

In the fall of 2008, the U.S. government guaranteed $306 billion in potentially toxic loans that had been made by the bank.

During the 2008 presidential campaign, labor leaders pinned their hopes on the Employee Free Choice Act. The act as proposed would have made it easier to unionize, in part by eliminating the need for an election if a majority of employees signed union cards. The bill was intended to extend Franklin Roosevelt's 1935 Wagner Act, which tried to protect unions against unfair company practices (although that act was weakened in later years). Both acts aimed to put more money in the hands of workers. Wal-Mart was opposed.

"There was talk of such a bill during Lyndon Johnson's term when Democrats controlled Congress, but labor was told it would have to wait till after the Great Society programs. That will happen again. They will say the time is not right for labor," said Dr. John Russo, now co-director of the Center for Working-Class Studies at Youngstown State University, when I interviewed him on the eve of the 2008 election. As predicted, this headline appeared in the *New York Times* on July 17, 2009: "Democrats Drop Key Part of Bill to Assist Unions."

2008 Wal-Mart employed 1.4 million workers in the United States.

2008 General Motors employed 92,053 workers in the United States.

2008 General Motors projected that it would employ 72,650 workers in the United States by 2014.

2008 It took $1.3 billion to make the Forbes 400 list of the richest Americans.

2007 The average CEO in the United States was paid 275.4 times what an average

12 REINDUCTION

Twenty-seven years and one month after our first hobo trip, I walked into what had been the Western Pacific rail yard in Sacramento. The previous day, I'd watched my mother die after a prolonged illness in the suburban Sacramento home that my parents had bought after they retired. That final night, I dripped one-tenth of a milliliter of morphine sulfate into my unconscious mother's mouth every fifteen minutes in the hope that she'd absorb enough of it to numb an unfathomable pain. In between, I escaped from the horror of the situation by flatbed scanning old family photos, losing myself in the images, among them pictures of my father's tool grinding shop behind our house in Cleveland. He had built the shop in 1970, when his business outgrew the basement. In one photo, I'm working at sharpening end mills with a Harig Air Flow fixture on a Covell machine. My thoughts were filled with metal and sparks and dust and how I grew up—another life.

That day after Mom died, I was in a state and didn't want to talk with anyone. I could think of nowhere else to go but the old yard.

The Western Pacific Railroad no longer existed. Years before, it had been taken over by the Union Pacific. The engine repair shops had been torn down. Only the mainline track and a few sidings remained. Many rows of track had been pulled up. Gone was the boneyard where I'd met No Thumbs. Those acres of former rail yard were thick with overgrown grasses and weeds. The icehouse had been razed and was now a parking lot for a community college. There weren't even any hobos around.

Up the line, a mile or so north, was the *Sacramento Bee* building. The paper still published good work, but both the staff and the physical size of the paper had shrunk. Today, if I were a young man living out of a pickup truck, it's highly unlikely that I could replicate my 1980 experience and get hired there. And the odds would be against an editor sending me and Michael out to ride the rails for six days to do a story on today's hobos and hard times.

A southbound Union Pacific came down the mainline. It was going slow enough to catch on the fly. I ran alongside, holding on to a grain car's ladder. I felt the power of the train and the pull of the past as my feet kept pace. All I had to do was lift up. A voice inside me said, "Go, *go!*" Oh, did I know that old road. Stockton. Fresno. Pixley. Bakersfield. The sugar beet and cotton fields where Michael and I had once chopped weeds in 110-degree heat back in 1983 when we went undercover and did a farm labor camp story. I was gripped with a moment of terror because a piece of me wanted to get lost in all of that. I released my hold on the steel ladder, stopped running. I knew better. There was no escape on that road of denial.

The train picked up speed. I closed my eyes. The sound of metal thunder was as fresh as if I'd jumped on trains only yesterday. The smell hadn't changed either: a blend of tar, creosote, spilled diesel, chemical cargo, rice, wheat, and who-knows-what from a century of use.

I opened my eyes after the train clattered away. There were three rows of sided rolling stock—"convertibles," boxcars, grain and rock cars. Many cars were covered with "spider writing" and spray paint art from *cholos* and white taggers. There were also small monikers written in chalk, the signs of hobos. I didn't recognize any of the names, most themed to the male gender: "Wild Man," "Bookman," "Broken Man." And there was Rowhoe, who wrote: ROWHOE'S LAST RUN.

I wondered about Herbie, Charley Brown, and Bozo Texino, names in chalk that we always saw on train cars nearly thirty years ago. Two cars later, I came across a graffito bearing one of those names.

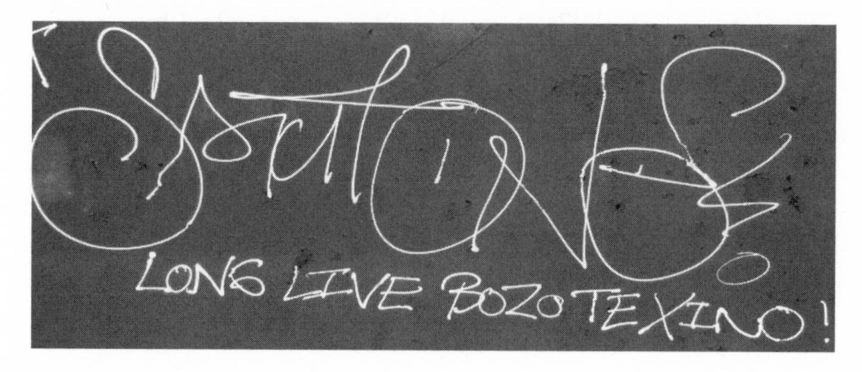

There's dispute over whether Bozo was or is a living man. We'd never met him on the rails and didn't know of anyone who had. A few guys claimed to be him. Bozo was as much a ghost as the past depicted in the pictures from my blue-collar days that I had scanned as my mother lay dying, or the past of No Thumbs and our hoboing all over the American West in the 1980s. Is it a waste of time to visit ghosts?

I thought of Ambrose Bierce, who fought in the Civil War; he was shot in the head by a Confederate rifleman. He went on to author *The Devil's Dictionary* and dark short stories rooted in the experience of his wartime trauma. On October 2, 1913, at the age of seventy-one, he departed Washington, D.C., bound for Mexico and its revolution. He wrote to his niece: "Good-bye—if you hear of my being stood up against a Mexican stone wall and shot to rags please know that I think that a pretty good way to depart this life. It beats old age, disease, or falling down the cellar stairs. To be a Gringo in Mexico—ah, that is euthanasia."

En route, Bierce went to Civil War battlefields: Orchard Knob, Missionary Ridge, Chickamauga, Snodgrass Hill, and Hell's Half Acre. At Shiloh, he sat alone for an entire day. He was reportedly dressed entirely in black. It appears he was visiting ghosts.

He traveled on and made it across the border. His final letter was posted from a town in northern Mexico. He then vanished. Some believe he came north and shot himself at the Grand Canyon. Others are sure that he died of disease and was buried in a mass grave in Marfa, Texas, or that he indeed ended up in front of a firing squad. His fate remains a mystery.

In his 1985 book *El Gringo Viejo* (The Old Gringo), novelist Carlos Fuentes imagines the last days of Bierce, conjuring his ghost to tell the secrets. On October 15, 1987, I had dinner with Fuentes. I tried to explain why I liked the novel, but I'm not sure that Fuentes clearly understood. The sentiment of the novel struck a nerve that captured my state of mind. I was just a few years removed from riding the rails and still had a lot of hobo remaining in me. To be a hobo, watching from the boxcar door as America rolls past, amid the illusion of so much wealth, is to be like that gringo, alone in a strange culture at a dangerous time in its history. No Thumbs, Sam, the Alexander family, most everyone we'd met in the 1980s—all were outsiders who felt alone in a nation that didn't want to acknowledge them. The new legion following in their footsteps along the rail lines and in the tent cities in the America of this new century dwell with this solitude that is like a form of euthanasia.

About two months before revisiting the Western Pacific yard, I had been in Detroit, in the vast ruins of the old Packard car factory. It's a favorite of hipster adventurers who come to explore and make statements in spray paint; to them, Detroit is an urban horror Disneyland. I found the graffito shown here.

I'm not sure what the author intended. If it means we're impotent against the huge forces arrayed against us, he or she is wrong. It isn't an oppressive society that creates the crawling dead. The people documented in this book, the hipster spray painter, me, you, the reader—*we* are society. I blame political and business forces for what has happened economically but not for what we have become. We've been dealt a bad hand, for certain. Yet we can't let that defeat us. We don't have to be a nation of old gringos, believing that we are alone and dead. Only we can make it be otherwise.

I began thinking about the 1930s and writers who had published works during the Great Depression. Back in those days, most of the Americans these writers interviewed blamed themselves for their hard times. That's not true today. Most people I interviewed, with one or two major exceptions, blamed Wall Street, corporations, globalization, and other overarching forces. That doesn't mean they were any more politically active, however: American workers are prone to withdraw rather than taking to the streets as their European counterparts often do.

And in many ways, the jobless and the homeless of the 1930s were just as much outcasts then as they were in the 1980s and as they are in the present day, at least in the eyes of a conservative sector of society who expressed open antagonism toward the poor. Forget the TV folklore of *The Waltons* that we were "all in it together" during the Great Depression. John Steinbeck wrote about an uncle who believed that Roosevelt's Works Progress Administration was a boondoggle. The uncle claimed to have seen a group of WPA men standing idle, watching one man shovel dirt, and he called them "lazy." In reality, they were taking turns. Steinbeck bet this uncle five dollars that he "couldn't shovel sand for fifteen minutes without stopping. . . . At the end of three minutes his face was red, at six he was staggering and before eight minutes were up his wife stopped him to save him from apoplexy," Steinbeck wrote in a 1960 issue of *Esquire* magazine. According to my wide reading on the Great Depression, the divisions in the American electorate then were about the same as they are today: roughly 20 to 30 percent on the right and far right, about the same percentage moderately liberal to very liberal, and the remainder in the middle.

Despite the hostility expressed by many conservatives toward the unemployed and homeless during the 1930s, by April 1939, when *The Grapes of Wrath* came out, something had flipped in the American psyche, and enough of the middle had tilted toward feeling compassion for cotton pickers and the displaced poor. *The Grapes of Wrath* flew off store shelves—in its first week, it sold close to a hundred thousand copies. By September, it was in its ninth printing. Twentieth Century–Fox signed a $75,000 check over to Steinbeck for rights to the novel—the largest sum ever paid for a book up to that point. Darryl Zanuck made the epic motion picture, which was released the next year.

Many Americans remained conservative, but their hostility had by now been marginalized. In Steinbeck's 1939, a majority of Americans were on the side of feeling compassion for their fellow citizens. It was a sentiment that lasted for a long time. In 1960, Steinbeck wrote that the "most rabid, hysterical Roosevelt-hater would not dare to suggest removing the reforms, the safeguards and the new concept that the Government is responsible for all of its citizens."

If Steinbeck had lived past his sixty-eight years and made it into the 1980s, when we started our journey, I suspect he would have retracted that statement.

As we set out to update our work, we first traveled to Youngstown, Ohio, with the hope that sometime in the coming few years we would once again be able to find Steinbeck's 1939.

13 NECROPOLIS: AFTER THE APOCALYPSE

On a chilly March afternoon in 2009, we drove into Youngstown and felt the desolation of this lost city. There were miles of burned-out and abandoned homes amid meadows that once were neighborhoods. In my mind's eye, the empty floor of the Mahoning Valley, almost all field and forest, looked naked in the absence of over 20 miles of steel mills. The blast furnace area of the Brier Hill Works, the "Jenny" in Bruce Springsteen's song, had long since been demolished, as had the Campbell Works. No blimp factory was ever built. The biggest job creator had been the construction of four prisons.

The town felt unfamiliar. So much had decayed and grown over. Then we went to the home of Ken Platt in the town of Girard, adjacent to the city of Youngstown. Michael and I exchanged hugs with Ken on the porch of the same house where we'd first met him over a quarter of a century earlier, in 1983. There was something comforting about the familiarity of Ken's living room.

We had visited Ken again in 1985, while we were on a book tour, and he had proudly shown us a Radio Shack computer that he was fooling around with at the time. That tinkering set him on a course to defy his own assertion that all he knew was a 20-pound sledgehammer. He learned computers, and when we next saw him, in 1995, he was working at Youngstown's Butler Institute of American Art. He was traveling all over the country showing other museums how to electronically archive artwork.

"Why me?" he asked in 1995 about his high-tech fortune. "Who am I? Most of it is luck. I know people with ability who work hard. For some reason, God looked on me."

When Ken traveled, he was treated like a rich man. On one trip, he was put up at the venerable oceanfront Hotel Del Coronado in San Diego. He was embarrassed that he ate meals costing $20-plus. "Who would ever think a guy who came from where I came from would stay at a place like that?" He found California beautiful, but he felt out of place. Yet he was now repulsed by the unkempt nature of Youngstown. He was lost between worlds.

In 2009, Ken was still working for the Butler Institute. He had nineteen years in—the longest time he'd held a job without being laid off. Gone was his talk about the guys he once worked with; he had lost touch with people from the mill. We got the strong sense that Ken had moved on—as if the man we found in 1983 and in the 1990s had been living someone else's life. He was as jovial and easy-going as ever, though.

Ken was worried about his son, Ken Jr. Despite all odds—and despite his father's concern in 1995 that Ken Jr. might have to join the military—the son had gotten a job as a steelworker at a time and in a place that seemed impossible. He worked as a millwright at McDonald Steel, a small hot roll mill. "They make a product no one else in the country makes," Ken said. "Bridge decking pieces, tire rims." Ken Jr. lived with the same uncertainty faced by steelworkers in his father's time: orders were down, and layoffs were happening. Would the job survive? It was anyone's guess.

Ken telephoned his son, who owned a home across the street, and he came over.

Michael had taken a picture of father and son in 1984 (it appears on the cover of this book). Redoing that picture at the now-vanished blast furnace was not going to happen. "And you aren't going to be holding him in your arm," Michael quipped. As Michael took the updated picture on Ken's front porch, he noted that Ken Jr. was now the same age as his father had been in that image of twenty-five years earlier. Ken, Michael, and I exchanged uneasy glances. Time sure has a way of speeding past.

Ken Jr. had to leave for work, and the three of us went back to the living room. Ken talked about some plans proposed by the city that he'd read about in the papers.

"They're trying to get millions to tear houses down. It's like the destruction of the city has become a major industry."

Ken laughed and added, "If you don't laugh, you're going to cry."

People he knows find hope in the smallest things: "They are excited about a Wal-Mart opening up."

Desperation is constantly evident.

"There isn't a trash day that goes by that I don't see multiple people driving up and down my road looking at my trash for scrap," he said, referring to those who sell this scrap to recyclers. "They take the manhole covers off in the night. You're driving down the road, and there are places where there are no manhole covers.

"The rest of the country is down to where we are. The funny thing about it? In a way, it's kind of better being here in Youngstown, because we've been in it so long. It's 'normal' for us. It's bad out there. There's not a lot of future here, or anywhere. I probably know twenty people who are between forty and fifty living with their parents. Here, that's the norm. I'm glad I'm not a young person starting out. I worry about my grandkids. I don't worry so much about myself. I worry about the future. I don't know how people are going to achieve a good life in this country. There's no opportunity for young people. How can young people grow families on what companies want to pay?

"This country is changing so rapidly. Our expectations seem to be lowering as a nation. What do you say to a person in Youngstown who is eighteen years old, just out of high school? 'I want to go to college.' Go to college—what for? Look at, say, health care. Years ago, you saw a doctor and a nurse. Now there's a lot of downgrading in health care. There are lots of medical assistants that make eight bucks an hour. You can't live on that. It's scary."

I asked, "What's secure employment now?"

"I don't know. Maybe a log cabin somewhere up in the hills. You got all the firewood you need. If your health hangs in there, you can shoot rabbits, I guess. That's probably the only security you'll find left in this country. I don't know what the answer is. They talk about green jobs. How many jobs are created by the green movement? I don't know what you become. I don't know, I don't know. I don't think it's going to be a bright future."

As I did with everyone I interviewed, I asked, "What's the end game? What kind of country do we want to live in?"

"I guess we got to look at different things and find different satisfactions. Because we've pretty much given it all away to Mexico, as far as good jobs are concerned. You just hope your grandkids end up with something."

When I telephoned months later to say hello, Ken was fretting about the health care "debate." Thugs and screaming people were turning out at town hall meetings to call any change to the system "socialism."

"I'd like to see something happen to health care. I'm not sure that what they are talking about is the answer, but something has to happen. Health care is the big nut for me. I have diabetes. I'm fifty-seven. We got this right-wing radio stuff going. It borders on treason. It's very radical. It's not 'I disagree with you.' It's 'I hate you.'"

Joe Marshall Jr. came to the door of a suburban ranch-style home, giving us a big smile and a hug. He announced that he'd survived colon cancer and was now healthy. He was nearly giddy.

Joe's mood was in stark contrast to what we had found in 1995. Back then, he was working sixteen hours a month as a guard at the city's jail. "Working in the jail is worse than being in it," Joe had told us that cold night as he stood in uniform in front of a dance hall. He had three jobs: as a deputy, a hospital security guard, and a guard-for-hire. Joe had worked at the hospital the previous night. On three hours' sleep, he awakened to do his second job, at the jail, that morning. Now he was at his third job, providing security for a wedding.

Some years earlier, after we met him in 1983, Joe had married, bought his own home, and had children. But, according to his sister, Ellen, the stress of his multiple jobs had contributed to problems that ended his marriage, and he had moved back home with his parents. As we were about to leave that night in 1995, with well-dressed wedding guests walking past the dance hall, Joe added, "What I wish is that the mill was still open. I would have been there for life. In the mill, people were more friendly. Not like what I find now."

In 2009, however, he seemed to have made peace with all that life has thrown at him. The latest hit was being laid off from the sheriff's department job. He also lost the hospital gig. He was now working at a Christian call center, soliciting money by phone for various ministries.

"I never thought I'd be able to do that job. Oh, my gosh, I get money galore. I get people who say 'I'm broke, I can't give you anything.' Then I get twenty-five, thirty bucks out of them."

Joe was fifty-five, the same age as his father had been when the Ohio Works shuttered, and he was again living with his parents, Joe Sr. and Kay. The family had moved northwest of Youngstown after selling their house, which was not far from the former site of the Ohio Works. The elder Marshalls had trouble with the stairs in that old house—the new dwelling was all on one level. Joe Sr. was eighty-four; he and his wife were in their sixty-fourth year of marriage.

"This whole area was devastated," Joe Jr. said as we sat at the kitchen table. "But people had money everywhere else. Now the devastation's spread all over the country. We're used to living like this. I call all over the country on my job. It's unbelievable what happened in eight years. When Clinton left office, the country was prospering. I make these calls, and people are really hurting. People don't care until it happens to them. It's like having a kid. When you have a child, people don't understand how your life will change until the baby comes. Then every spare second of your time goes to that kid. Until you have a child, you can tell them that, and they won't comprehend it. And that's how it is with this."

I asked, "What can the rest of the country learn from you?"

"Save your money," Joe Jr. said, fast. "Put your money in the bank."

"And don't fix up your house," added Ellen. "Pay it off. Then fix it up."

"My generation was bad, but this generation is even worse," Joe Jr. continued. "You gotta put your money away. Don't blow it. Everyone thinks their money is going to last forever. It won't."

"Bring the jobs back from overseas," Joe Sr. interjected, in his gravelly voice. "Keep them here. Until they change NAFTA, it's going to be like this."

"And you wonder why nobody is working," Joe Jr. said. "They gave the companies tax breaks to boot. Remember they said, 'This is going to bring up their standard of living in other countries'? You know what it did? It brought all of ours down to theirs."

Joe Sr. talked about the Republicans being bad for workers, especially with NAFTA.

Joe Jr. cut in: "They all did it."

"It was a Republican Congress," Joe Sr. reminded us. "But Clinton signed it."

"Yeah," his son said.

I asked the elder Marshall about the Great Depression.

"It was identical under Hoover and under Bush. Trickle down—and there was no jobs. The only difference was [in the Great Depression] there were steel mills here, and people worked maybe once a month. Now you got no jobs to go to. It's worse. Bush was the worst president in history, in my estimation. You need the middle class to spend money, to buy cars, and then the economy will prosper. But when you expect the millionaires to trickle down—no way."

"Look how much money we owe to China now," Joe Jr. said. Speaking of the larger U.S. debt, he asked, "How are you going to get out of that? How you going to pay off $4.5 trillion? All you can do is pay the interest on what you owe. And you can't even pay the interest. How are you going to get out of that?"

"You remember that remark, 'What's good for General Motors is good for the country'?" Joe Sr. asked. "Now we're supporting them, but we shouldn't."

Said his son, "They didn't support us. My neighbors, friends, and stuff, we all need jobs. They give GM everything. Nobody ever gave us breaks like that."

Like Ken Platt, the Marshalls had lost touch with their former co-workers. In the case of Joe Sr., many of them were dead. For Joe Jr., he was focused on his own world.

"My first son, Joey, he's got a 4.0, National Honor Society, second in his class. I'm not worried about him. He'll get scholarships. He'll be a doctor or a pharmacist. He's headed for college, there's no doubt. My youngest, Andrew, he didn't want to go to college. But he's getting better grades now, so now he's talking about going to college."

I returned the conversation to Joe Jr.'s analogy of people having a child. Now that the nation is like Youngstown, will people become aware and come together?

"You're going to have one world order," he responded. "It will be controlled by one leader. You will have different sections, but it will be under one. The first Bush said 'New World Order.' I think that's where we're headed."

"Who? Who will that be?"

"It's all money. That's what I think. This was all planned. And there is nothing we can do to stop it. Ten years ago, if somebody would have told me that, fifteen years ago, I would have said 'You're crazy, you're crazy.' They want people to make nine, ten dollars an hour. That's what they want. You know what the number-one employer in the state of Ohio is? Wal-Mart."

14 NEW TIMER: FINDING MR. HEISENBERG INSTEAD

In late 2008, I found a telephone number of someone with Sam's surname in the small midwestern town where he'd grown up. In thirty years of reporting, seldom had I been so tentative about making a call.

I dialed.

The phone picked up. It was Sam's elderly father. Sam, the father said, lived in a nearby state, was "doing real well." We had a pleasant conversation. The father said he'd pass along my phone number.

Sam never called.

Maybe I was a reminder of a time that he wanted to forget. Or—

Who knows? I certainly had demons from that era that I didn't want to face.

Was he okay? How were his three children, now in their twenties and thirties, doing in today's economy? I decided against phoning a number that came up on the Internet. It seemed best that we simply drive to the Midwest and knock on his door so that the three of us could face our past and talk about this current grim economic time. Perhaps Sam would slam the door or punch us. Maybe we'd all get drunk.

Sam haunted us. For decades, Michael and I had talked about him. Occasionally, I turned to our first book and read the part about him. Especially searing was the conversation we had when we first met in St. Louis in 1983. "I hit the road," he'd told us that night when we took him to dinner. "It was probably an immature thing to do, but I had to do it. I'd rather be like a whale that goes off to beach himself—you know how some whales do that. I'd rather die alone than have people see me. I don't want people to see me like this. I want to go down alone."

After we rode the freights from St. Louis with Sam and got him a room in Denver, where we left him, we kept in touch. A few months later, after our final drive to Youngstown in 1983, we stopped in Denver to visit. Sam still lived in the same dive, but he'd gotten a job as a clerk at an upscale hotel. He now sported a mustache and was more upbeat about life. He was talking with his wife. Perhaps they would get back together? He had hope. Sam was doing much better, and he agreed that we could use his pictures. Our visit was all too brief. When I later tried to send a book, I couldn't locate him.

The late winter sun was noon high over the flat expanse of the Midwest. Roads were flanked by the brown stubble of last year's corn. We came to a town with a large manufacturing plant whose gates were shuttered. This factory's parking lot was empty, and a FOR SALE sign was in front. The town had the usual rundown central business district, numerous church steeples bright against a blue sky, and Norman Rockwell–era homes beneath the naked limbs of hardwoods. It was a typical Midwest place.

We arrived at a modest and well-kept white clapboard house on a back street and pulled into an alley next to it. Michael turned off the engine. I sighed.

Drapes were drawn. I came around front, took a deep breath, and went up the walk of the home that, from my database search, seemed to be the best possibility for where Sam was living. It was Saturday.

I stood at the front door for a prolonged period of time, as if facing a firing squad instead of a brass knocker.

We'd explained to documentary filmmaker Ron Wyman, who was traveling with us, about the weight of our history with Sam. Ron was filming out in the street, a good and respectable distance away, yet I felt suddenly awful about that. Ron is a fine journalist, a compassionate person, and a very nice guy. But the act of contemporary journalism—video rolling, multimedia being so "important"—suddenly seemed intrusive. Some moments should simply be experienced, no? I wished I were alone at the door, not even in the company of Michael, though in my state of mind I was not even aware of him being nearby. I then wished I were not here.

I knocked.

Nothing.

I peered in the window—the kitchen. Not much was visible besides a toaster and such. We walked around the house. The garage door was closed. I went to some nearby homes. My knock went unanswered at several. Another was occupied by a woman who had just moved in that week and didn't know her new neighbors.

We traveled on. I had some eight or nine possible addresses from my database search. Sam may or may not have owned at least one or more of the properties. All were within three contiguous counties. Some addresses were certainly old. I had tested the database service using my own name, and it showed a half dozen locations, including an Iowa town where I once lived while working on a book project and my family's home back in Ohio. No dates of residency corresponded to any addresses.

We went to the next address on the list, in a town half an hour away. We followed the same drill. A knock. No answer.

Another town, another knock—

No one was home anywhere. Ron filmed it all. Most homes appeared to be rentals. One was a rundown duplex; another, tiny and containing raw lumber, was being remodeled. Two of the homes, on suburban-style streets at the edge of town, were nice, in stark contrast to the two addresses that were apartments. One of the apartments was above an insurance office, in a century-and-a-half-old brick building in the center of a town, with cheap, tattered drapes in the windows. Another was in a complex that resembled public housing: bleak buildings, ratty cars in the parking spots, life-weary residents. Two men with Dust Bowl faces, working on a beater truck near what had been Sam's unit, according to the database records, glared as I approached. I asked if they knew Sam. "Nah," one said. The tenor of the response indicated that even if they did know him, they were the kind of guys found in the kind of place where no one knows anyone, ever.

Amid this, I called a phone number attached to one of the addresses. A woman answered. I asked for Sam.

"*You* have the *wrong* number," she abruptly said. It was too curt to be an ordinary response.

"It isn't like that in the Midwest," I said to my traveling companions. "People aren't that rude. Something was off about that."

I wondered aloud if Sam had been watching us from behind a curtain at that first house.

We searched on into the evening. There was one final address in a tiny town to the south. It was a long drive on a winding road. My stomach hurt. We didn't talk much.

The house was empty of furniture.

We stood next to our rental car, silent. I had nothing to lose. I put a file folder on the hood, found the telephone number for Sam's father, and dialed. The father remembered me and said that his son did indeed live in the first town we'd visited, though the dad identified the town only as being west of another city; he didn't recall the town's name until I reminded him.

"Do you have Sam's number?"

"Yes."

Rustling in the background. I stood next to the driver's side fender looking at the sun, orange and diminishing, near the horizon. The father returned and gave me the number. It was in none of the database information that I had. I read the number back twice to be certain I'd written it down correctly.

I hung up, paused, then dialed right away for fear that I might not follow through if I didn't act fast. It was precisely 7:30 P.M. on March 21, 2009, according to my phone's time stamp. Michael edged close, ear next to my cell phone. An electronic voice answered that read back the numerals; then a beep. No name was mentioned; I had no sense whether or not it was Sam's phone.

"Hi, my name is Dale Maharidge, and I'm looking for Sam—I, well, we—" (a nervous chuckle) "rode a freight train with him from St. Louis to Denver, back in 1983. I'm not sure if this is the right Sam—" (I waffled because it clearly was an unlisted number and I didn't want to explain that I'd gotten it from his father, from whom he had been estranged back in 1983) "—but if it is, it would be great to talk with you. My number is—"

There was a clicking sound: click, click—

Someone was picking up. Michael's eyes widened.

"You have the wrong number!" a loud voice said.

"Are you sure?" (A stupid thing to say, then I rebounded.) "I mean, do you know Sam?"

"You DEFINITELY got the wrong number!"

Click. He hung up.

"That was his voice!" Michael cried. "I know it from listening to the tapes! That was him!"

Still, I wondered. Maybe it was someone else. Ron and Michael said, "*No way!*" in unison. "His father gave you the number!" Michael insisted. "And that was his voice!"

"He's denying to us who he is," I said. "That says something. I just don't know what."

Michael told Ron that Sam had become mythological to us, as had a few other people in *Journey to Nowhere,* such as the Alexander family. "We told his story on TV so many times because he captured it," Michael said of the terrible saga of the newly homeless that we documented in the 1980s.

"Sam wasn't even really real anymore after a while. He became an icon of the book."

My head reeled. My stomach hurt worse. Oh, do I remember that self-made book tour. The Dial Press had gone through a corporate downsizing by the time we were published in 1985. We ended up in the hands of its parent company. Our alleged publicist at Doubleday dismissively laughed when we said we'd do our own media after she declined to promote *Journey to Nowhere.* "Nobody will have you on a show," she told me. Part of her reluctance was that the recession had officially been declared "over" in 1985—supposedly it was now a boom time, and all was well in the world. Jim, our editor, gave us a hundred books, and we set out on our own with help from Michael's friend Dorothy Kupcha. We sent out books and landed dozens of TV and radio bookings, including Studs Terkel's radio show, CNN, and a host of regional TV programs such as *Morning Exchange* in Cleveland and *Pittsburgh Today.* I'd told Sam's story so many times that he became an apparition in the nightmares I had about the project.

I mumbled that for a long time we didn't want to face our demons, "and maybe he doesn't want to face his." It was growing chilly. I shivered. We drove off. Michael turned us onto a road that faced us head-on into the final minutes of the sun before it dipped over the horizon that was the road itself. The orange glow made us blind to all but the silhouettes of silos and farmhouses. I babbled. "Maybe he's doing okay. Maybe not. Some of those places, they were dives. He might own one, or did own one, maybe not. Some were pretty nice. Who knows?"

I grew lost in thought, recalling all the times Michael had speculated about what might have happened had we not run into Sam that cold night in St. Louis. Just maybe, Michael would say, we came along at the right time and saved Sam. "He gained confidence as we rode the train to Denver," Michael said. "He was coming off that low." This was true, for sure: we had visual evidence as we watched Sam cease squeezing that rag he carried. "He might have died on the streets if we'd left him alone." Perhaps. But I wouldn't describe anything we did as "saving" him any more than he would have been "saved" by that dime-a-dozen Bible banger in the mission that night.

A good friend of ours, actor Ann Cusack, says that we were just twenty-six and twenty-seven at the time we met Sam and that we were muddling through, figuring it out on the fly. Ann has a point. But is youth supposed to excuse us? What was the proper thing to have done? Should we have driven him to Denver? Should we have walked away and left him alone? A student at Colorado College, where I once spoke, wondered if we should have gotten him to a shrink, but that young woman didn't understand that there was no such help for the impoverished Sams of this free-market world in the United States of the 1980s—nor is there today. There was nowhere to take him, nowhere to seek assistance. When

New timers, Western Pacific Railroad yard. Oroville, California, 1982.

(overleaf) Squatters, the night before eviction, in a former Pacific Gas and Electric building. Sacramento, 1982.

(above) Hobos riding southbound on a piggyback car, Western Pacific Railroad yard. Sacramento, 1982.

Ken riding the Denver and Rio Grande Western to seek work. Glenwood Canyon, Colorado, 1982.

Michael Williamson. Feather River Canyon, California, 1986.

Dale Maharidge, on a grainer somewhere on the Southern Pacific Railroad line in the Central Valley. California, 1982.

Brier Hill Works. Youngstown, 1983.

Items left in the locker room on closing day, Jenny blast furnace, Brier Hill Works. Youngstown, 1983.

Lobby, Weirton Steel. Weirton, West Virginia, 1984.

U.S. Steel's Ohio Works. Youngstown, 1983.

Joe Marshall Jr. and Joe Marshall Sr., U.S. Steel's Ohio Works. Youngstown, 1983.

Sam, somewhere on the Missouri Pacific Railroad line. Kansas, 1983.

Hobos. Denver, 1983.

The Alexander family in their "living room" with the neighbors. Houston, 1983.

Jim and Bonnie Alexander. Houston, 1983.

One o'clock in the morning in a cash machine lobby, as a customer enters and remarks, "It's a New York party." New York City, 1990.

Bruce Springsteen at the Jenny blast furnace, Brier Hill Works. Youngstown, 1996.

(overleaf) Edge Man George crutching across the Mojave Desert. Old Route 66 near Chambless, California, 1995.

(above) Frances and Frank in their shanty beside the Colorado River, after their nighttime shifts at a Nevada casino. Bullhead City, Arizona, 1995.

Baby with her brother in a food bank line. Austin, 2000.

Maggie Segura Fonseca with her daughter Mary Frances in a food bank line. Austin, 2000.

Two boys share food that was just brought home from a charity pantry. Pigeon Forge, Tennessee, 2000.

The Murray boys near the tent that was home, where they lived with their jobless father. Broderick, California, 1989.

Two blocks from the White House. Washington, D.C., 2002.

you hit that low, the best you're going to get, if you're lucky, is a cot in a homeless shelter.

Moral questions apply each time I commit an act of journalism that goes beyond the basic "who, what, when, where, and why." I cannot simply say, "So be it." The moral question comes down to an equation that might be described as a social cost/benefit analysis. Our motive for traveling with a human being who had been damaged by the economy, in so fragile a state, was to use his story of quest and struggle to inform the larger world so that attitudes and policies might change. That may place a value on the worth of what we did.

Yet our track record in the intervening quarter of a century in effecting change (and by "our" I mean a very large contingent of writers, academics, film makers, artists, musicians, and so on) has thus far been dismal. Sam was a well-read man when we knew him, someone who grasped the power of the written word—he had those two thousand books stored at his parents' farm. You see him pictured in Michael's second section of photographs reading a book in the bed of a pickup as we rode the freight train across Kansas in a snowstorm. But Sam may have consciously or instinctively understood that opening old wounds by talking with us might not make one bit of difference; so why bother? Why continue being an iconic figure?

Are we fools to forge on, telling stories of people such as Sam? Was Sam collateral damage? Were we collateral damage? Maybe Heisenberg's Uncertainty Principle was incomplete as it applies to journalism: yes, the act of observing someone or some event changes the observed, but perhaps the observer must change as well. Was our angst really a reflection of our self-absorption with how difficult that project had been and how it affected us, and Sam simply a representative of our own inner turmoil for all these years? Maybe we—

"He's dealing with something heavy," Ron said. "I feel like you guys are mourning a death."

We headed in silence into the darkening evening. A lot of road passed beneath us.

Then—

"It's like we went through a war together," I said.

15 HOME SWEET ~~TENT~~ HOME

I'd kept in touch with the Alexander family after 1983. In one letter, Bonnie wrote some hopeful words.

We decided we'd go back to school and make something of ourselves. No more tents for us. Especially in a tornado!!
Call or write sometime.

Love,
Jim, Bonnie & Kids Alexander

But when I sent the family a copy of *Journey to Nowhere,* which contained their story, the book was returned by the post office—the address was no longer valid.

When I set out to find them for this book, I had more Internet search tools than I did during that second brief attempt back in the 1990s. Sadly, I came across an obituary for Bonnie, who had died from a brain tumor a few months earlier. She was fifty-eight. This article gave me the name of a town. I found a phone number and rang a few times. There was always a recording, and I didn't want to leave a message. But on the fourth try, I began a message, though I was fumbling my words as I had done with Sam. The phone picked up midway. It was Jim.

"For years, we talked about you guys," Jim said. We chatted a bit and had a great conversation. The family had never seen *Journey to Nowhere.* As soon as I hung up the phone, I put a book in the mail. Weeks passed. I heard nothing. I feared the cold reality of print had depressed Jim. Then I got this e-mail from Matthew Alexander, who had been eleven when he lived in a tent with his family. It said, in part,

> I went to visit my dad on November 14th to spend some time with him and do a little deer hunting. He showed me the book and I couldn't believe my eyes. . . . Chapter 9 was so real and vivid, it brought back the reality of what we experienced over those 13 months. I have been telling friends and family for years that poverty is a reality in America. I have made my two older kids read chapter 9 mostly so they can see when dad says to finish your food or to be thankful for what we have it is for a reason. You never know when you're gonna find yourself facing economic hardship.

Now it was early 2009, and the sub-boreal forest of north-central Michigan, dotted with glacial legacy ponds, came at our windshield. I watched the scenery. It's the kind of place I'd want to live if I'd been through what Jim has experienced in life. I knew that we would be warmly greeted. Yet I was apprehensive.

We came to a town and quickly found Jim's house, set among trees, with a gambrel roof. Jim was out in the side yard—he was recognizable despite the graying of his hair. He was with Matthew, who was visiting from downstate. We exchanged hugs. One of the first things Jim told us was that he'd built this house with his own hands, from foundation to rafters: he and Bonnie had vowed never again to go into debt. "No mortgage. I built it with cash as I went," Jim said.

Matthew sat near Jim, who was now sixty, in the living room. Jennifer, Matthew's sister, who lived nearby, was on her way over.

"I got another job after you guys left," Jim recalled, speaking of that summer of 1983. The job was just a half mile from the KOA campground in Texas where the family was living in their three tents.

"Then a tornado came in. And that's when I made my mind up: if I'm going to die, I want to die in my own state. That storm come in there, and it lifted sheet steel that thick," Jim said, indicating about an inch with his fingers. He was at work when the storm hit. "The lights went out. I ran to the side door, and the wind was so bad it almost pulled us out. I was watching it twist. Telephone poles and treetops were going right toward the campground. I barely made it to the car. There was hail and rain and lightning. It was just horrible. I got to the campground, and it was some kind of deal. You had campers spun around—"

"Mom had woken both of us up," Matthew said. "And all you could hear was the wind. We were barefoot. She had us run across the rock on the roads. We ran as fast as we could to the bathrooms, which were all the way at the front of the campground." The bathrooms were made of cement blocks.

"I made my mind up that night: 'We're getting out of here,'" Jim said. "Any way possible. We sold what we could. Once we got back to Michigan, we went to stay with family. It was a touch-and-go situation.

"Bonnie went to business college. And I went to a community college. We got some more education so we could get a little more employable."

It took them a year and a half to get back on their feet.

"I went in for industrial robotics, but I never finished it, because I ended up going back into welding. Then she got involved with a construction business, as a field inspector for the Michigan Department of Transportation, for a private company that contracted with the agency. That carried us for a long time. She made a real good wage, and I was doing pretty good at welding.

"Then she ended up teaching what she'd learned about bridges and highway construction. She was employed by Ferris State, in Grand Rapids. She would go down there and give testing to the people that did the job she used to do. We diversified our abilities, so if it got soft in one area, we could switch."

Jim said that he sometimes told his story of the family's time in Texas to people he worked with.

"You know, to people that became my friends. I didn't tell everybody about it. It was an embarrassment. But I related that story to show that you could fall, that you could go from having a horn of plenty to a can of beans overnight. People say, 'Wow, that won't happen. I've got a job, I make good wages, I own this, I own that.' But the problem is, it can disappear. One time, I made good money as a welder. We were living high off the hog. And it just went poof!

"Texas had no welfare system. You fell on your butt there, you had to pick yourself up, or you'd stay on your butt. There was no help. When the bottom fell out there, with no safety net, and we found ourselves displaced . . . I thought, 'Wow, we're in a world of hurt here.'

"We had just enough finances to get us there to the KOA. We bought the tents at Montgomery Ward. I was getting pretty desperate at a couple points in time. I probably would have used the firearm to secure food. But I'd never shoot anybody. My whole attitude in the last thirty years has changed about that. I would try to help out anybody who's in the same spot I was in. You know, people can fall on hard times through no fault of their own. It's not because they're lazy, don't want to work, whatever.

"For a life experience, we did learn from it. It did pull Jenny, Bonnie, me, and Matt tighter together. It got us through everything beyond that. For what we went through, a lot of people would have just thrown their hands in the air. But that experience in total toughened us up. We actually come through it better, with more knowledge of how to prevent a situation like that."

When Bonnie got an office job near the house Jim was building, they began living there full time. Matthew was a senior in high school by then, and he went on to graduate with a degree in theology from Christ for the Nations Bible Institute in Dallas, Texas. To pay his way through school, he worked as a doorman at the Hyatt Regency. After graduation, he came back to Michigan and got a job at a church. He married and went to work at Spartech Polycom, a plastic compounding plant in St. Clair, Michigan. The company makes different blends of plastic pellets, with machines the "size of this house," Matthew said. Other companies use the pellets to make tire additives, roller blade wheels, and plastic windows in mailing envelopes.

"In 2000, the economy started really fluctuating," Matthew said. "A lot of the polymer and plastic type companies started to take a big hit. Our company had sixty-six plants worldwide. All of their plants ended up cutting down to half staff. I got my pink slip in December of 2000."

He was out of work for nine months. In April 2001, a friend recruited him to join the Michigan Air National Guard "to try and make a little money." That gave him two months of income as pay for basic training. "After that, it was back to the unemployment office." He got a few weeks of carpentry work at his church, which was building a gymnasium. He installed metal doors and built a balcony. On September 11, he was laying flooring in the balcony when an electrician yelled that everyone had to get to a television set, fast.

Matthew watched live footage as the second plane went into the tower. Forty minutes later, a telephone call came from his commander at Selfridge Air National Guard Base, in Harrison Township: he was activated. For two years, he was part of Operation Noble Eagle, providing security here and abroad, including some time in the United Arab Emirates.

His commander felt that Matthew was a hard worker and gave him a tryout to be a federal technician, a full-time job with the National Guard.

"I worked my butt off," Matthew said. "The drive inside me was to not let my kids go through what I went through." He "shined" and was hired permanently.

And so Matthew has a job, but it's contingent on his staying in the National Guard. The downside is tours of duty. He was scheduled for a six-month stint in Afghanistan that coming fall.

"I can serve until I am sixty," Matthew, thirty-seven, noted.

These union government jobs have been scaled back by half—guys with twenty-five years in were pushed into early retirement. Matthew figured he could hang on to this job for a while. But the tours of duty were difficult, because he has four children: Alexis, thirteen; Nolan, ten; Wade, six; Andrew, four.

Michael turned to Jim: "So he didn't follow you into the marines."

"I actually said, 'I'll drive you to Canada,'" Jim said. "I didn't want him to be a ground padre, getting close to it.

"What a dip in my life," Jim added, referring to Vietnam. "How it changed me as a person."

"He still gets nervous," Matthew said.

"Now, I go to counseling," Jim explained. "I go to a Vietnam veterans group. There's Korean War vets in there, too. We go there and help one another. That's how we are dealing with long-term post-traumatic stress disorder. We had no idea what was bothering us. We come to find out later that it manifests itself in so many ways. And we're dealing with health issues with Agent Orange."

Not everyone has been approved for benefits. Jim said fourteen guys get help for Agent Orange; the remaining guys have been denied.

"The rest of them, they just let you die." Jim laughed sardonically. "It's really a sad fact that a lot of the guys that I know, a lot of them are dying. You go there, and there's a guy missing. It's tough. I feel bad for these guys coming back from Iraq. They recycle them too quick."

Michael took some pictures. I ducked outside to get a lens that he had left in the car. I looked up and saw the plaque on the front of the house.

I stared at it, overcome with emotion. It had been a long journey from that tent in Texas to this wall on which the Alexanders could attach a nameplate that signifies what a home is supposed to be—not an investment, not something to use like a cash machine, not something to be chopped up and "securitized" on Wall Street.

"I wish Bonnie was here to meet you guys," Jim continued when I returned. He spoke again of their life in the tents in Texas: "She was a lot easier with what happened than I was. Jenny and Matt—for them it was different; they loved it. Bonnie could survive it. I hated it. I lived in tents in Vietnam, and I didn't want to do it again. But we were doing what we had to do. Eking out the best we could. I even worked day jobs. I was not—"

Jim paused.

"—one of those people you would classify as not willing to work. I took everything and anything I could get. It was tough. When people said, 'Where do you live?' you didn't want to tell them."

"Me and my sister, we were both sort of easy-going. Resilient," Matthew said.

"How were you treated at school?" I asked.

"You were the odd kid out, for sure," Matthew recalled. "I can remember the school nurse coming in one day and pulling me out of class because I had a bunch of mosquito bites. I accidentally left my tent door open one night. It looked like I had pox or something. That was kind of hard to say, 'I live in a tent.' I'll never forget the fourth-grade teacher I had. It was Grace Raymond Elementary School, in Aldine, Texas. Mrs. Korff. She knew my situation, knew we were in dire straits. She was a great teacher. Many mornings, I'd come into school and she'd give me breakfast cereal from the cafeteria. She made sure I had food in the morning. A couple of times, she offered to do laundry. She would also protect me from the kids in class that would incessantly hit me and kick me for being poor and a Yankee.

"They could tell by your accent that you weren't from Texas. You tried to act like you're from Texas, but it never worked. You're too close to Canada to talk 'normal' for most Texans. You got picked on a lot. There were a few times in Houston, we ran home pretty fast. We got to be good runners and hiders.

"The day I came up here with my son and Dad had told me about the book, as soon as I opened it, there was that picture of us on the picnic table—that's my son, Nolan!" he exclaimed about the picture of himself as a boy, looking just like Nolan does now.

"It's crazy. He's got the same hairdo and everything. I said, 'Look, it's you.' He was kind of shocked. I made him read it. Forever, I tell my kids, 'Finish your food. Don't waste things. Take care of your stuff.' And this is why. They say, 'I know, Dad, you grew up poor—blah, blah, blah.' But when they read that book, especially my thirteen-year-old daughter, she was, like, 'Wow, you weren't kidding!' This was real. It actually brought my family, my wife, a little bit closer to me, just talking about it. I had told her some pretty good details of it. Experiences, good and bad. The tornado and stuff. People just don't understand. Home, it becomes—"

Matthew searched for words.

"—your refuge, something you feel protected in. When you don't have that, you have to improvise mentally, emotionally, everything. It just changes your whole chemistry. But, obviously, I feel I wouldn't be as strong as I am if we hadn't come through that. And we've been, since day one, the tightest family ever.

"When I read it, I just teared up. Wow, this stuff is so detailed and so accurate. I told my dad I couldn't believe how much detail you captured in our story. I'll always remember that Mom had pulled a clipping out of the *Sacramento Bee,* and she kept that. I always remembered Sacramento, California."

I had forgotten that I'd mentioned the family in that newspaper story and had sent them a copy.

"I didn't exactly realize what you guys were doing down there," Jim said of our book. "As bad as we had it, compared to some, we were better off. We were pretty much dry. We had clean clothes. We had showers there. People were amazed how much it cost us at that time to pitch a tent. It was outstanding money."

"There was a candy bar thing," Matthew remembered. "It was Mars. If you collected sixty candy bar wrappers, they would send you five dollars in the mail. Well, I had done that, and things were getting real tight. It had been a couple of days, Dad hadn't gotten his job yet, and we didn't have a lot of money. I can remember mom was, like, 'If I can get five bucks, all I need is five bucks, for some eggs and potatoes, we can make something.' And here comes, through the mail, a five-dollar check from the Mars Corporation. We ate because of that. I looked at it as God providing for us. Mom and Dad, and I, we had our faith in God, and that brought us together. It helped us get through those things. We could see God providing help every step of the way. Like Dad said, we felt we were better off than a lot of people we had seen and heard about."

"Yeah, all those other stories," Michael said. "But your story got in our heads. We'd go to sleep at night, and your story would be there. We needed people like you to let us into your lives, to tell your story, for this book to do what it had to do. You took the risk that it could be an embarrassment. . . . I want to thank you because it worked only because you folks let us in."

Michael grew emotional as he recalled that Matthew had been eleven when we met the family in 1983—about the same age Michael had been when he lost his mother.

"I saw a kid on a stoop, that age, my age," Michael said of the moment he snapped a picture of Matthew and Jennifer holding the puppies (included in the third section of photographs). "And I thought, 'This is going to break you or make you.'"

There was a beat as Michael wiped away a tear.

"What's the lesson?" Michael asked. "We're doing a story for now. What can we learn as a society? What are we as Americans? Are we our brother's keeper? So that the next group can learn. Once again, we're naïve enough to think that now, thirty years later, we have to do something different. We're not 'every man for ourselves.' We won't survive as a country if we keep that attitude."

Jim and Matthew thought long about this before answering. First, the men said, people have to rely on the power of family, if they have family.

"What I would say to people right now is that you can't count on anything that you don't do yourself," Jim said. "If your hand don't put it there, and you don't provide for your own family yourself, by your own intelligence and by your own means, you can't count on anybody else to do it for you."

Matthew cited the church as a powerful tool to help people. "You are going to see more and more faith-based organizations getting involved." For awhile, a church housed his family before he went off to basic training.

"Did the experience in Texas change your life?" I asked Matthew.

"Absolutely. In 2000, when my wife and I were a young couple, with two kids, I found myself in the unemployment line. It was bleak. There were still jobs you could pick up. I found that I was still very resourceful. Mom and Dad were willing to help out. You learn to stretch. To make things go, to make things last. And I still—you still kind of stockpile a little bit."

When Matthew goes on a rotation with the National Guard, he's noticed that other soldiers sometimes won't eat their Meals Ready to Eat rations, especially the vegetarian entrees. "It's good for ten years, I'll take it," Matthew said. He has a closet filled with them. "My wife says, 'Why do you have all those MREs?' You never know when that rainy day is going to happen. You got the emergency food, the candles, the lights."

Matthew and his wife, Lisa, own a house in Fort Gratiot, which is near Port Huron, Michigan. Their three boys sleep in one room.

Jim shook his head at the prospects for working people.

"Jobs in Michigan, they're like—*bllptt!* Gone," Jim said. "The way I see things today, it's more widespread, and it's going to affect more people. When it finally comes down, it's going to come fast, quick, and bad.

"And, you know, I've been telling Matt and Jenny for years, doom and gloom, do this and do that, because of that experience. You can have chicken today and feathers tomorrow, that's what my mother always told me. She went through the Depression. It's a good thing to hold back. Good advice. We used to fluff that off. 'It can't happen'—till it does happen. It changes your whole persona. They were right, oh, man. I just talked to Bonnie's old man the other day. He's in his nineties, his wife is in her upper eighties. And we were discussing the very thing we are talking about now. You do learn, or you burn."

"Is it worse now than back in 1983?" I asked Jim.

"Oh, yeah, oh, yeah, by far," Jim replied.

"It's broader," added Matthew.

"Those who are really well educated and got into a bracket of making good money, it's starting to come apart for them," Jim said. "It's not just blue collar. People like me, you go to the bottom a couple of times, you can bounce back. My feeling is a lot of people that's never felt or been in the spot me and Bonnie and the kids were in, how are they going to deal with it? I feel these people are going to have a lot harder time to adjust than I would. We do a lot of living off the land.

"If the food stops going to the stores, if people can't get food, no matter how much money you got, you're in trouble. I honestly believe that if it turns to anarchy, if it goes sour, the cities are going to be tough. And people may resort to violence. It's a sad fact. But I don't think this administration, or the last one, or the last one—go back to whatever—really understands the desperation of the American people. It's going to get real rough. I think of the little kids. That's who I worry about. I'm older now, I've lived enough life to where I ain't worried about it. But it's those little kids, Jennifer's little kids, that's who I have a heart for. What are we leaving them? What legacy? They're just piling debt on them—"

Jennifer arrived. She had turned thirty-eight the previous day. She was now Jennifer Spicer, married and living not far away with Brad, her husband, and their children: Shaun Weaver, eighteen; Abigail Alexander, twelve; and Tabitha Alexander, eleven. Brad works in the oil fields; earlier that day, some of his co-workers had been laid off. Jennifer is now in nursing school but had to take time off for surgery on her neck. She is also an artist who paints in oil.

Jennifer and Matthew opened *Journey to Nowhere* and thumbed through pictures of the family.

"I probably couldn't smoke that day," Jennifer said when she saw the picture of her, confessing that she would sneak off and smoke half a pack of cigarettes each day at the age of twelve.

"My tent was here, and Jenny's tent was here. Right behind us was the water," Matthew said.

"The guys from Ohio were next to us," Jim chimed in. He didn't know what happened to them. "After the tornado, they went back to Ohio. After you guys left, I bought a little travel trailer, because I was making a little bit of money. At least we got a little air-conditioned travel trailer; it was better than the tent."

"See that briefcase right there?" Matthew pointed to the picture of Jim with a sidearm in the tent; the briefcase held the weapon. "I have that. I have a whole bunch of nostalgic stuff in it. When dad had taken off to go up to Michigan ahead of us, we had another storm. All of our pictures got soaked. We lost so much stuff in that second storm. But I was able to keep the briefcase."

"It's hard to look at them pictures of Bonnie and the kids, especially with Bonnie passing," Jim noted. "It's pretty tough. But we're tough people. Me and Jenny, we had her here in hospice. We took care of her to the end. It was hard. But we did it. That was our way."

Bonnie had volunteered at a food pantry up to the time she fell ill.

"She ordered food for it," Jim said. "Packed it up for people. She had a lot of empathy for people."

Speaking of their thirteen months living in a tent, Jim pointed out that Bonnie "came from a middle-class family, ate solid every day. Nice house. I didn't think she—she probably survived that better than I did. It devastated me."

"It was probably one of the better times in my life," Jennifer added. "I did a lot of growing there."

"As I said, Bonnie didn't have the problems with that situation like I did," Jim reiterated. "Not so much pride. I felt like a failure. I let my family down. I didn't want it to happen again."

"Afterward, even years later, we have to reassure dad that it was all right," Matthew said.

Matthew added, "We came through it strong, you know."

Jim looked at me. "I felt worse than they did."

"He did an outstanding job coming back and getting his head straight," Matthew said.

"It's been a journey," Jim replied. "You know, the title of your book was just so spot on."

Jim laughed softly.

"A lot of people can't believe it happened. People working the Big Three, making good money, they have vacation homes. I became friends with a lot of them. I relate the story, they freak out. They ask: Why? How? They just didn't understand. They'll sit there and look at you with a faraway unbelieving look."

Jennifer told us that her daughters had taken *Journey to Nowhere* to school for "show and tell."

"In the eight months since Bonnie passed away, I've been kind of secluded," Jim told us. "A lot of our friends died, too. A lot of people we knew have passed away already."

Jennifer said that everything that happened, from being homeless to her mother's recent death, has had a profound influence on them.

"We've always been a different family," Jennifer asserted. "Between my dad and mom and Matt and I, we're a nucleus, and it's not going to be divided. That's how it's always been. We've been close."

While Jim was talking with Michael and Ron Wyman, Matthew went to Jim's computer to show me pictures of his children on Facebook. Matthew whispered that what happened in the 1980s continues to be very hard on Jim, who constantly second-guesses how he might have avoided having his family live in a tent. That guilt is combined with the continued fall-out from his experiences in Vietnam.

"You came at a good time," Matthew confided. "He needs to know that he didn't fail."

"Of course he didn't," I said. "What he did, it was heroic."

I recall Jay, whom we met right after leaving the Alexanders, and his utter submission to the overlords who ran that Texas slave labor camp. Jim has doubted himself, but he stuck it out; he didn't go over the brink into despair the way Jay did. I think of what my father always said about his experience fighting in the Pacific during World War II: "You survive." Not only did Jim survive both Vietnam and the nightmare of being homeless, he also kept his family together.

But the flip side of surviving a nightmare is a dark legacy. Dad made it back with a Purple Heart for his near-death wound, but he was not quite whole; he remained a bit broken till the day he died. I saw the same thing not only in Jim but also in his children. We were witnessing a family still coping with what had happened over a quarter of a century ago. There is no escape from history; we are what we have lived. We must deal with our demons to ensure our future narrative, which the Alexanders were doing. Their story is both redemptive and cautionary. Those who become homeless now and later in the 2010s face a journey similar to that taken by the Alexander family.

Jim took us to a shed behind the house and showed off a new purchase—a Yamaha V Star 1300 CC road motorcycle. He fired it up. The air was filled with the sound of metal thunder. Jim revved the engine a few times and described how he was going to ride alone through the woods of northern Michigan in the coming summer. I could see his face with the wind tearing his eyes as he throttled fast on the highway, where he could forget, if only for a little while.

We took the family out for dinner at a local pub. I told Jim twice during the meal how proud he should be for all that he went through. "You are a success story from our book," I said. And I meant it.

Then I looked at Matthew, sitting farther away from me at the long table, and I imagined him in Afghanistan at the end of the year. And I thought about the forces that were arrayed against the Alexanders, so many of the things that had wreaked havoc with this family: the exploding inequality and the heedless trade policies and the looting from the top that had precipitated economic crisis; the mistake of Vietnam and its horrors; the pointlessness of Afghanistan. And I thought about how nothing has changed as far as class is concerned in this nation. The rich continue to be pampered, taking care of their own. The rugged individualism of the Alexander family is admirable, but family alone can't do it. An economy, a society, has to be created that skews toward working men and women and families, so that people don't have to join the National Guard in order to survive.

16 MAGGIE: "AM I DOING THE RIGHT THING?"

Irene, age four, wearing a purple t-shirt with the word "Princess" on the front, watched television with her older sister, Mary Frances. Without prompting, Irene jumped up and, with a smile on her face, ran to Maggie, who was seated at the kitchen table talking with us.

"I love you," the little girl said.

Maggie hugged her daughter.

"She always does that," Maggie told us.

Maggie had been talking about the past nine years since we'd last seen her, for the *George* magazine assignment in 2000. It had been a rough time for her, both emotionally and financially. Maggie was married in 2001, and she had changed her last name to Fonseca. Not long after Irene was born, her husband left her for a much younger woman. She was once again a single mother.

Now, at age thirty-three, Maggie was rebuilding her life. Foremost was the well-being of her daughters.

"The thing of it is, they're fine," Maggie said. "They're never any problem. Of course not. I'm raising good girls here. They know better."

Maggie pointed to Mary Frances.

"She's A and B honor roll all the time. She's the only child in her school that got a perfect score on the science test."

When I had seen Mary Frances in 2000, she was two and was still under a doctor's care for her congenital health problems. Now, just a week from her eleventh birthday, Mary Frances was perfectly healthy, except for her teeth, which had been damaged by one of the drugs that saved her life. Maggie faced some expensive dental bills.

Maggie's Habitat for Humanity house off Montopolis Drive in Austin, Texas, where the family still lived, had a feeling of warmth and pride. The home was tidy and filled with simple possessions. There was fresh paint on the walls, the kitchen had a new tile floor, and the lawn was nicely mowed.

On the good news front, Maggie was passionate about helping children and elderly people through her state job. And she had advanced to a higher position.

"It's now called the Texas Department of Family and Protective Services. I've been in the Diligent Search Unit for five years. We're involved when children are removed from their parents and a report has to be written up. I do Internet searches to find missing parents, to find relatives to possibly place the children with, or to find the relatives of elderly people who need help. To me, it's important. It makes me feel good. I'm the lead of my unit. I lead six people.

"Yeah, I make more money, but things didn't stay the same price as they were nine years ago. And I have another child. It's still a struggle. Being a state employee, you basically are on a fixed income. I get paid month to month. And when it's gone, it's gone. I feel like I'm barely holding on. I'm barely making it all these years later."

When her husband left in 2005, he declined to divorce her. Support from him for Irene had been sporadic. Maggie had to hire a lawyer.

"We were left high and dry. What I had to do at the time to get by was short my mortgage. So now I'm having to pay more every month to get out of the hole I had to put myself in. I know it was wrong, but I didn't have a choice. I mean, it just has been—" Maggie sighed, "—a rough few years. I'm still trying to get over it personally."

Maggie was still working two, and sometimes three, jobs. Between December and April each year, she works for a tax preparation company, readying 1040 forms. Other times, she will clean homes for pay or bake desserts for hire.

Maggie remained as frugal as she had been when I first met her, standing in a food bank line for the first time in her life. She spends $210 a month on food for the three of them: $2.26 per person, per day. She can make a meal from three chicken thighs.

"I can get a big pack of chicken and make four dinners out of that thing. You know how much ground meat fits into a sandwich bag? That's a meal. That will be spaghetti or whatever I decide to make for the girls. You just figure it out. It's what you have to do."

She goes to the food pantry at her church, Dolores Catholic, which is supplied by the Capital Area Food Bank. She is allowed one visit per month.

"Last week, I got two dozen eggs. A small turkey breast—that's for sandwiches. A few canned goods, fruits, and vegetables. My grandmother, she goes to the rec center for the senior citizens program, and they always give them way, way lots of stuff, so she spreads it around. It really does help."

"How many days does it last?"

"Hmm. Probably not a week's worth. Enough to get a couple of meals out of it. I'm frugal. I mean, I'm like way frugal."

The previous day, I'd been at the Capital Area Food Bank. Its president and CEO, David Davenport, reported that need had exploded. The food bank was working at capacity, and Davenport was frustrated—many of its 335 client agencies in twenty-one counties, covering 20,000 square miles of Texas, didn't have enough food to distribute. "It's sort of the dog chasing its tail," Davenport remarked, describing their efforts to keep pace with need. In 2000, when I first met Maggie, the Capital Area Food Bank distributed some 10 million pounds of food. By 2008, according to Davenport, this total had grown to 17 million pounds; and in 2009, the projected distribution was 22 to 23 million pounds. Nationally, Feeding America, to which the Austin food bank belongs, gave away 1 billion pounds of food nationwide in 1999 and 2.6 billion pounds in fiscal 2009.

Besides the food bank, her mother's garden helped Maggie feed her family in the summer. Mary Frances liked working in the garden, and she was good at it.

"Every year, their garden gets a little bigger. And we do use everything. We eat off the garden. They grow tomatoes, okra, onion, jalapeños, cilantro," Maggie said. "I learned from my mother to not live beyond my means. I totally don't. Not only because my needs are little—my daughters', too. Our joys are not in material things. The recession? I do realize that people, their worlds, are crumbling; I feel for them. That's not anything new to me. My life has been a recession. I've always had to do with what I have. If I needed more, that meant I went and waited tables, or I cleaned somebody's house. You definitely have to learn to live within your means. I've just learned to really work with what I have."

She had a little credit card debt: clothes for the girls and school supplies accounted for most of the charges.

"God forbid my mower breaks down. Things like that totally throw a wrench in it. I had to get a brake job—something so simple as a brake job messes up my whole month. My daughters have severe allergies because we're in Texas. They could get nasal spray and a prescription, but I had to choose, because there were no funds for both. That's just how it is. It's a very hard choice to make. It's awful to be in that situation. Thank goodness the nasal spray works.

"It's overwhelming for one person. It's really hard sometimes. My mother, she always tells me when I get down, or get this lost feeling, 'As long as you do right by the girls, everything else will fall into place.' I live my daily life that way."

Maggie's grandmother and her now-retired mother babysit the girls. And other relatives help in other ways.

I asked: "Without family, you'd be sunk?"

"If I didn't have them, I don't know what would have happened to me and Mary Frances," Maggie said. She began crying, and apologized. "It makes me very emotional. It's emotional for me, because it's her birthday month. When I look at her—"

We were now outside on the porch. Maggie gazed through the glass pane of the front door at her eldest daughter.

"It hasn't been easy. And it's still not easy. It can get real rough. It's hard. Very hard. I was raised with a lot of pride. I am raising my daughters to be proud to be who they are. That's what we get from my grandmother."

I asked who, or what, she blames for her situation.

Maggie thought—ten seconds, fifteen, nearly a half a minute.

"That's hard for me to say because—" A long beat. "I'm all about responsibility. I take responsibility for myself. I do believe that if more self-responsibility was taken by everybody, that would fix a lot of problems that are out there right now. I might not have always done the right thing, made the right choices. I have regrets. I should have gone to school. I could have gotten myself a college education. . . .

"I just question why everything has to be so hard. Why? Why does everything have to be such a struggle? Again, going back to Mary Frances, it's pretty sad. She's already becoming a young lady. I was telling you about her teeth. The teeth that came in, they're damaged too. It's just sad. Why does everything have to be like that?"

It bothered Maggie that the Texas state employees' health plan was inferior to the health benefits kids on welfare got.

"I would love Medicaid. Children get to go to the dentist as they are supposed to. Get their shots like they're supposed to. It's pretty sad when dental is just not there."

At one point, Maggie did apply for food stamps.

"I was told I made twelve dollars too much to qualify for food stamps," she said, referring to her monthly salary. "I couldn't imagine being worse off."

Maggie was no fan of welfare, however, and she based her views on what she saw in her job.

"I think the whole welfare system . . . I feel that it's kept people down more than helped them. In my most frustrated moments, don't think that I haven't thought about it. It would be so much easier if I just took the easy way out and gave up my job, took everything that would be given to me freely for not doing anything. More help would be offered to me if I quit my job.

"But I have hope," she said of her children. "I'm going to do everything in my power to have them more prepared for the world than maybe I was—with education. Mary Frances, I just know that she was made for big things. You go in that house and ask Mary Frances when she can move out of the house, and she'll say, 'Twenty-one, when I'm out of school.' When she is ready to go to college, I'll be done paying the house. I will do just whatever I have to do."

The family celebrated good news that summer: Mary Frances was accepted into Harmony Science Academy, a rigorous college preparatory school in Austin. (Months later, Irene would also be admitted to this same school's kindergarten program, stoking Maggie with hope for their future.)

"Mary Frances wants to be a marine biologist. We love the ocean. She loves the ocean."

Each summer, Maggie takes the girls to the beach at Corpus Christi, three and a half hours away on the Gulf of Mexico. She never went on vacations when she was a child. "I save all year so I can take them for a week. I start paying on our little condo that we rent—I make payments."

Her girlfriends are amazed that Maggie's daughters would rather stay home and eat than go out for a hamburger.

"My children are happy. We need each other. If there's one thing I can teach my girls, you have to be happy with yourself. Material things are not going to do it for you. The girls make my world go around. It's what gets me up in the morning. In my struggles and down times, you know, things are real shitty sometimes. I question, am I doing the right thing? Do you think I'm doing the right thing?"

17 MAGGIE ON MR. MURRAY

I had interviewed Charles Murray, the author of *Losing Ground,* in 2000 for our *George* magazine assignment. But the interview material didn't make the cut after the magazine piece was scaled back. So, at the time, I didn't call Maggie to get her reaction to his terming the children of single mothers "illegitimate" or to his dismissal of her specifically when I began explaining to him how she was working and losing ground.

Now, nine years later, on a warm summer afternoon in Austin, I told Maggie what Murray had said.

"You know," she began, then stopped. She thought a bit. "It's just easy for people to say. Really, you know—"

Maggie was as stunned and befuddled as I had been back then that anyone could say such a thing, and it took her time to react.

What would she say to Murray? "Tell me what to do," she finally replied. "I would like to know. I'm not a burden to society or anything like that. I work night and day. I mean, there's nothing I wouldn't do for my children. I provide for them. Not because I chose to be a single mother—that's just how it played out. I wouldn't be a single mother if a man hadn't left me.

"I'm out doing the best I can. I don't have days off, I work two jobs five months out of the year. I clean houses, whatever. When I can, I bake cheesecakes; I get orders. You do what you got to do. I'm not, never have been, able to get any kind of government aid. I just—it's a struggle.

"I just think that somebody would really have to walk in my shoes, I guess, to understand. Even for one day. I wouldn't be a single mother if I didn't get left to be a single mother. It's not a blame game. It's a responsibility thing. Come home, do the homework, get them to bed. I do the yardwork myself. I'm my own husband. Who would choose that?"

Maggie didn't want something for nothing. She just wanted a living wage and decent health care.

"I work damn hard for everything that I have. I've not had anything handed to me. Everything I have, I had to scratch and fight and bleed for."

PART 5 **AMERICA WITH THE LID RIPPED OFF** THE LATE 2000s

You need to know that our whole nation cares about you—and in the journey ahead, you are not alone. . . . Throughout the area hit by the hurricane, we will do what it takes, we will stay as long as it takes to help citizens rebuild their communities and their lives. . . . We'll not just rebuild, we'll build higher and better.

—President George W. Bush, September 15, 2005, in a televised speech from the darkened French Quarter of New Orleans in the aftermath of Hurricane Katrina

Have you heard of the 99ers? . . . Some of these people, I bet you'd be ashamed to call them Americans. They think that 99 weeks on unemployment benefits just aren't enough. . . . Go out and get a job. You may not want the job. Work at McDonalds. Work two jobs. There's been plenty of times in my life I've done jobs I hated, but I had no choice. Two years is plenty of time to have lived off your neighbor's wallet.

—Glenn Beck, August 16, 2010, on his Fox News television show

We have a tight focus on spending as market activity increases, operating more effectively and minimizing rehires where possible. We're not only holding headcount levels, but are also driving restructuring this quarter that will result in further reductions.

—Charles D. McLane Jr., chief financial officer for Alcoa, quoted in the *New York Times*, July 26, 2010

Don't let those little punk staffers take advantage of you, and stand up for yourselves.

—Senator John Boehner (R-Ohio), March 2010, counseling members of the American Banking Association to resist the efforts of Democratic lawmakers and legislative staff to regulate banks

Eight out of ten jobs created between 2009 and 2016 will be low paying, according to the U.S. Department of Labor; five of the ten will pay less than $22,000 annually; three of the ten will pay between $22,000 and $31,000.

Wall Street bonuses at the big investment banks averaged more than $340,000 per trader in 2009, according to Johnson Associates, a pay consultant; for senior traders, the pay average was estimated to be $930,000. In 2009, David Tepper, a former Goldman Sachs worker who is now head of the hedge fund Appaloosa Management, was paid $4 billion, an all-time record for his field. Because of a special tax privilege for the wealthy, he paid 15 percent federal tax on that money on Tax Day in 2010, half the rate paid by the average American middle-class worker.

In July 2010, the *New York Times* reported that many U.S. companies were seeing profits soar, were awash in record levels of cash, and yet were still laying off workers. Alcoa, for example, has laid off thirty-seven thousand workers since 2008, despite rising profits and a 22 percent jump in revenue.

About 1.4 million workers have been out of a job for 99 weeks or more, the point at which unemployment benefits run out in many states. These unemployed workers, dubbed the "99ers," have been attacked as lazy, irresponsible, and un-American by Glenn Beck and other right-wing pundits. Glenn Beck Inc., Beck's company, took in $32 million between March 2009 and March 2010, according to *Forbes* magazine.

18 SEARCH AND RESCUE

You might believe that the authorities in post-Katrina New Orleans, where there are some seventy thousand rotting and abandoned buildings, would make a concerted effort to help the thousands of squatters who are now living in these buildings. You might expect that there would be concern about the fate of so many left homeless in a major American city.

You would be wrong.

Help for the displaced comes down to two men, Shamus Rohn, twenty-eight, and Mike Miller, twenty-nine. They are outreach social workers for UNITY of Greater New Orleans, described as "a collaborative of sixty agencies working to end homelessness." It's funded on a shoestring. Its mission statement: "Working to End Homelessness, Bringing New Orleans Home."

But the title of "social worker" does not fully explain the job description of these two men. They're the U.S. Marines of the social assistance world, first to hit the backstreets of despair, armed not with weapons but with Magnum flashlights, on the front line of a lonely battle to help people in dark places. They've made it their job to comb through the seventy thousand empty structures. They section off fifty to sixty square blocks of the city at a time and catalog each abandoned juke joint, apartment, school, and house in that quadrant. They enter buildings whose security has been visibly breached—plywood ripped off, doors open—and try to help the squatters inside. Then they move on to a new zone.

In one year of work, they've gone through thirteen hundred of the decaying buildings. They do what they can, sometimes with the help of other outreach workers. In the process, they're bringing some people home.

I met Shamus at UNITY headquarters on Canal Street in March 2009. He was tall and quiet, with short-cropped hair. He wore a "uniform" of black gloves and a short-sleeve blue polo shirt with yellow lettering over the left breast that read: "UNITY, Welcome Home New Orleans."

"Let's go to the City Hall annex across the street," Shamus told me. He said little else. I followed, expecting that we were going to meet an official. Suddenly before us was the five-story annex, the bottom window glass and doors covered with plywood, other windows blown out. Shamus handed me a weighty flashlight, and we entered the pitch-black interior. I recognized the smell of post-Katrina New Orleans: a moldy rot unique to the city.

"Hello! UNITY!" Shamus shouted into the darkness. His words echoed. "Anybody home?"

Silence. I followed Shamus to a stairwell. Flashlight beams danced off walls. As we shuffled through broken glass, he explained that in multistory buildings, squatters prefer the topmost floors. It's safer—the squatters can hear danger coming. Here, people live on the third through fifth floors.

"We've never had a violent episode," Shamus said. "But this isn't the kind of place where I need to run out and try to find an exit."

"It's a long way out," I noted.

The third-floor hallway was littered with debris—people have sledgehammered walls open for pipes, copper wire, and other metals to sell for salvage. Shamus had been trying to meet the inhabitants of this floor for weeks, to no avail.

"You've got a number of different implements here," Shamus noted. "Crack pipes. I don't want to get stabbed by that. Or that," he said, pointing to hypodermic needles on a bed and floor.

"From my experience with our clients, a lot of them are working, and a lot of them are using drugs. You don't have great labor practices here. You'll find people who are making thirty-five dollars a day, cash, from odd jobs. It doesn't pay for a hotel. You want to eat? You end up living in a place like this. There's a very good chance the person didn't complete school. Or they were in special ed. Or they have mental health issues. This is what they have had to come home to for three years, and they're just getting by. You find a lot of substance abuse. If you've been living in one of these buildings for two years, it's often where you end up going to set your mind at ease."

We approached an abandoned juke joint in the Seventh Ward.

The triangle-shaped building appeared impenetrable. A metal grate door covered the side entrance, but a pull swung it open. Shamus shouted. No one was home. "Probably out working," he said.

In a back room, posters were scattered on the floor from when "Blues Legend" Little Milton, with Buddy Ace, played here on November 27, 1993. A ball cap with "Big Easy" on the front lay amid the posters.

"It looks like it was a pretty good place to catch a show, before the storm," Shamus said. "Not so good a place now."

Our flashlight beams raked the bar, illuminating empty liquor bottles coated with dust. In the dining and drinking area were four beds, made of cardboard and blankets set on the floor. People once sang the blues here. Now they live the blues inside these walls. On a table, carefully stacked, was a pile of pay stubs from a day-labor operation, all in the name of Mr. R.

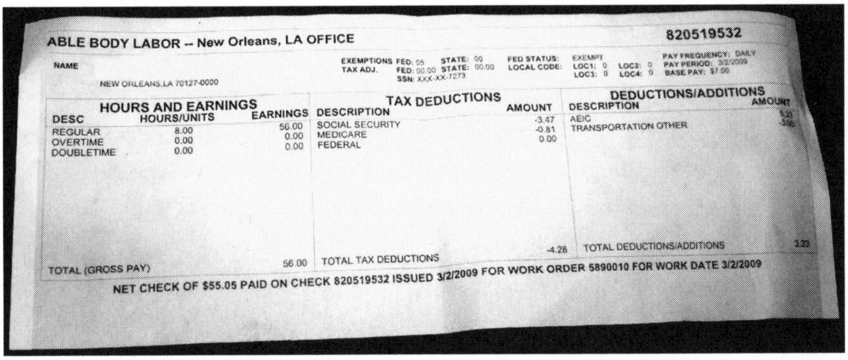

ABLE BODY LABOR -- New Orleans, LA OFFICE

820519532

NAME

NEW ORLEANS,LA 70127-0000

EXEMPTIONS FED: 05 STATE: 00
TAX ADJ. FED: 00.00 STATE: 00.00
SSN: XXX-XX-7273

FED STATUS: EXEMPT
LOCAL CODE: LOC1: 0 LOC2: 0 LOC3: 0 LOC4: 0

PAY FREQUENCY: DAILY
PAY PERIOD: 3/2/2009
BASE PAY: $7.00

HOURS AND EARNINGS

DESC	HOURS/UNITS	EARNINGS
REGULAR	8.00	56.00
OVERTIME	0.00	0.00
DOUBLETIME	0.00	0.00
TOTAL (GROSS PAY)		56.00

TAX DEDUCTIONS

DESCRIPTION	AMOUNT
SOCIAL SECURITY	-3.47
MEDICARE	-0.81
FEDERAL	0.00
TOTAL TAX DEDUCTIONS	-4.28

DEDUCTIONS/ADDITIONS

DESCRIPTION	AMOUNT
AEIC	[illegible]
TRANSPORTATION OTHER	[illegible]
TOTAL DEDUCTIONS/ADDITIONS	3.33

NET CHECK OF $55.05 PAID ON CHECK 820519532 ISSUED 3/2/2009 FOR WORK ORDER 5890010 FOR WORK DATE 3/2/2009

Next to these papers: crack pipes.

Shamus leafed through the stubs. "Looks like he's getting three or four days most weeks. March 13, March 12, March 10. Ah, March 11. He worked almost the entire week." One of the vagaries of day-haul labor is that some mornings one does not get hired. Mr. R. nets, it appears, between $700 and $800 a month.

Shamus eyed the rest of Mr. R.'s possessions, drawing inferences as an archaeologist or a detective might. He spotted a razor and a mirror. "He's shaving. Keeps his appearance up. That's the thing that blows people's minds," Shamus said. One can't recognize squatters on the street—they don't always appear to be homeless.

"This is a guy who's not going to a shelter, I'll tell you that much. If he wanted one, he'd be there by now. Their hours don't work for a guy who's working." Shamus mentioned the shelter rules requiring residents to be inside the building at certain times—often the same times a person would have to be at a job. "The crack pipe suggests there is a substance abuse issue that we need to address, too. But our experience suggests that is secondary to the need to find affordable and safe housing."

Mr. R. has never been home when the UNITY team has visited. Shamus planned to come back to this bar at night, which added a level of scariness, to meet the guy. "We're still trying to figure out what the safe way to do that is."

Before we left, Shamus restacked the pay stubs. "I'll put it all back, or I'll piss him off."

In other squats, we found crack pipes and evidence that their owners had jobs.

The pipes bothered me. Back in 1995, I'd gained new understanding of the long-term, and often addicted, homeless who had once been part of society but had lost their connection both to others and to reality, when we met that wasted old homeless man from Youngstown, then living on the streets of Houston. And I understood

Edge Men. But this was different. I'd never witnessed this kind of drug abuse among the working homeless.

Later, an explanation came from a former student of mine who grew up in New Orleans. Both rich and poor in that city, he said, were still crazed in the years after Katrina. They each medicated anxiety in their own way: "The rich drink. The poor do crack." His parents were wealthy. "They drank. Still drink. They put on twenty to thirty pounds after Katrina."

Still, the crack pipes didn't make sense. I didn't truly understand.

Next we entered an abandoned house.

Shamus shouted as we went up the stairs of the wretched house. There was no answer.

"Most people would be terrified to walk into these buildings," I ventured.

"Physically, I'm a fairly big 'predator' among the range of people I meet in a day," he replied. "The people I meet are fragile. They're just not thinking that way. They're weak. They're sick. They need help. Our philosophy, the philosophy of outreach, is to reach out to people who are not showing up at your doorstep. And if we're afraid of them, we can't expect anyone else to take a chance to meet them. So, yeah, you be careful, you pay attention—but, overall, you get used to it, you hope for the best. We have a running bet on the first body we find. The second guy in the room has to pay a hundred dollars. That's for the bar tab. We're going to go out and get really drunk."

Most commonly, squatters are welcoming.

"We hear people say, 'I was praying just before you showed up. Thank God, I don't know where to turn for help. You must be angels.' Religion is strong here. They pray. Then we show up. As an agnostic Catholic, I say if this works for them, we're happy to hear that."

He dissed himself about being an angel: "If they only knew what we do on our off time!"

Shamus's cell phone rang—it was Mike Miller, his co-worker. As we drove to meet him, I asked Shamus if the upper class was aware of what was going on in the seventy thousand empty buildings.

"My impression is that people don't really want to know," he answered. "I don't know how much of it is willful ignorance or how much it's just not on people's radar. People are commuting to work, taking the expressway past all of this. You don't even see the buildings."

Shamus has been working with the downtrodden since college. He graduated with a degree in political science and public policy from the University of Notre

Dame and then got a master's degree in political science from Tulane University. He talks about his path from idealism to the reality of the New Orleans streets, yet he remains at his core an idealist.

One of his biggest frustrations is the older people who run government programs. "Seeing your age group, the fifty-year-old bureaucrats who got into this work thirty years ago to help people—they found it was a lot more work than they thought it was going to be. They're sucking up a state paycheck. They're not doing anything to make a difference."

"Do you think there's a big difference among those in your generation and younger?"

"I'm pretty critical of my generation. I actually have a tattoo that says 'American Malcontent.' It's like a name tag."

I realized later that I didn't really understand this, so I asked Shamus to explain in an e-mail. He replied:

> I got the tattoo October 25, 2008. It stems from a conversation in a bar sometime in winter of 07–08. Some friends and I were talking about the term "American Badass" that many in my generation self-apply. I got off onto one of my tirades stating that our generation is not one of badasses—those were earlier generations that really had to rise up against some sort of oppression or struggle, like the Okies during the Great Depression, much of the WW II generation, etc.—but one of self-centered whiners. "Malcontents" popped into mind. That then led me to change tune and talk about how the entire country was founded by malcontents unhappy with taxation and British rule, and that our country exists exclusively due to the actions of a group of drunken malcontents from the late 18th century (most people call them the Founding Fathers).

I then changed track again to talk about how that makes malcontention the most patriotic stance there is, which led to more rambling about how Bush-era restrictions on First Amendment rights related to the war on terror (Patriot Act [mostly] came to mind) were the exact opposite of being patriotic due to the fact that they quash the malcontention and dissent that result from critical thought.

I realize that's not perfectly lucid. But you leave me in a bar with a little too much whiskey, beer and my fractured understanding of history, and that's what you get.

Shamus spied Mike standing on a streetcorner. Mike, who had a full beard and a deep-pitched voice, hopped in the truck and joined the conversation. I quickly learned that in terms of disposition, Mike is drummer Keith Moon to Shamus's acoustic and gentle-voiced Dave Matthews. It makes them a good team. Mike tends bar two nights a week and makes "double my salary" in tips, he noted as Shamus took us to another squat.

We continued our conversation about generational differences.

Mike spoke about his family: "My parents—I don't know how you feel, Shamus—they bought into the system. They got a 401(k), they still get to keep the benefits of the free market. They were anti-establishment while absolutely benefiting by buying into the establishment."

"Absolutely," Shamus agreed.

"Unfortunately, in our time, we don't get the benefit from market economies that our parents did," Mike said. "That's why we're not just paranoid and disillusioned—we're also jaded."

The sky blackened and rain began to fall, hard as a tropical shower. We dashed through the downpour into an old hotel, the courtyard littered with sinks that had been ripped out by salvagers. Rain sheeted off the roof.

Mike told me that he had come to New Orleans from Chicago to attend Tulane University. After graduation, he rented a tiny apartment with six-and-a-half-foot ceilings for $500. Then Katrina hit.

"I lost all my shit except for my top shelf—I had my saxophone up there. It was wild, dude, wild. But I kept my sax. It was, like, the only thing high enough."

Back in the truck, we talked about how a lot of agencies aren't exactly eager to help the squatters. The duo finds people in need, and then other service providers drag their feet, doing little or nothing. The "easy" homeless, the ones freshly fallen onto the streets, the ones without mental health problems, are "creamed" off the top and taken care of, while the difficult cases languish.

On top of this, UNITY has been waiting months for a federal program, funded but not yet activated and long overdue, that would get some five people per week into homes. They have a waiting list of eight hundred "gravely disabled" squatters. So far in this year, fourteen people on the list have died. (The federal program would come through later in the year.)

"The whole point of our outreach department is to make sure the hardest of the hard, the sickest of the sick, actually get served," Mike said. "Because if you're not, fuck it, you're helping people who really don't need help, the people who can figure homelessness out on their own."

We got back in the truck. Mike wanted to meet a man living in the Carter G. Woodson Middle School. We spent an hour roaming the school, which had been ravaged by salvagers. In an exhibition of stunning energy, whole sections of block walls had been sledgehammered out for the pipes, to sell for scrap.

"You see people on crack doing amazing things. Like ants," Shamus observed.

The sprawling school was full of squatters' beds, with the ubiquitous pornography next to each one. We got back in the truck and eventually dropped Mike off before heading back to UNITY headquarters.

I asked Shamus if he was burned out from the intensity of this work. He's been in New Orleans since 2003, when he first came down from his native Grand Rapids, Michigan, to work for AmeriCorps.

Quite the contrary.

"I actually was supposed to start law school at the University of Michigan last fall. So I agreed to come back for nine months and go to school this coming fall. But last week, I made the decision to delay law school again and stay here another year. I don't know if I'm law school–bound a year from now."

He felt that his work in New Orleans was not done.

Our day ended. We hadn't met a single squatter. I told Shamus that I would have to return to see and learn more. I wanted to understand those crack pipes.

Inside the Canal Street headquarters, I met Martha Kegel, UNITY's executive director. She pointed to Shamus and Mike and said, "Four years after Hurricane Katrina, they're still doing search and rescue."

Shamus and I left the building together. In the parking lot, he shook his head.

"If somebody had done it when it needed to be done, maybe we wouldn't be here."

19 NEW ORLEANS JAZZ

We were driving to the beat of Jivin' Gene's and Neil Pellegrin's show "'50s R&B" on WWOZ, 90.7 on the dial—

Annie is back, back, back,
in a brand new Cadillac . . .

Little Richard was singing John Anderson's "Annie Is Back," blasting from the speakers of the UNITY van. Mike was kicking it in the shotgun seat, right foot on the dash. Shamus gunned us up the sky-reaching steel truss arc of the U.S. 90 bridge over the Mississippi River. A dizzying panorama of the Crescent City: for a moment it felt as if we were about to soar over all that lay beyond and around the skyscrapers, the seventy thousand secret nooks where squatters dwell—

Now she's lookin' good,
Now she'll know how to act . . .

WWOZ provided theme music for this twelve-hour day and night. I'd been here in March, and now it was July. I was back, had to come back. I couldn't let NOLA go. It's America with the lid ripped off. I had to see more of what's inside. I had to see the squatter's night.

Night, cruising down a boulevard—

Mike cried, "It's ———!" when he spied a huge square beast of a vehicle parked in front of the nasty rot of a building. We rolled up behind the 1988 Lincoln Town Car. A dude who has had a job all his life emerged from the car. Shamus and Mike greeted him and talked about how they were pushing the levers of bureaucracy to get him into housing. *It's gonna take time, and we can't promise anything. We're working it hard, man—* Oh, did the dude want to get off the street. *I can't wait to get back into a house! Yes, that will be a glorious day.* And Mike promised that when that happens, *we gotta go driving in this big old beautiful car to celebrate.*

"I'll give you the keys!" the dude said excitedly.

"No, no!" Mike protested. "No, man, YOU'RE driving! We're gonna ride in this Town Car down BOURBON STREET, and I'm gonna be HOLLERIN' out the window! We're gonna celebrate! We're both gonna be HOLLERIN'!"

The dude smiled. We moved on and left him dreaming of a better future in the present of his homeless night.

Now we were traveling some badass streets that I'd likely never go down alone, no way at this time of night.

At an abandoned service station surrounded by a chain-link fence, a large group had gathered at the fence gate. People were sleeping on cots, on the ground, and in a smashed-up motorhome. Shamus shut off the engine of the van, and WWOZ fell silent. He and Mike were greeted with joy by old black men sitting on chairs. One had a cane. Another guy's right foot was in a walking cast. "Diabetes," he said.

We approached a gray-haired man we'll call Cig, as in Cigarette. He was someone who had been sleeping here till Shamus and Mike got him into housing six months ago.

"Coming back to hang?" Mike asked. "How you doing, man?"

"If you're breathin', you're doin' okay," Cig replied. He laughed, really a chortle with a life's worth of living behind it.

Two crazy women lived here. One was huge, and she hugged all of us. My arms barely reached around her middle. The big crazy woman began dancing, and Mike danced with her.

Off to the side, Shamus was talking gravely with a man whose eyes were wide with worry. The man told him about his job driving a delivery truck and recounted in exacting detail how a guy with a .357 Magnum revolver had tried to rob him recently.

"Says, 'I'm gonna shoot you.' I said, 'Why would you want to shoot me! Why? I give you what you want.'" The man described putting his truck in gear, just before a bullet came through the window. "I'm layin' in the seat like this as I take off," the man said, leaning sideways. "Then the other bullet hits back here." He pointed to what would have been the rear edge of the truck's cab.

"I survived for a reason! I survived for a reason! There's a reason I'm still here!" The man was nearly in tears. He had no idea what that reason might be.

Shamus asked questions and discovered that the truck driver was still residing in a nearby home, but barely. He was on the brink of financial disaster. The man was pre-homeless—outside the job description of the UNITY team. Shamus couldn't let it go, though. He gave the man a business card. Shamus meets a lot of folks, so he told the man to "call me and remind me of shots being fired." He could hook the man up with an agency that might be able to help with his utilities and prevent him from becoming a squatter.

As we were saying goodbye, three New Orleans police cars roared up a half block away, lights blazing. Cops emerged from the cars; they handcuffed a woman.

Canal Street, more cop cars.

The New Orleans night was lit by strobing flashes of blue light. A man we'll call Skinny was out riding a bike. Skinny flagged down Shamus and Mike center-street in the west lane. Shamus told Skinny to meet us on the east side of Canal; we hung a U at the first legal left.

Skinny talked alone with Shamus while we sat in the van. I couldn't hear the conversation, but Skinny's body language was frantic. Shamus and Skinny came back to the UNITY vehicle. Shamus sat behind the wheel, and Skinny leaned on the passenger door. Skinny's face was deeply lined at age thirty, though he didn't look old—that will come soon if he lives long enough. His face was simply hard-lived; it was like a Mardi Gras mask with elastic eyes. He jerked his arms and spoke fast. Skinny has four tickets from the cops for blocking the sidewalk on Canal. "What do I do?! What do I do!?" He swore he was just standing on the sidewalk. This, however, was the least of his problems.

Mike and Shamus had gotten him into housing. But it was in a bad neighborhood, and not long after he moved in, a gunman attacked him. He ran, hoping his feet would do their stuff.

He showed us how bullets whizzed past his ears.

"It was like this, *phewww! phewww!*" he said in a rush of words, using left and right fingers to show bullets going past one ear, then the other.

He didn't dodge them all: he took one in the chest. I couldn't make out how seriously he was injured, but there is no good way to take a bullet. He was frightfully thin.

Now he was again homeless, in the Canal Street area, because he was too scared to go back to that house. Shamus and Mike told him they would push to have him moved.

The stream of frantic talk continued. Skinny didn't want us to leave. Goodbyes were exchanged five, six times, and he talked on. Mike listened, his right foot up on the dash like he had all the time in the world, which he didn't. Mike and Shamus convey the illusion of having time for people who get little attention from anyone else.

"Homeless people," Skinny said to the men, "you know what they do? Give you their last food, dog."

There's a whole lot more to the night. Rats in alleys. Climbing a five-story fire escape next to The Roosevelt New Orleans, a Waldorf Astoria hotel where the best Internet out-the-door rate for a double room was $181.67, seeking a couple who slept and made love on a roof in view of hotel guests. Nearby, a woman in her twenties was in a doorway curled beneath a blanket. "It's ———," Mike said. "She's that 1 percent I was telling you about." He meant that she was among the rare homeless individuals they run into who don't want a home. The woman was bipolar, and the men feared she would suffer rape or assault. She was a high-priority case.

"She's going to run on us, just watch," they warned. I was hanging back. Shamus and Mike talked with the woman, and she didn't bolt. She agreed to meet again when someone came back in the daylight—the men planned to send a female outreach worker. Mike and Shamus were happy: just getting her to agree to meet was one small victory.

It had been a long day and night with few measurable successes—a routine day and night. Success in New Orleans for those working with the displaced is gauged in weeks at best, months, multiple months—years. Our day was just one day in a process. It had begun in the afternoon in the abandoned New Orleans City Hall annex that I'd first visited in March, where Shamus and Mike had since made contact with some of the third-floor residents. It was an afternoon that would answer the question that had nagged me about the New Orleans squatters.

We entered the now-familiar dark stairwell and clicked our flashlights on. On the second floor, we walked out into an open courtyard, where graffiti artists had painted a panel of swimming sharks and two large birds with bits of lyrics from "Surfin' Bird," the 1963 song by the Trashmen.

Back in the stairwell, light beams darted; we heard barking dogs that sounded fierce. Growls echoed as we neared the third-floor landing.

"Jazz?! Trent!?" Shamus yelled. "Homeless outreach! Mike and Shamus!"

A male voice. The door opened a sliver. Weak light sliced the darkness of the landing. More barking. The voice ordered the dogs to shush. The door opened, and we faced Trent, a short, bleary-eyed, bearded man. We shook hands.

Trent hollered to his wife that Shamus and Mike were visiting. It was lucky to find the couple in during the day. They usually leave by 6:30 in the morning and don't come back until dark.

A woman came into the room. "My name is Ludmilla," she told us. "My street name is 'Jazz.' As in jazzed-up. I used to have such a bad temper when I was young." She'd come to New Orleans seeking work after Katrina. "I am from Gallup, New Mexico. I am a Navajo, full blooded, off the reservation."

She had gotten work, but the place closed. That began her descent.

My biggest first impression of the couple was that they seemed very fragile, as Shamus had told me squatters in general tend to be.

Jazz wore an oversize t-shirt. She invited us into her room, where she sat on the bed. The dogs joined her. One dog has been with her for ten years; its Japanese name, which I missed, translates to "Emperor Autumn Dog." The other dog, a stray the couple had recently taken in, was simply named "Sherman Tank."

On a bulletin board next to the door hung a small American flag, a rosary, a pressed dried flower Trent had given to Jazz when they were courting. The couple had been married by a homeless ordained minister three months previous. On a stand was a novel Jazz was reading. She was also studying Japanese.

"It's a wonderful language," she said. Jazz abides by Japanese and Hindu spiritual practices, "because these characteristics taught me to keep my anger under control. It's trying. There was a time when I came under the influence of crack. But I have been clean for a year now."

"Congratulations," I offered.

"Thank you very much. But crack brought back a lot of my anger. And hate. And after so many years of working toward keeping it under control and finding this way—"

I asked whether the couple wanted to get into housing.

"Oh, *yes!* Duh!" Jazz cried out. "Duh!" Trent shouted. The couple talked over each other about how they desperately wanted to get out of this squat.

"Okay, a stupid question," I allowed.

"We have rats as friends," Jazz said. "And every now and then, we find a little poopie on the bed."

"So if you get housing, you're there?"

"Yes, sir," Jazz said.

"Most definitely," Trent added.

"When was the last time you were in housing?"

Trent laughed. "Good question."

"For me," Jazz said, "about a year, maybe a year and a half. I worked and I worked and I worked, but the dude who owned the place, he went under. So we just lived there. It went down, and it got bad. There's—"

Jazz paused for a long time.

"I would like to live, thank you, in a place with locking doors and good windows. Where I wouldn't have to stay awake at night, where we wouldn't have to take turns sleeping."

"It would be wonderful," Trent said.

"It would be nice not to have to worry about people coming downstairs, and upstairs," she continued.

Another worry, not as immediate, was the approaching hurricane season.

"I think we'll do better than most people because we're used to living on the rough," Jazz predicted, thinking about the potential of a hurricane. "We have no air-conditioning. We have nothing but the wind coming through. People who suffer most are people used to air-conditioning and twenty-first-century utilities. We are living just like we would on the reservation. We haul our own water."

She held up one of the eight one-gallon jugs next to the bed. Trent cannot help haul the water—he has Buerger's disease, which restricts blood flow in his legs. It's all he can do to get himself up the stairs.

"We don't do bad for a couple of homeless people," Trent offered.

The couple had made a bathtub of sorts in the second-floor courtyard with debris to channel rainwater. Jazz talked about the graffiti, the sharks, and the birds.

"Have you heard the word?" Jazz said, alluding to the Trashmen song.

"About the bird," Trent added.

"The bird is the word," Jazz said.

The couple heard the visiting artists working on the paintings and went down to ask them to dinner. They declined. Amid this conversation, Shamus left the room. He returned with a poster that had been tacked on the wall outside Jazz's door.

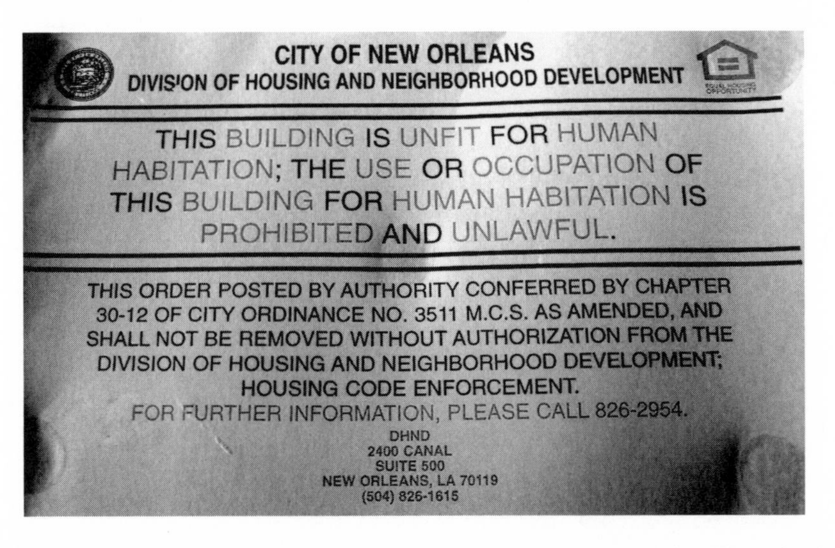

"How stupid to put this sign up!" Shamus exclaimed, angry. "They don't have any money to help, but they can spend money to put this shit up. What a waste of time!"

The couple gave us a tour down the hall of their "dining room," an open office area with large windows that afforded a great view of the city, from the French Quarter to the east.

"It's a wonderful place to watch a lightning storm," Jazz commented.

I mentioned that Shamus had taken me up to the roof in March. "It's beautiful when you're up there," I said.

Jazz and Trent shuddered. I had touched on a bad topic. They never go above the third floor.

"We got beat up big time, one time, up there," Jazz told us.

A squatter on the top floor "picked up his girlfriend by the throat, threw her against the wall," said Trent. Trent is so small and frail that it's hard to imagine how he might have stopped the violence. But he tried. "I jumped up and said, *'NO!'* I grabbed him by the throat—"

"The thing of it was, he was stomping on this dude who was already unconscious from being drunk," Jazz added. "He was stomping on his head. So we stopped it. We got our asses beat. Big time."

"Big time," Trent echoed.

"Big time," Jazz said. The couple showed us scars from that beating. "Six of them against the two of us. They hang out on the upper floors. I don't go up there. I don't know if you've noticed, but I have this little area cordoned off. Booby traps."

"I better watch where I step," I said.

"No, no, nothing like that," Jazz reassured me. "We don't want the police to be irate if they raid. I've got little cans hanging up. I can hear things. Alarms."

We started to leave. "We'll keep our fingers crossed for you," I said. "I hope you get into housing soon."

"We would like it a lot," Jazz replied. "It would be so nice to be able to bathe. And just be able to lock the door. You know what would be extra nice? To be able to sleep through the night without having to be on guard and taking shifts, and having everybody just sleep.

"If we panhandle fifty dollars, we can take the weekend off. On Sundays, we know they're not going to raid. We try to have a day of rest. Usually that is the day we sleep. It's so tiring. You're always on guard. You're afraid. You hear something, you jump up. It's frightening sometimes. You have to be awake. You always have to hear. It's not a foolproof way, the dogs. It's not good. It gets scary. There could be dead bodies lying around, and you wouldn't know. We're trying. We're doing the best that we can."

We descended into the dark stairwell. Our flashlight beams swept across the walls smashed open by scrap scavengers.

I left town. Some thirty hours later, I got this e-mail from Shamus:

> Apparently, a woman's body was just found in the same stairwell we used to get to Jazz and Trent. . . . Throat was slit . . . I think this helps to verify the level of violence and danger that Jazz and Trent told us exists in some of these buildings.

The woman was dead in that stairwell one day after we were there. For the next two hours, I feared the victim was Jazz. Then I got another e-mail from Shamus:

> No. Jazz found the body. Jazz had a 9 A.M. Municipal Court hearing. Mike was going to meet her there at 8:45. He showed up here at the office at 9:15 A.M. saying Jazz was a no show. What actually happened is . . . she ran into a different outreach worker who has ties to the police department. She took him to see the body and he called it in.

There was a brief article the next day in the *New Orleans Times-Picayune*. The following day, reporter Ramon Antonio Vargas wrote in his lead: "A woman found dead inside of a vacant building once used as the City Hall annex under strange circumstances Thursday morning appears to have committed suicide by slitting her neck and wrist, but the New Orleans coroner's office won't yet classify the death, officials said Friday."

The woman was identified as Angela Erin Ball, twenty-nine. Blood was all over the landing, and "smears of blood led up and down the space above the stairwell's handrail," Vargas wrote. Shamus said the woman was from Kansas and had been in town "a few months."

Officials kept alluding to suicide. The cops wouldn't return my calls. Vargas dug deeper. His story that ran on August 7, 2009, raised doubts about suicide.

According to Vargas, Ball was a stripper who worked long hours in a few clubs on Bourbon Street. She sometimes prostituted herself to make more money for her sons, to pay for the hotel room where they lived. On July 21, her birthday, she put on a tight white dress and took a gold purse, a present from a friend. That night she made $94. She telephoned a friend who was babysitting two of her four children and said she was going to remain out longer to make more money. (Jazz found her body on the morning of July 23.) Friends say they suspect robbery because her purse was missing. And a coroner's investigator noted that Ball's body was not near any knife-like weapon or shard of glass. In her hand was a strand of hair.

Vargas interviewed some of Ball's friends, who said she treated her boys well. After working some nights from 4 P.M. to 6 A.M., she would get up at 11 A.M. and take them to the zoo or the aquarium. The last thing a friend saw her do was kiss the boys after celebrating her birthday in the hotel room where the family lived, and then she headed off to work. Ball hated going into dark rooms, another friend said. Those who knew her could not understand what would have led her to enter the City Hall annex on her own.

Months passed. In December, the coroner finally ruled the death a homicide.

I have a nightmare. Screams. I am in the stairwell when a murderer has finished stabbing Angela Ball. All I see is the slashing knife. I am unarmed, dodging the blade.

I awaken, hot, not quite dripping sweat. I think of No Thumbs and what it must have been like when the assailant or assailants came into his hobo camp. Because he wasn't shot, I wonder if he'd been stabbed first and then the gunfire began to kill the witnesses, his two hobo buddies. And it was then that all their throats were cut to make sure they were dead.

Michael and I have been at the edge of violence in all our thirty years of doing this work. Luck was with us all that time, as we went into the secret places where the desperate dwell. In New Orleans, a simple change in schedule of one day, something that could have easily occurred, given the vagaries of how the trip was planned, might have meant my dream becoming reality. Maybe I would have faced that blade. Luck, good or bad, is all about timing.

But that's not the point of what I learned from Jazz and New Orleans. I had new understanding about those who live in squats and do drugs or drink. I intellectually understood what Shamus had told me about the squatters self-medicating their pain. But I now understood it emotionally. It would be amazing if most of them did not somehow numb themselves. You may dismiss them. If so, ask yourself this: can any of us with a solid lock on our doors really understand the impact of living through night after night of unsettled sleep amid constant danger?

My uncle Robert Kopfstein once told me about labor unions—he was a professor at a community college and was involved with the faculty union. He explained that sometimes weak members are unfairly shielded, but he insisted that it was okay. "By protecting the fringe, the center is made much stronger," he said. Sure, the squatters may not be as "sympathetic" as other people in this book who are in the center—the Alexander family, or Maggie, for instance. But they are human beings, American citizens, and we are all made stronger if we protect those on the economic fringe.

20 SCAPEGOATS IN THE SUN

May 12, 2009, began typically for Leopoldo Arteaga, owner of Mesa Groundskeeper, a landscaping company in a suburb of Phoenix. At 6 A.M., Leo, in his mid-sixties, and a worker began trimming 400 linear feet of oleander, a bush that grows aggressively in the Arizona heat. By eleven o'clock, the men had filled an 8-by-20-foot trailer with oleander clippings. Leo began towing the trailer to the landfill in nearby Pima County.

He was driving east on Apache Trail Road and was about to leave the city of Mesa when he stopped at a red light. On the green, he started to move forward but noticed a Maricopa County sheriff's unit with its roof lights blazing behind him.

Leo pulled to the side of the road. He looked in the mirror and saw three sheriff's cars, followed by a U.S. Immigration and Customs Enforcement van.

A deputy named Thompson approached.

"He asked for my driver's license and my insurance," Leo recalled months later when I interviewed him. He'd seen immigration sweeps by sheriff's deputies, and he knew they were profiling Latinos. But Leo figured he'd be okay—he'd initially come into the country with proper papers, and then he became a U.S. citizen after the 1986 amnesty. He also spoke good English.

"So I say, 'Why did you stop me?' He says, 'You were speeding.' I was unhappy with that answer. I told him, 'Mr. Thompson, there's no way I can be speeding,'" Leo related, noting that the light had just turned green and he was starting out with the heavy trailer. "'What is the reason you are stopping me?' Thompson got upset. He opened up the door, holds my hand, and twists it backwards. He tried to pull me out of the vehicle. But he didn't see my safety belt that was on. So he keeps pulling me, yelling, 'Get out! Get out!' I say, 'Wait, let me show you my papers.' He says, 'It's too late.'

"Mr. Feagan came along, and he pushed my chin back really hard. He hurt my neck. I could hear a cracking sound. He did that to make some space between the steering wheel and my body to undo the seat belt. Once they undid my seat belt, they pulled me out, they twist both of my arms backwards and keep me against the pickup. They turned me around, and somebody tripped me, put his leg in front of me, and those two guys pushed me forward."

Leo was slammed to the pavement, which was sizzling in 107-degree heat. Blood poured from his nose. His lip was cut, forehead scraped. His belly burned from the hot road. He pleaded with deputies Thompson and Feagan to allow him to stand. Someone said, "Chicken," and Leo heard jokes being made about him. He lay on the hot ground for ten minutes.

Officer Thompson, who tried to justify using force because of the "danger" that Leo, a man of slight build, posed, wrote in his report that "numerous tools [were] in the vehicle that could be used as weapons." He referred to garden implements. Singled out was a loose bar from a chainsaw—minus the chain. The 14-inch-long, wafer-thin steel bar weighed a few ounces.

Blood was everywhere. Leo asked to see a doctor. The officers called an ambulance. He was treated and then taken for booking.

The intake clerk asked, "Are you illegal?"

"No, ma'am, I'm a citizen of the United States," Leo responded. The woman smirked. She asked him if he was illegal two more times and smirked some more when Leo insisted that he was a citizen. She then joked with a deputy about Leo, implying he was lying. He was booked for criminal speeding and failure to show identification.

The next day, at his arraignment, the judge let him go. No charges other than speeding were filed. Leo had to pay $720 to get his truck and trailer out of the impound lot. He hired a lawyer at a cost of $700. After three court appearances, the lawyer advised him to plead guilty to speeding. Leo pleaded not guilty. The court fined him $180. The hospital sent a bill for over $7,000. In total, Leo ended up spending over $9,000. Eight months later, he still has severe neck pain and wakes up hurting in the morning.

The day that he recounted the incident to me, he wore a tattered ball cap with USA written above the bill, the big letters surrounding an American flag. He is a devout Mormon. He has seven children, all citizens, as well as thirty grandchildren and fourteen great-grandchildren. He is a soft-spoken man and has the weathered skin of someone who has spent years toiling beneath the sun.

Leo is but one of many stopped in sweeps by the Maricopa County Sheriff's Department. Between late 2007 and the end of 2009, thirteen major sweeps were conducted in Latino neighborhoods. In several cases, sworn officers were aided by volunteer civilian "posse" members from the American Freedom Riders motorcycle club. (On its Facebook page, this club wrote that its members are "hard working, tax paying American . . . motorcycle riding patriots who believe in the rule of law and the principles which have made our nation great, and who realize that the time has come to aggressively combat the catastrophic consequences of continued illegal immigration.") In these sweeps, officers arrested 669 people, about half held on immigration charges. In total, the department brags that it has arrested more than 35,000 undocumented people in a few years leading up to 2010.

It's common for U.S. citizens to be caught up in the sweeps. Simply driving while brown is a dicey act in Maricopa County.

Leo has joined a class action lawsuit against the sheriff's department alleging racial profiling, filed by the American Civil Liberties Union and other groups. If the suit is won, Leo will have a sense of justice, but it won't mean that he will get back his $9,000. To do that, he'd have to file a civil action lawsuit on his own. No lawyer will take the case, explained ACLU staff attorney Annie Lai; the damages aren't big enough to work on contingency. There are even worse cases than Leo's.

This is the story of two men—Leo Arteaga, and Joseph Arpaio, the former born in Bahía Kino, Mexico, the latter born to parents who immigrated to the United States from Naples, Italy. Each is a type, as much as one human can represent a larger group of people. Theirs is a story of the west and of the south, the dream of someplace like America, and two kinds of people who came to live that dream in a land of eternal summer.

For those of European ancestry, their arrival in Phoenix resulted from a mix of historical drives, influenced as much by Sir Thomas More as by Huck Finn. The whites came on rivers of Eisenhower-era concrete to seek utopia in this ever-expanding metropolis. From 1 million residents in 1970, Maricopa County grew to nearly 4 million in 2000. Housing developments materialized as fast as dandelions flower after spring rains back east. Values went in one direction—up. Some older newcomers were in flight from northern winters. For those younger, they sought a new way of living. Their children grew up with a sense of privilege: when they became teens, many considered it beneath them to flip burgers or do yard work. They got jobs at Starbucks or started blogs, dreaming of landing advertisers. That was the cool money, the easy money.

And so another kind of dreamer came, this one from the south, another land of sun that for too many had become an impoverished waste of *el monte,* empty mountains. There was money to be made doing the jobs in Phoenix that the citizens considered themselves too good for.

Joe Arpaio was among the older white people who retired here. He had grown up in Springfield, Massachusetts. He served in the army from 1950 to 1953 and then worked as a cop in Washington, D.C., and Las Vegas, Nevada. After that, he became an agent for the U.S. Drug Enforcement Agency, working in Turkey and Mexico and eventually being promoted to head agent for the DEA in Arizona. He remained in Phoenix after retiring. He and his wife, Ava, opened a travel agency. Joe offered to sell trips into outer space on a ship called the Phoenix E at a cost of $52,000 per passenger. "If you can afford a Mercedes, you can afford to go into space," Joe told a reporter for the *Phoenix Gazette,* in an article published May 5, 1985.

In 1993, Joe came out of retirement to run for sheriff. He conducted an intense campaign and won. The county jail was decrepit, and voters had repeatedly turned down ballot measures to fund a new one. Spending money on prisoners was not popular; they were easy targets. He began a series of now-infamous moves to humiliate and degrade inmates. He bestowed on himself the title of "America's toughest sheriff." He opened a tent city to house twenty-five hundred inmates, where temperatures inside the tents rose to 135 degrees in the summer. He put a blinking red neon VACANCY sign on the guard tower. Skin magazines were banned, along with cigarettes and coffee. He served inmates bologna dyed green. "The average meal costs about 15 cents," Sheriff Joe brags in the third person on his department's website, "and inmates are fed only twice daily, to cut the labor costs of meal delivery. He even stopped serving them salt and pepper to save tax payers $20,000 a year."

To make detainees feel their hunger, one of the few television stations allowed is the Food Network.

There was more to come. Sheriff Joe instituted chain gangs and made inmates wear striped uniforms. Later, he made them wear pink underwear and pink flip-flops. Music blares at the tent city prison—at Christmas, Alvin and the Chipmunks are commonly heard.

It must be remembered that people held in a county jail have not yet been convicted of any crimes—they are awaiting trial or deportation.

Sheriff Joe has shrugged off criticism. In the sheriff's department, there's a top-down message of condoning harsh treatment that has led to a culture of thuggery of the kind Leo Arteaga endured. Inmates have died being stun-gunned while in restraint chairs. In one case, a video revealed fourteen guards assaulting an inmate named Scott Norberg; he was shocked twenty-one times while handcuffed in a restraint chair. Norberg suffocated to death after a rag was stuffed in his mouth, apparently to stifle his screams. The county paid $8.25 million to his family in a pre-trial settlement. In another case, a paraplegic was stun-gunned while in the restraint chair. That cost the county $800,000.

The *Phoenix New Times* reported that between 2004 and 2008, the county jails in Chicago, Houston, Los Angeles, and New York, all of which house some sixty thousand inmates combined, were sued over jail conditions forty-three times. Maricopa County, with ten thousand inmates, was sued twenty-two hundred times. As a result, the county has been forced to pay out a lot of that salt and pepper money—$43 million in settlements so far.

The sheriff has never apologized for rogue actions. Often, the officers involved gain promotions. Instead, Sheriff Joe has gone after his critics. He had deputies raid the homes of *New Times* editors and arrest them on charges of leaking a grand jury investigation. (The district attorney declined to prosecute.) He has also raided the offices of county officials who oppose him. Once, deputies arrested five people who clapped when someone spoke against Sheriff Joe at a Maricopa County Board of Supervisors meeting. They were charged with disorderly conduct but were acquitted in late 2009.

Many of the refugees from northern winters and a sizable number of Californians who have fled the Pacific edge are not enamored of the brown-skinned people in their midst. This is no multicultural California where Latinos and other minorities comprise an ever-increasing share of the electorate. Dr. David Hayes-Bautista once argued that, with regard to their attitude toward nonwhites, white people fell into one of two categories: Puritans or Quakers. The "Quakers" embrace cultural change and live in multicultural communities, while the "Puritans" flee such change to live in the mountains or isolated suburbs behind walls with gates. In terms of voters, Phoenix is a city of Puritans.

Yet in his early years in office, Sheriff Joe didn't go after Latino immigrants with gusto. In fact, he even defended them. A database search turned up one story revealing this. In 2005, an army reservist back from Iraq saw seven Mexicans at a rest stop on Interstate 8. He pulled a revolver (which he legally carried on his hip under Arizona law), made the immigrants lie on the ground, and telephoned officers to arrest them for being in the country illegally. The officers complied. However, the reservist was also placed in the Maricopa County jail. "Even law enforcement has to have probable cause before taking people out of their cars and telling them to lie on the ground . . . he threatened to kill them," Sheriff Joe was quoted as saying.

But Maricopa County prosecuting attorney Andrew Thomas declined to charge the reservist. Thomas, a Republican up for election, called it a lawful citizen's arrest.

A nationwide anti-immigrant sentiment had begun to build. It was especially pronounced in Arizona. Along the border, various vigilante groups sprang up. Among them were different factions of the Minutemen, civilians who armed themselves and patrolled the border. One rancher took to holding immigrants at gunpoint, catching more than two thousand of them on his ranch. In early 2009, Shawna Forde, leader of a Minutemen faction, was arrested on murder charges when a Mexican man and his nine-year-old daughter were killed in a raid by the group in Arivaca, Arizona. The charges allege that Forde believed the victims were drug dealers. Forde had two accomplices, one of them with white supremacist ties; he also faces charges of fatally stabbing a homeless Latino man for sport in 1996. The trio, according to the charges, wanted to rob the family and use the money believed to be in the house to fund their vigilantism.

The 2005 rest stop incident and the subsequent wave of hostility toward immigrants appear to have been a turning point for Sheriff Joe. Once he saw that going after undocumented immigrants was popular with voters, the Maricopa County Sheriff's Department became an aggressive enforcer of immigration laws.

Arizona has the harshest anti-immigrant laws in the country. Immigrants have certainly been targeted in other places and have even been the victims of hate crimes: in suburban Suffolk County on Long Island, east of New York City, teenagers stabbed an Ecuadorian immigrant to death in 2008, part of a decade-long pattern of teens attacking Latinos for sport, which they called "beaner hopping." But what makes Arizona far worse is its state-sponsored bashing, along with violence by individuals. Most police departments don't want to be responsible for enforcing federal immigration law, nor do they want to be seen as the arm of federal authorities—rather, they want immigrants to feel comfortable talking to police about real crimes. The *East Valley Tribune,* a suburban Phoenix paper, won a Pulitzer Prize in 2009 for a project showing that violent crimes were not being investigated and that response time to calls had lengthened because of Sheriff Joe's focus on immigrants.

In Phoenix, however, because of his actions, and not in spite of them, Sheriff Joe, seventy-seven, is incredibly popular. He keeps being reelected by conservative voters.

The reasons for the backlash against undocumented immigrants are many, but a major driving force is the economy. While anti-immigrant sentiment began peaking a few years before a recession was officially declared, many of those who became most vociferous were already living in hard times despite the allegedly booming economy. Later, when housing prices went south, foreclosures mounted, and unemployment topped 9 percent in this once ever-growing sunbelt city, immigrants became easy scapegoats.

In writing my book *Homeland,* which examined fear in post-9/11 America and argued that it was anchored in economic anger, I spent time with members of far-right groups such as the National Alliance and the World Church of the Creator. And even before that project, I had gotten to know people in the Christian Identity and Freemen movements. I found them furious about economic disparity. It isn't that their rage has no merit—they have valid beefs about what the economy has done to them. But, for some, this anger morphs into racism and anti-Semitism.

The National Alliance, the most powerful of these groups, has since fragmented, following the death of its leader, Dr. William Pierce. Matthew Hale, the leader of the World Church, is in prison, convicted of plotting to kill a judge. Some of the members of both groups have become part of anti-immigration organizations, according to Eric Ward, who studies these groups for the Chicago-based Center for New Community.

Phoenix is another dark epicenter to gauge what is going on in the country. Traveling to New Orleans and spending time there with the outreach workers had revealed official indifference toward those in need. In Phoenix, as I soon discovered, the core of the story is rage.

Rage blared on the car radio on the long drive down from Northern California. You can listen to commentators with the names of Beck and Hannity and Limbaugh, and the answers are facile, always negative. At three o'clock in the morning, I passed a sign for the Maricopa County line. A few hundred feet later, I got a sense of the size of Sheriff Joe's 9,226-square-mile fiefdom—a sign announced that it was still 75 miles to Phoenix.

In two days, on January 16, 2010, there would be a protest march against Sheriff Joe, who is often compared with Bull Conner, the sheriff in Birmingham, Alabama, who used police dogs to maul civil rights demonstrators in the 1960s. Sheriff Joe's campaign against immigrant Latinos doesn't involve canines, but it was described by Phoenix mayor Phil Gordon in a 2009 *New Yorker* article as "a reign of terror."

The next day, I went to a corner in downtown Phoenix where opponents of Arpaio have held a daily vigil each lunch hour for the past sixteen months. I found eight people holding signs, two of them taking turns using a bullhorn to invoke facts in a denunciation of the sheriff, whose office was above, atop a skyscraper.

Passersby were a mix. Some listened to the protesters, amazed by the stories of abuse. Many were disdainful and openly hostile. "I like Joe!" was repeated numerous times. While most of the supporters were white, two Latin-looking men wearing suits shouted, *"Viva Arpaio!"* in English-accented Spanish as they got into a car across the street.

I asked Orlando Arenas, who was holding up one end of a large banner, about the origins of the antipathy against Latino immigrants.

"It began in 1994," he told me.

"Why?"

"NAFTA. When NAFTA was signed, we saw more people coming to Phoenix."

He explained that NAFTA had grievously harmed small corn farmers in Mexico—they couldn't compete against American conglomerates, whose products came flooding into Mexico. "All the mom-and-pop stores in Mexico, they were taken out by the Wal-Marts and Home Depots" that moved into Mexico. The result was an influx of economic refugees coming north. Orlando said that workers on both sides of the border were screwed by NAFTA.

"Detroit and Chiapas, Mexico, they are connected," he continued. "They are the same. What I'm seeing is the free-trade police state. The Minutemen and nationalists, it's a misunderstanding. We have a common future. We have the same enemy. Their jobs are being sent down south. There needs to be a dialogue between the undocumented and the patriots. Why don't we work together to end NAFTA? Right now, Mexico is run by corporations for corporations. I'm not asking for us to hold hands with them as we go after NAFTA. But we want to work with them. We've got to work against the neoliberal people who are fucking up this world."

As for Sheriff Joe, Orlando said, "He is going to be remembered as bringing the police state to America, not as America's toughest sheriff."

The following day, I showed up at Falcon Park on 35th Avenue in Phoenix, an area heavily populated by Latin immigrants. About five thousand participants had gathered for the march. By the end of the 3-mile route to the tent city jail, the march had grown to ten thousand people, according to the *Arizona Republic*. Many came from surrounding states.

There was a lot of anger evident against Sheriff Joe, but the march was largely peaceful, save for a small group of people dressed in black, with black bandanas hiding their faces, who provoked the cops by throwing water bottles and constant jeering. They were pepper-sprayed, along with some innocent marchers. After the spraying, there was a tense moment when helmeted officers faced off against the protesters. Someone held a sign with a quote from Martin Luther King Jr., invoking Hitler's Germany.

All through the march, a man wore a papier-mâché head caricaturing Sheriff Joe. The head was 3 feet tall.

I wanted to meet this menacing man.

Sheriff Joe has a public relations staff of five—by all accounts, he lives for press coverage and especially likes being on national television. His office is a media machine. But I was a university professor writing a book, not exactly big media. Because of a former student of mine who worked at the *Arizona Republic,* I had the cell phone number of Lisa Allen, Arpaio's chief flak. I called her. She blew me off. A while later, I called back, and she gave me Sheriff Joe's number. He blew me off. I called again and convinced him to meet.

After getting behind a phalanx of cops guarding Sheriff Joe's command post, about 300 yards from the action, I found a man who by appearance and manner could be anybody's genial grandpa, not that ugly papier-mâché head out there amid the ten thousand marchers. This is the persona that voters like, the man they simply refer to as "Joe" even if they don't know him.

For our entire conversation, a staff member videotaped me doing the interview.

I opened with an easy question. Why was he going after immigrants?

"Because it's the law," Sheriff Joe said. He went on to talk about how the U.S. Department of Homeland Security had taken away his power to arrest people on the street under federal law. (This was a result of his abuses.) "There's a new state law, and I'm enforcing that one. We still arrest illegals under the state law. They don't like my crime suppression when I go into the cities and arrest people pursuant to our duties."

He looked over the backs of dozens of distant officers and the protest beyond.

"They come out here, always demonstrating, using the media, hype it up. . . . If they want to change the law, go to Washington. Don't use me."

"I interviewed a guy named Leo Arteaga yesterday," I said. "He was a citizen who was arrested. Some U.S. citizens are getting caught up in your sweeps, aren't they? I—"

"Who arrested him?"

"Sheriff's—your guys."

"Yesterday?"

"No, back on May 12, 2009. It was in Mesa."

"Oh, they got all their allegations." Sheriff Joe paused. "It's all hype. So, uh—"

Sheriff Joe fell silent for an uncomfortably long time. I asked, "What do you think of your visitors today?"

"Same movie. They imported a few extra actors. Same thing."

"They sure don't like you."

"Hey, I got eighty percent approval rating. I don't need theirs."

"So you represent the voters of Maricopa County?"

"They keep reelecting me. I just raised, in eight months, 1.4 million dollars. . . . I think I'm doing pretty good. I don't think they could raise that money. My polls are high. I could get the governor's office if I wanted to. That tells you the people support me. So, hey, you can't get a hundred percent, right?"

I asked what he feels about NAFTA.

"We go into workplaces and we arrest illegals, especially those with phony identifications, and that opens up positions in the workplace for U.S. citizens. I'm really helping the economy. Every time we raid a workplace, people come running down and say, 'I want a job.' I don't think it's right to come into this country illegally and get a job when we have U.S. citizens trying to find jobs. Especially today with the economy."

"Are people going for those jobs?"

"People will work," Sheriff Joe said. He mocked politicians who say U.S. workers won't take menial jobs. In a slight falsetto, he mimicked them: "'Nobody will do this, nobody will do that.' That's garbage!"

Lisa Allen, standing nearby, spoke to the sheriff. "Most of the press is gone now," she said. "Your PIOs are leaving."

"Okay," he said of the departure of his public information officers. "They're gone? Is the T.V. gone?"

"I would imagine," Lisa replied. "They might still be getting some stuff, but they're done with you."

Meeting Sheriff Joe was evidence of the longstanding truism about the banality of evil. He is unremarkable in person. If he were not in office and were still selling rides into outer space, you might find him mildly amusing.

But he is in power. And yet he is not, ultimately, the problem. Sheriff Joe is merely a shrewd opportunist. In his own words, albeit in the third person and with bad punctuation, his website declares, "Arpaio knows what the public wants, 'The public is my boss,' he says, so I serve the public."

What that repulsive papier-mâché head depicts is not really Sheriff Joe, but the face of Phoenix. What's going on in Phoenix is much larger than just this one man. Sheriff Joe represents a type of Phoenix resident: he is a mouthpiece for the rage of the 730,000 citizens who voted him back into office in 2008 for a fifth term. That public wants him to bash Latino immigrants.

I talked about this with ACLU attorney Annie Lai over coffee after the march that day.

"How does an elected official get this bad? Are things really going to change in Maricopa County even if he goes to jail?" Annie asked. "No. Someone else who gets in could be just as bad."

Annie's jail reference was regarding two investigations against Sheriff Joe. The U.S. Justice Department apparently was looking at discrimination and illegal search and seizures related to the sheriff's immigration sweeps, in violation of civil rights laws. And a federal grand jury was examining allegations that Arpaio had intimidated county workers by having deputies show up at their homes at night to discuss budget cuts. He had also criminally charged two county supervisors and a judge, with the support of county prosecuting attorney Andrew Thomas. Sheriff Joe may have crossed a line when he started going after people who can fight back. He might indeed end up behind bars—or in one of his miserably hot tents.

No matter how pleasing that image might be, what Annie hopes for is that the U.S. Justice Department mandates fundamental changes in how the Maricopa County Sheriff's Department does business. It could order written policies that provide transparency and make officers provide details of each traffic stop, including the race of the driver. In this way, there would be quantifiable evidence to hold the department accountable, no matter who is sheriff.

Annie noted that this is how things were changed in the South during the civil rights era. “What you saw was, there is a boundary you can’t cross.” She added: “A lot of it is scapegoating. Here, you have political leaders saying things that are not possible in places like California and New York. The important thing about scapegoating is that it can happen to anyone, any group. Who’s next?”

I drove west. Even though I’m white and shouldn’t have been a target for Sheriff Joe’s deputies, I felt brown that evening. I was happy to cross the Maricopa County line as the sun set over the Arizona desert. I drove into the California night with rage on the talk radio dial for company.

Sheriff Joe had told me that you now find more whites working in fast-food restaurants. Perhaps he is correct about those menial jobs; maybe U.S. citizens will take them. Yet in a decidedly unscientific survey of several fast-food restaurants in different parts of Phoenix after the march and before I met with Annie Lai, there were few non-Latinos to be seen working in these establishments. I heard Spanish spoken behind the counter at two restaurants. Maybe undocumented workers should not be here and U.S. citizens should have those jobs. One can argue that point. But what is going on under Sheriff Joe in Phoenix is not the answer. It is ugly and frightening.

How Latinos are being treated in Arizona echoes the situation of Jews in prewar Europe. We can blame “those people,” as “those people” have always been scapegoated all through history. Or we can take a harder look at something more troubling—ourselves. I wondered about Annie’s comments about the need for some rules to check the sheriff’s power. But that won’t stop the rage that exists in Phoenix, or in a lot of other places in this nation. It could grow even more fierce.

Months later, the Arizona state legislature, on a party-line vote dominated by Republicans, passed its most repressive law to date, SB 1070. The new law made it a misdemeanor for noncitizens to fail to carry immigration registration documents with them. During a stop or an arrest, the police are obligated to try to ascertain a person’s immigration status if there is “reasonable suspicion” that the person is an undocumented immigrant. The law allows officers to arrest people who can’t prove on the spot that they are legal citizens. It also authorizes anyone to sue the police or a city or county if he or she does not believe these entities are enforcing immigration laws.

(The law was battled in the courts in the coming months, and more large protests were held in Arizona. Sheriff Joe remained defiant. He twice arrested, on absolutely no grounds, a leader of Puente, an immigrant-assistance group; the leader was merely standing and watching protests. In the 2010 midterm elections, Sheriff Joe went around the country endorsing Tea Party candidates.)

After signing the Arizona bill into law, Republican governor Jan Brewer insisted that law enforcement officers needed this "tool."

"We have to trust our law enforcement," Brewer said in a statement.

21 THE DARK EXPERIMENT

> We have an explosion of homelessness caused by the loss of fifty-one thousand rental units. But just as dramatic as the actual homelessness are people who are in such horrendous living conditions. Severely overcrowded—not just doubled up, but quadrupled up. And living in such substandard conditions that it can only be described as Third World. Just the other day, a baby was killed in the family home by a rat. A three-month-old baby. Killed by a rat. Those are the conditions people are having to live in. They tried to slap some drywall to cover the holes, but they hadn't succeeded in securing the house from rats. It's just horrible. The crisis of homelessness, the crisis of horrendous housing conditions. . . . It's as if you ran an experiment. What would happen if you took a city with a very high rate of poverty, destroyed fifty-one thousand units of rental housing in one fell swoop . . . [and] at the same time jacked up the rents on what was left, 50 percent overnight? Did not increase wages. This is a city with many thousands of people . . . making nothing but federal minimum wage. This is what would happen.
>
> —Martha Kegel, executive director of UNITY, a collaborative of sixty organizations working to end homelessness in New Orleans, interviewed July 21, 2009

Martha Kegel could have been referring not just to New Orleans, but to the United States of America.

It's as if someone decided to run a dark experiment to see what would occur if the government did everything in its power to ensure that high-paying, middle-class jobs would be destroyed and replaced with low-wage, service-sector jobs. If the rules were changed so that the rich could amass more wealth, including trillions of dollars of welfare in the form of bailouts and tax cuts. If wages for most workers stagnated as they did between 1980 and 2005, and 80 percent of the total increase in income went to the top 1 percent, the already wealthy. And if, in the midst of all this, the cost of everything skyrocketed.

A 2010 Brookings Institution report, citing 2008 data, revealed a startling fact: one-third of all Americans, 91.6 million people, fell below 200 percent of the federal poverty line, which was $21,834 for a family of four. The fastest-growing poverty

Abandoned home across from an idled blast furnace. Warren, Ohio, 2009.

Ken Platt and his son, Ken Jr. Youngstown, 1984.

Ken Platt and his son, Ken Jr. Youngstown, 2009.

The Marshall family. Youngstown, 1983.

The Marshall family. Youngstown, 2009.

Jennifer and Matthew Alexander. Houston, 1983.

Jennifer Alexander Spicer and Matthew Alexander. Michigan, 2009.

The only water in town. Bayview, Virginia, 1998.

Praying for better times. Bayview, Virginia, 1998.

(overleaf) A rental home. Bayview, Virginia, 1998.

(above) Border crossing. El Paso, Texas, 1994.

El Paso, Texas, 1994.

Nogales, Arizona, 1994.

Thirty-five hundred people waiting as long as fourteen hours to seek health care from the Remote Area Medical Volunteer Corps, an organization that once served only the desperately ill poor in Third World nations but now operates in the United States. Wise, Virginia, 2008.

Health care by donation, collection jar in a convenience store. Gun Barrel City, Texas, 2009.

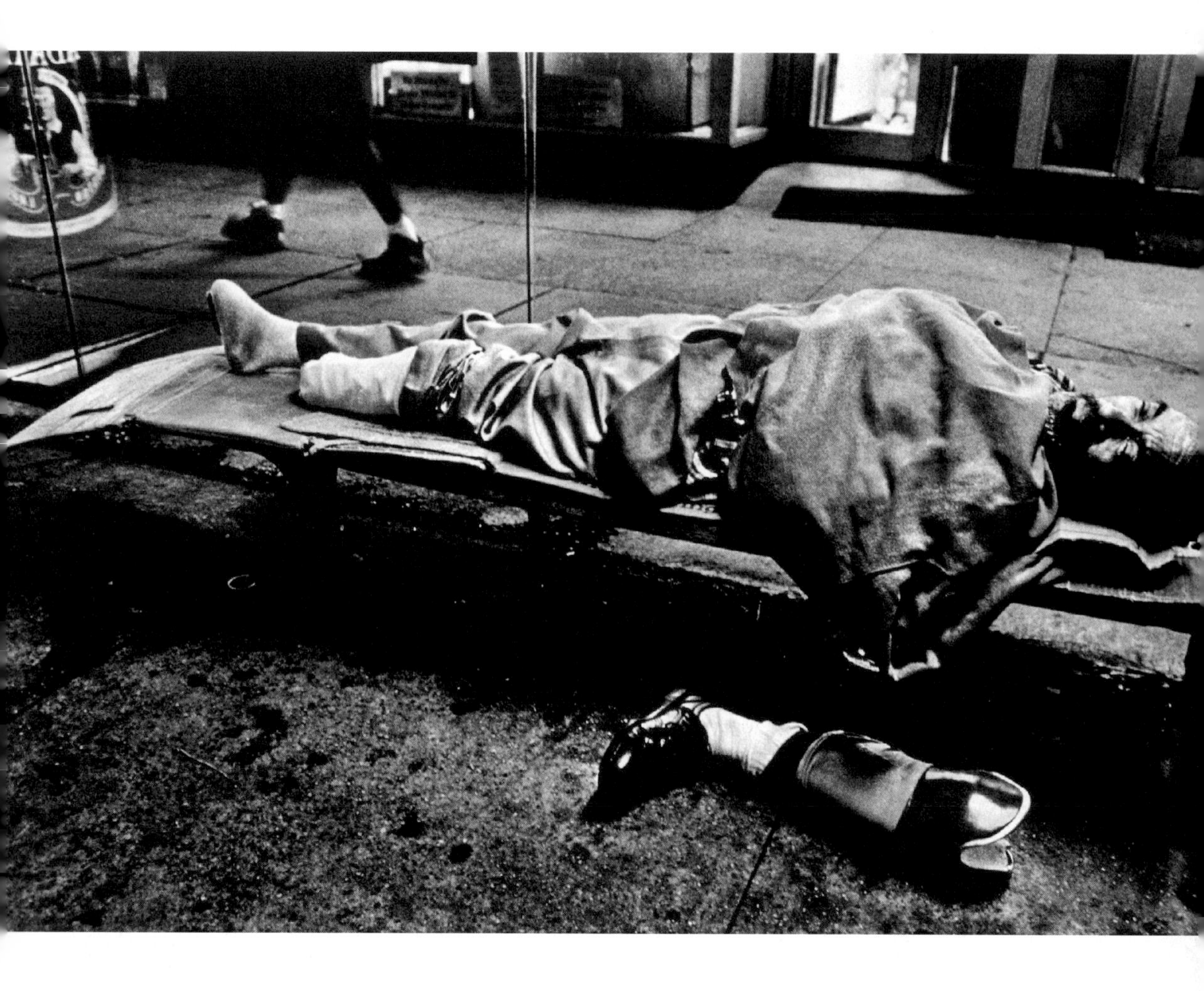

A diabetic man who has lost his leg, his job, and his home because of a lack of health care.
Adams Morgan section, Washington, D.C., 1993.

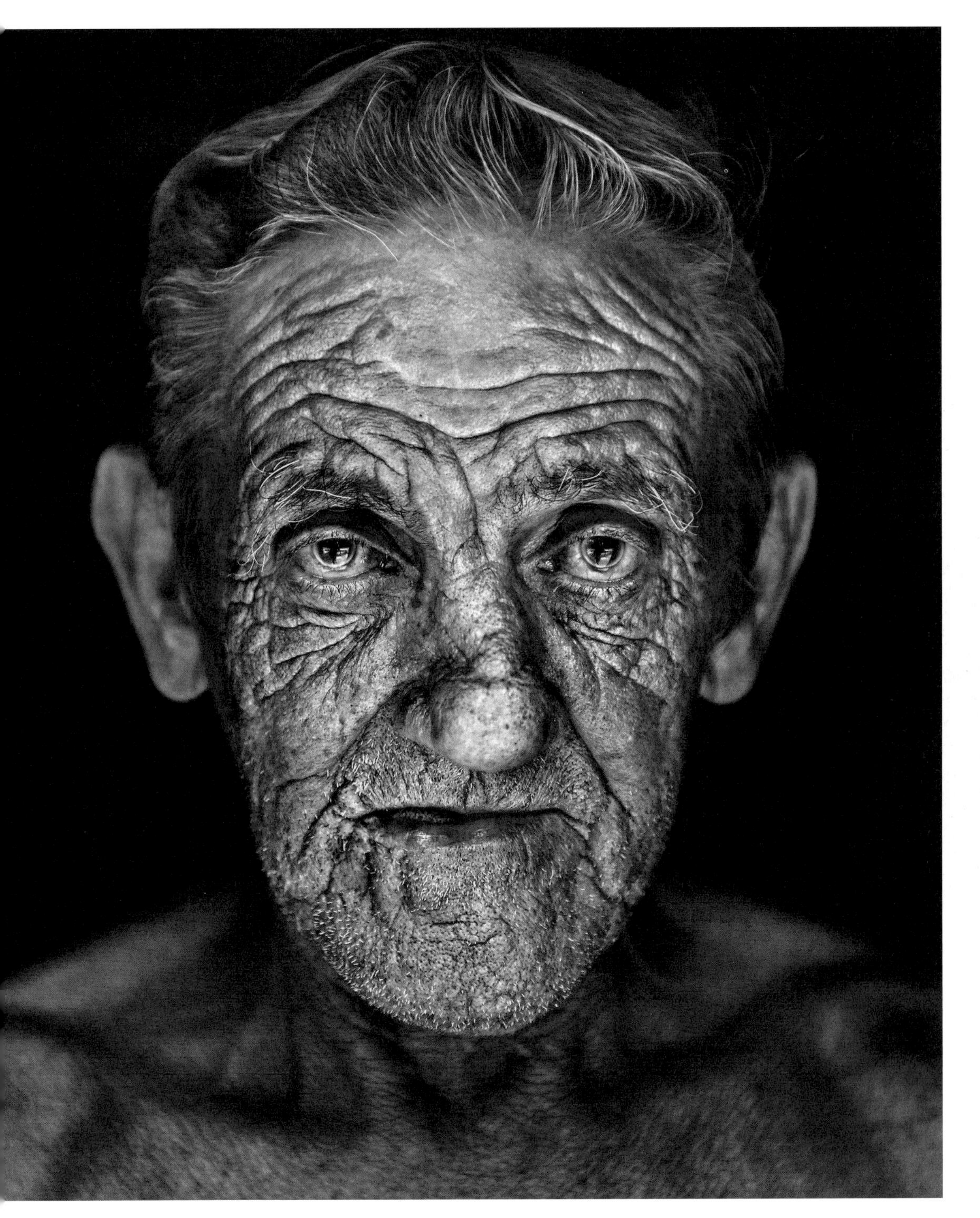

Robert Morris, unable to work any longer because he needs surgery for a work-related injury but cannot afford it. Esmont, Virginia, 2010.

Roanoke, Virginia, 2009.

Suspended development. Brawley, California, 2009.

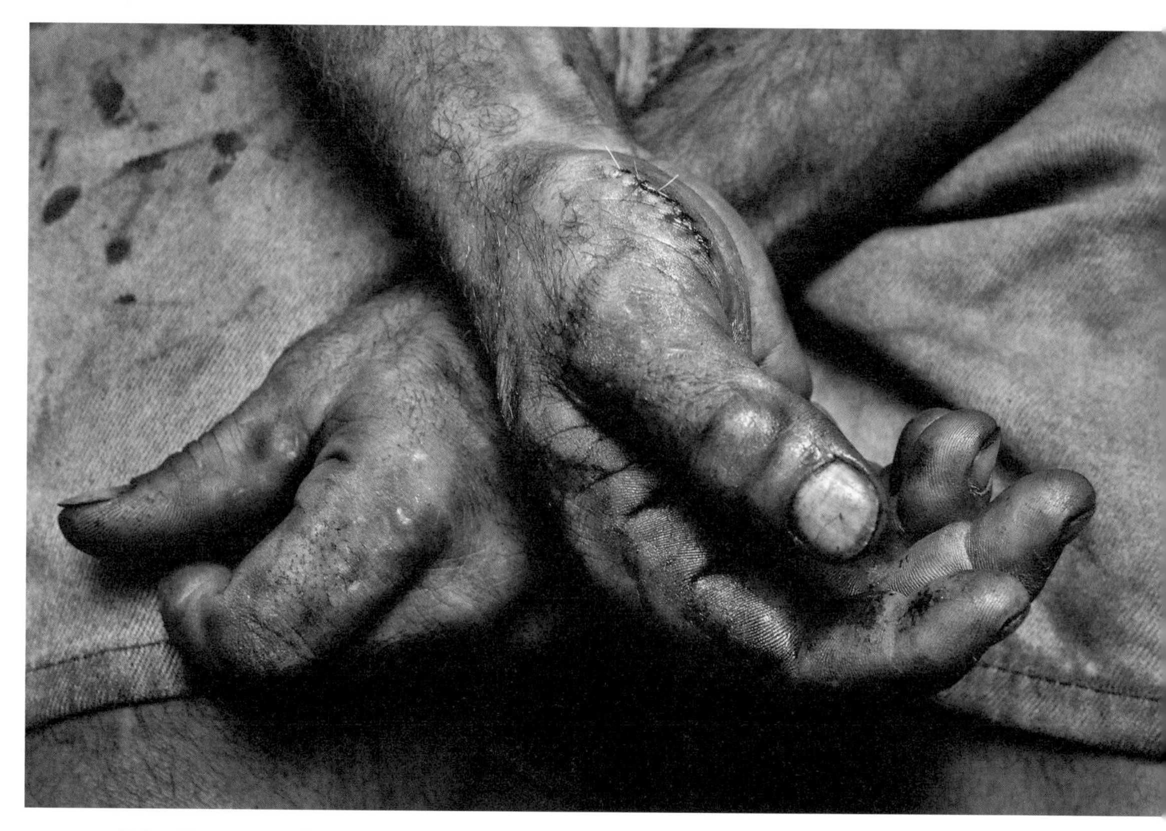

Robert Strong, a part-time mechanic, who had cut his hand working on a car but had no medical insurance. Esmont, Virginia, 2010.

Louis, from Jamaica, who has been following the apple harvest for twenty-five years. Clear Brook, Virginia, 2010.

Pushing paper, Cascade Flats paper mill. Gorham, New Hampshire, 2009.

One in twelve Americans has worked at McDonald's. Roanoke, Virginia, 2009.

America's largest employer, located on the site of a former surface coal mine. Logan, West Virginia, 2009.

Outreach worker Shamus Rohn seeking squatters. New Orleans, 2009.

Florence, whose base wage at Denny's is $4.25 an hour and whose tips have fallen; she never expects to retire. Fort Lauderdale, 2009.

Dolores Johnson, first in line at a job help center after fifteen months of joblessness, despite having "wallpapered" the town looking for work. Las Vegas, 2009.

A year and a half after President Barack Obama's inauguration. Near Howard University, Washington, D.C., 2010.

rate was in the suburbs—with 2.5 million more falling into poverty between 2000 and 2008. Americans were so broke that on Tax Day in 2010, 47 percent didn't owe anything. Yet at an April 15, 2010, rally of Tea Partiers in Washington, D.C., at Freedom Plaza, Dana Milbank of the *Washington Post* reported that Representative Louie Gohmert (R-Tex.) chastised that low- or no-income 47 percent for "not helping on Tax Day." When radio personality Neal Boortz again brought this up, the crowd booed the Americans who were too poor to owe taxes. Milbank wrote, "The wealth advantage of the Tea Partiers helps to explain the rather un-populist message emanating from Freedom Plaza: Tax the wealthy less and the poor more."

Witnessing the human impact of this dark experiment over the previous thirty years has been a long, intense journey. From the beginning, one of the people I have always looked to for guidance in gauging the impact of American decline has been Dr. John Russo, co-director of the Center for Working-Class Studies at Youngstown State University. I was eager to touch base with John. One afternoon in 2009, Michael and I sat with him at an Italian restaurant in Youngstown. When my wedding soup arrived, I reminded John just how pessimistic he had been in 1995.

"—The worse it gets, the better it gets," he said, quoting the old Communist Party slogan.

"And now the worse it gets, the worse it gets," I added, recapping what he'd told me about the right wing ascending. "How do you feel now?"

"They did ascend," John said. He added that he hadn't factored in positive progressivism coming from the newly disenfranchised middle class. "I think there's this populist division that's developing."

"Conservative populism versus liberal populism?"

"Remember, it's not a political spectrum, it's a parabola. Left and right meet at the bottom of the political parabola."

Left-wing and right-wing populists both hate free trade, John noted. "On a number of issues, you can have agreement between very liberal and very conservative people."

Today, the blue-collar working class leans toward conservatism much more so than it did in the 1980s, John said, while members of the middle and upper-middle class are becoming more progressive. He pointed out that Barack Obama won the presidency in a different way in 2008—in the suburbs, in places like northern Virginia. Reporters who came to Youngstown and went to bars for interviews, for example, missed the story. Working-class support for Democrats has been decreasing, John believes.

"I think what's happened now is that the middle class got gored. That's been the big change. Progressives swung northern Virginia for Obama, yet Youngstown became more conservative during that period. The working class has become more conservative. And that makes for a very interesting dichotomy now in terms of class resentment. The right meets the left. They're fighting over language. They're fighting over nationalism. It goes to trade theory. It goes to questions about taxation, unfairness. It's a contested terrain among the populace right now."

The right is loud and shows up at town hall meetings. Right-wingers focus on crazy things, like the repeatedly disproven rumor that President Obama was not born in the United States, rather than using their energy to go after a very real issue such as welfare for Wall Street. Progressives are angry and wounded, but they're not taking to the streets and town hall meetings as the Tea Party movement has done. (More than a year later, suburban progressives and the young would stay home in the 2010 midterm elections, allowing the right to dominate.) John feels that while many people are angry, they focus inward—trying to survive without a job or with less income if they are working.

"That's not necessarily an activist model. There has been a shift, but it's not strong politically. Certainly, the right is more virulent. A lot of fascism is bubbling."

Michael wondered whether the broad public had lost faith in free-market ideology.

"I think those sets of neoliberal ideas are clearly in disrepute," John said. "There's no set of ideals that's going to come in and settle this other than a neo-Keynesian set of ideals that have redeveloped. Now we're fighting over the meaning of the 1930s again.

"There's no easy way out of it. The brunt of it is that for thirty years, we've let our manufacturing base, we've let a good part of our middle class, be eroded. What happens when you keep getting rid of the middle class? What happens to demand in the economy when we're just getting by on consumption, credit cards, housing inflation—and all that ends? You've wiped out a good part of the infrastructure in manufacturing and other businesses that were important to America. The dot-com bubble burst, and then the housing bubble burst. We're left with thirty years of neglect in terms of economic policy."

What might be happening is what economists call a "long wave" theory, John explained. "That is, within every business cycle, there are longer influences that happen every fifty to seventy years within capitalism. Maybe this is one of them."

This theory was posited by Nikolai Kondratiev, a Soviet economist (executed on Stalin's orders in 1938), who argued that capitalistic societies have natural cycles of boom, followed by collapse into depression.

"And now about sixty, seventy years later," John said, "here we are again. A generation or two forgets. Okay, nobody gave a hoot about steelworkers in Youngstown,

Ohio, or Pittsburgh, or Gary, or autoworkers in Flint. Until it started to impact middle-class workers and white-collar workers—and then, suddenly, all those ideas about 'creative destruction' were in disrepair. Even conservative economists are changing their tune.

"I'm not very good at predicting what's going to happen. But I can see the contested terrain that's going on politically and in the minds of working people and in the country itself right now. It's still being fought out."

Months later, I phoned John to talk with him about solutions. What could the government do to help get us out of this dark experiment?

John laughed.

"You want that in how many column inches? A solution?"

When compared to the 1930s, he told me, "The issues are much more difficult. The situation is much more severe because we're in a global economy. Is there any way to recover manufacturing in this country? I'm not sure. What's after the stimulus? If you go back to the 1930s, a lot of people said the same thing. What happens after the Works Progress Administration? What happened is war. That's what got us out of the Great Depression. But war isn't the same today as it was back then. Wars are fought differently."

Today, wars don't put America to work building tanks and ships, as happened in the early 1940s. In the 1980s, Michael and I often heard older people musing about the hard times and how maybe "they" had to start another war to get people back to work. But in recent years, we haven't heard that once in all our travels.

"There doesn't seem to be a clear path," John said. "Where's the wealth for working-class and middle-class people that could create demand for products? There are only so many windmills we can make. But the question of it is that we have to make things. There's only so much information sharing that you can do. In the long term, I ask, what are we going to make? What always strikes me when I talk with people in China and India is that there is a real sense that, 'You guys had your century. This is our century. We're going to be the generator of wealth in the world.' You've got this grim story going on, yet the stock market is going up. It's a con game. I think the future is a leveling down. It's not a leveling up for American workers and American society. People are trying to get by on less, live more frugally."

"Can we be happy that way?" I asked.

"You tell me," John replied. He referred to the questions I raised in *Homeland* regarding the struggle between the left and the right: "That breeds a type of resentment," he said. "Who harnesses that resentment? The left or the right? That is the question. It's what happened in the 1930s."

Rahm Emanuel, chief of staff to President Barack Obama, stood in the hallway a few feet away, guarded by what appeared to be Secret Service agents. Or perhaps they were Capitol cops. He was backstage, as I was, waiting for Bruce Springsteen to come out of his dressing room at the Verizon Center in Washington, D.C.

All the previous week, Emanuel had worked hard to lobby Congress to weaken the Sarbanes-Oxley Act, nicknamed "Sarbox" in business circles. This act had been passed in 2002, after the WorldCom and Enron scandals, to protect investors against fraud by ensuring proper auditing. It became law under George W. Bush, when Republicans controlled the U.S. House of Representatives, and was termed the most "pro-investor" act in a quarter century. The Obama administration, wanting to appear friendly to small business going into the 2010 midterm elections, was backing a proposal to exempt smaller corporations (those whose market value was less than $75 million, about half the companies in the country) from Sarbox requirements. Arthur Levitt, the former chairman of the Securities and Exchange Commission, told the *New York Times* that he found it "surreal" that Democrats were trying to destroy that reform. Without giving investors transparency, Levitt said, "the whole system is worthless." (The next day, the House Financial Services Committee would accede to Emanuel's lobbying.)

I studied Emanuel, who was wearing a sporty dress shirt without a tie, standing in the hallway. He carried himself with the timeless air of omnipotence that befalls Washington power types, though even among them, he stood out as being more inflated by it than others. The agents were part of that power trip—historically, not all cabinet-level guys like him got protection. He reportedly had asked that his security code name be "Black Hawk." He had the appearance and reputation of a man ready for a brawl.

That persona was honed in his role as an advisor to President Bill Clinton, when he was nicknamed "Rahmbo." According to press reports, at a victory dinner after the 1996 election, Emanuel became so enraged at the thought of Clinton's enemies that he plunged a steak knife into a table after reciting the name of each foe, screaming, "Dead! . . . Dead! . . . Dead!" He left Clinton in 1999 to become an investment banker at Wasserstein Perella, where he pocketed $16.2 million from deals in just over two years. He was then elected to the U.S. House of Representatives, taking campaign money from hedge funds and the securities and investment industry.

And now here he was, pushing for a dark victory that could harm ordinary investors, working Americans, through their 401(k)s, because a weakened Sarbox might lead to more scamming.

I wished for a moment that I were more like Norman Mailer or Ernest Hemingway, the kind of writer who would find pleasure by provoking Emanuel into a fistfight, culminating in a few well-landed blows to his coifed silver-haired head. But I'm not that kind of writer. I simply wanted to walk over to Emanuel and ask about the pampering of Wall Street. But then Bruce's door burst open, and he went down the hall and shook a few hands, among them Emanuel's. Then Bruce spotted us and invited Michael and me into his dressing room. When we emerged ten minutes later, Black Hawk was gone.

What would Emanuel have said, anyway? His action on Sarbox was just one of many cave-ins on the part of the Obama administration that coddled moneyed interests and ignored the working class. Even later, in 2010, when Obama was pushing Congress to regulate derivatives and enact other measures to rein in banks and Wall Street, the proposals were far from thorough. Derivatives had been a major contributor to the 2008 meltdown, but the Senate bill on derivatives that finally passed was filled with loopholes. Paul A. Volcker, the former Fed chairman and an advisor to Obama, had called for tougher regulation. He was quoted as saying he'd give the new law a B grade, not even a B-plus.

No consideration was being given to reinstating the Glass-Steagall Act, which would separate commercial banking from the investment business to keep government-insured deposits away from speculation. (As Paul Krugman, the Nobel Prize–winning economist, notes, there were no truly large bank bailouts between the 1930s and the 1980s because of such strong regulation.)

And even though "too big to fail" is simply too big if we have to pay for their shenanigans, lawmakers didn't consider breaking up the big banking companies. Additionally, the financial reform legislation "deliberately narrows the central bank's focus to Wall Street alone," wrote Thomas Hoenig, president of the Federal Reserve Bank in Kansas City, in the *New York Times.* Hoenig argued that such focus would violate the historical role of the Fed, which should also take into account Main Street's economic concerns when making policy. Oddly, the International Monetary Fund, often criticized by liberals for being on the wrong side of money politics, was talking tougher than anyone in power in America. A leaked IMF memo called for a Financial Activity Tax, or FAT, to be imposed on excessive bank profits and bonuses. This would "mitigate excessive risk taking," said the IMF, and could "tend to reduce the size of the financial sector." Smaller banks would be a good thing, the IMF argued.

This lack of strong regulation means that we are destined to see a repeat of the banking crisis of 2008—whether it happens in 2012, 2015, 2020, or who knows when. Greed and avarice will surely not cease.

The Democrats, bad as they were by acting "Republican light," looked like Marxists when compared with the Republicans, who were being absolutely avaricious. Most Republicans, citing faux populism and the lie that reform would mean more bailouts, were simply shilling for the banks and Wall Street. Many Republicans still favor free-market policies, though I find it hard to fathom how anyone can promote these with a straight face after the corporate welfare giveaways of 2007 and 2008. Adam Smith's invisible hand was indeed at work—picking our pockets clean.

In late 2009, not long after the one-year anniversary of the crash, as the Dow industrial average crept back over 10,000 and official joblessness topped 10 percent, one of my students, Denver Nicks, went to Wall Street to look for a story. He ended up at a bar called Ulysses Folk House, in the shadow of the Goldman Sachs tower, a rock's throw away if you have a good pitching arm. This watering hole with its oxymoronic name draws primarily male money dealers and women who want to date them. Denver knows what he's doing as a reporter, and yet he was repeatedly rebuffed. Those who talked with him uttered only practiced nothings.

The word had gone out: avoid the press. Look what had happened earlier that week when Goldman Sachs CEO Lloyd Blankfein, who some years takes in as much as $68 million, talked with the *Sunday Times of London*. He told its reporter, "I know I could slit my wrists, and people would cheer." Then he defended himself and his minions by claiming they were "doing God's work." This was on the eve of bonus season. The 32,500 workers at Goldman Sachs were projected to earn an average of about $700,000 each in de facto welfare checks. (The average was cut in 2010, for public relations purposes, to "only" about $595,000.)

A few days after Blankfein's comments, I went to Ulysses, with Denver as my guide, to study God's workers at the bar between Pearl and Stone streets. Maybe I'd talk with some of them, I thought, but that wasn't my goal. To really get inside their heads is a different book and would require an entirely different kind of reportage. I'll leave it to others to document the yachting class. I merely wanted to spy.

This bar, down the street from where Herman Melville was born, was filled with portraits of James Joyce. The many faces of Joyce, with his round spectacles, stared at over a hundred patrons. A sign offered four ages of single-malt scotch:

Balvenie 10 yr

Balvenie 12 yr

Balvenie 15 yr

Balvenie 21 yr

The bartender informed me that a single shot of the twenty-one-year-old Balvenie was $25. We ordered Brooklyn Winter lagers.

In walked a suit, wearing a tie with gold squares on it, who took up a station across from us at the long, oval bar. The man, in his fifties, was among the oldest present. He focused on a twenty-three- or twenty-four-year-old that came not in a bottle but in a dress. He talked with the brown-haired hottie, who was with three other equally attractive women.

We studied the suit. He had dark and deepset eyes that suggested lack of sleep because of depression or ceaseless hours before a trading computer or both. The man's hair was receding, to about a quarter of the way back on his head; the short hair that remained showed gray. His custom-tailored threads cost at least a grand. The frame on which they had been sized was thin, with sloped, diminished shoulders and pencil-thin arms.

"He has a body shape that says he's been doing nothing for a long time," Denver said.

The women now talked among themselves. The suit turned to chat with a couple. His jacket came off. A half hour later, it was off with the tie. In another half hour, he removed the tailored shirt. Beneath was a long-sleeve, tight-fitting body shirt. Amid this, he alternated talking with the group of women, but whatever money he had wasn't helping: they seemed not all that interested. He looked ridiculous in the body shirt.

Next to us materialized three young suits, one whose head was shaved bald. Another was baby-faced, wearing a well-fitted dark blue suit and a flaming red tie knotted a little too tightly.

A few weeks earlier, writer Calvin Trillin had published a story about why Wall Street had become so pernicious. Trillin wrote about a money guy he met in a midtown bar. Before the pay grew so heady, this guy told Trillin, only those at the bottom of their Ivy League university class went into money dealing. Those at the top of the class became lawyers, judges, professors, or other occupations with status but less pay. But in recent years, the top graduates had begun to eschew status and go for the money. That, Trillin wrote, is why the deals are so complex today and regulators are left in the dust. These new money dealers were the "best and the brightest," in the dark manner that David Halberstam dryly meant that oft-misapplied phrase.

The latest ploy concocted by these maliciously creative dealmakers would pay off the elderly in cash for their life insurance, say $400,000 on a $1 million policy. Then these policies would be "securitized" in packages of hundreds or thousands and sold to investors who would collect when people died, profiting on the balance. The Wall Street suits were also cooking up other exotic deals that no mortal could understand, making money from fees and doing nothing to create jobs for regular people.

Those three men next to us were Ivy League. Babyface was a Princeton frat boy. The men were drunk and probably stoned, too, involved in a heated discussion about how long marijuana remains in one's body. Princeton, swigging fast on a Corona, had lost a job recently, maybe today. He was looking for work and worried about the urine test. The conversation grew heated, and I could discern only pieces of it.

"What was the downfall of your company?" the bald man asked Princeton, who mumbled, growing irritated.

"—I'm not trying to give you a hard time!" the bald man slurred loudly over a thumping Michael Jackson song. "I frequently hire people for a hundred fifty thousand a year! You should appreciate my advice!"

There was more arguing that I couldn't make out. The bald man angrily stalked away.

Denver and I left and went to 85 Broad Street. It was after midnight. There were no signs indicating that the building was Goldman Sachs's headquarters. An American flag, large enough to cover the side of a cottage, was on a wall behind the security desk in the otherwise bleak entryway. Most low windows were blackened. I craned my neck, face taking a misting rain—a lot of lights were still on. A line of black Lincoln Town Cars, some twenty deep, stood idling in a block-long row. They were drivers waiting for suits to get off work. One of God's workers emerged from 85 Broad Street. Was he armed? *Bloomberg News* had just broken a story, quoting a New York police official, that requests for concealed weapons permits from Goldman employees had gone up. They feared the angry masses.

The suit rapidly strode to a Town Car, eyeing us nervously. The driver sped him away.

Another night at Ulysses. I was alone.

On bar left were two British suits and a dress who had flown in for some deal. One suit, a late twenties sandy-haired man I'll call Cheeky, told the other suit and the dress, who had a squarish torso, about his $250-a-night room at the Ritz Carlton, not all that expensive by New York standards. Perhaps this reflected a European sensibility. The dress talked about the project she was working on for the company—

"What services do you offer?" Cheeky suggestively quipped, with a smile. A beat. "I mean, professionally."

Laughter all around.

"—you do a deal for ten million dollars—"

"—best trading program—"

"TMG is everything—"

Two Americans, one bald, entered and greeted the trio.

"You New Yorker!" Cheeky said to the bald suit, no more than thirty years old, gripping his hand with enthusiasm.

What's with this bald thing? There was the guy the other night, and tonight a number of young suits with heads purposefully shaved bald walked by on Stone Street, visible out the nearby window. The passing ivory domes in the light of the streetlamp looked no different, save for the lack of fight scars, than neo-Nazi skinheads. These $kinheads in Armani aren't making a racial statement. But they share the same projection of power as their cousins in leather and chains.

The bald suit smiled easily when Cheeky made frequent but lame jokes. Talk turned to the travails of business road warriors. The young Brit looked at his male colleague and asked, "Does your wife mind you being away so much?" A beat. "Does your wife even know you are away?" More laughter. Their conversation was facile, assured.

I gave up on eavesdropping. I surveyed the bar, studying the body language of other young money people. I realized that this crowd possessed something I had not witnessed for a long time in America: confidence. It was something I hadn't seen in the places I'd traveled over the previous year and the preceding twenty-nine. And that wasn't just because I'd been hanging out in food bank lines and the industrial cemeteries of our inland cities.

What I witnessed at Ulysses Folk House that night at the end of the first decade of the new millennium was the kind of body language I once saw in book publishing circles and newspaper gatherings back in the 1980s and into the 1990s. We had the same cocksure swagger, the same belief that we owned a piece of the world. We weren't making money like this crowd, for sure, but ours was a psychological income that came with decent wages. Now our swagger has atrophied. It's my field, the one I know best, and so that is what I see most vividly. But I imagine the same thing is happening in other professions.

Some writers and photographers I know are now doing the post-millennium version of selling apples on street corners, using websites to advertise their services. I recently Googled one of them, a news photographer once as self-assured as those around me at the bar, who was now shooting weddings. She had just a few samples on display; it was clear she wasn't getting much work. There was a plaintive, pleading tone to her site. The site of another acquaintance, a master wordsmith, simply had a phone number, an e-mail address, and the address of an office in a cheap building in a West Coast city—there were no published bylines for him in over a year. Another former colleague had told me in an e-mail that he was one of the 6 million Americans who survived solely on food stamps; he was desperately seeking any kind of work, from cleaning to carpentry to editing, but no one was hiring him. One laid-off journalist e-mailed me from a public computer in the Kingman, Arizona, library and related how much he appreciated reading our book *Journey to Nowhere* because he was now living it in a nearby homeless shelter.

When I now go to gatherings of my colleagues, fear and uncertainty dominate. At book functions, there is no boastful talk about the six-figure advances of days past; today low five-figure ones are desperately accepted. Among the newspaper crowd, journalists are gleeful if they've "only" had their salaries cut by furlough and have not been laid off.

Ulysses, in a nation beset by loss, is a throwback. I wanted to despise the people around me. Instead, I merely felt melancholy for a lost time.

I walked through the bar to exit on the Pearl Street side. The door was blocked. The street glowed day-bright from klieg lights. Someone mentioned that the people outside were filming a Matt Damon movie, *The Adjustment Bureau,* a science fiction tale somewhat based on a Philip K. Dick story. Only one woman stood at the glass watching. The rest of the bar didn't care to look out to see Damon go through the scene. Such nonchalance came in part from the blasé attitude New Yorkers have about the constant filming going on in the city. But part of it also came from the deals that had started in the towering buildings around Ulysses and the continuation of them going on behind me. The power of show-biz celebrity was nothing against the workings of the money machine.

I exited on Stone Street and walked to the number 2/3 subway station on Wall Street. As soon as the doors closed on the uptown train, a haggard black man walked down the length of the car, passing out sheets of paper.

The man attempted to talk, but his words came out like "Dub, duh, dah." If he was acting, he was good—real good. And if he wasn't, he was real. I handed him a dollar.

I thought of what I'd recently heard in my travels, listening to the righteous rage of a spectrum of Americans. It was a different anger than I'd found in the 1990s. It had broadened, suburbanized, as John Russo noted in our interview. A lot of it was directed at the Big Boys, as John Steinbeck liked to call the Wall Street and banking interests. And they still are largely boys, though today a significant number are women, usually holding lesser positions. (A year after my visit to Wall Street, three women who once worked at Goldman Sachs filed suit in U.S. District Court charging that few women make it to the top ranks in the company and that when they do break through the glass ceiling, they are paid far less. The lawsuit alleged that celebrations were held at strip clubs, where women employees felt excluded, and that one Goldman manager had hired near-naked female escorts wearing Santa hats to appear at a Christmas party.) At Ulysses, you didn't hear many women's braggart voices; those of the men dominated.

I am personally angry. Those Big Boys I had just left at Ulysses were the reason I have a rate of 1.2 percent on a "jumbo certificate of deposit." The Fed is keeping interest rates low to help the economy. But let's look at what this means. Later in 2010, when Citigroup posted a first-quarter profit of $4.4 billion and other banks raked in more billions, a lot of this money came from the U.S. government making loans to these banks at .50 percent interest. The banks then turned around and invested in U.S. Treasury bills at a 3 percent return—a markup of 2.5 percent.

Policy makers want to create the impression that all is well in the economy, in an attempt to bolster consumer confidence. We're supposed to look at Citigroup's $4.4 billion "profit" (welfare) and the resultant "boom" in the stock market, marveling at the pace of the economic rebound, and then spend, spend, spend.

But it has been a Viagra recovery. There's very little real about it. And the creation of this illusion harms a lot of ordinary people.

I think of my mother, who fretted terribly as the Fed lowered interest rates. She had some $200,000 in bank certificates of deposit, a lifetime of savings, vital to her. At 5 percent interest, that meant about $10,000 in additional annual income on top of Social Security. The notes were soon coming due as her illness worsened. The brick-and-mortar banks were paying around 1 percent—had she lived, she would have earned about $2,000 in annual interest. Mom would have considered herself in serious financial trouble.

Older Americans who saved their money were the ants that stored food, not the grasshoppers that fiddled away the summer only to die at the first frost. Yet in America, when winter came, the ants were punished by having their food given to the rapacious grasshoppers.

In Wall Street talk, we on Main Street took a "haircut" so that their party can continue.

I'd wondered in print in the mid-1990s, and again after 9/11, if we would get lucky and a president would come along who would be able to harness the anger felt by American workers into a progressive force, as Franklin D. Roosevelt did. FDR was combative. He didn't seek consensus with the right. He said in speeches that he welcomed their hatred and the hatred of moneyed interests. FDR pushed through reforms, awkwardly at times. His was not a well-oiled machine, but in the end, he prevailed because he had on his side the one-third of Americans who were liberal, plus most of the centrist third. Obama has been no FDR. His administration grievously misread the mood of the country. Timidity and capitulation to the Big Boys were the wrong approach. Then, in 2010, Obama tried to find his populist sea legs, dropping his "Gs" at the end of sentences. He still didn't sound like Roosevelt.

Later, the day after Republicans dominated the 2010 midterm elections, the Federal Reserve pumped an additional $600 billion into the system to buy Treasury securities and to lower interest rates even further. The stock market responded by going up some 2 percent. Word was that it would be a very good bonus season for the Big Boys in 2011. The Republican leaders talked excitedly about guaranteeing that nothing would get done in Congress so that they could topple Obama, not about how to create jobs for ordinary Americans. And the Democrats appeared to be poised to do what they typically do when faced with a chance to show some mettle: retreat and waffle.

Wall Street continues to gamble with our money. Some banks and insurance companies are still "too big to fail," and they expect Uncle Sam will ride to the rescue when their deals again sour, or the firehosing of free money no longer works.

Wall Street's Big Boys are not masters of the universe, but they are masters of the continuing dark experiment that tries to commoditize even death. It makes a handful of them rich while the rest of us lose.

The anger generated by this is profound and dangerous, and it will be captured politically by someone. Perhaps progressive populism had its shot with the 2008 election. We shall see where that goes after the big rightward shift in the 2010 midterm election. Perhaps dark populism will have its turn, in 2012, or 2016.

23 ANGER IN SUBURBAN NEW JERSEY

Lisa Martucci, her husband, and their ten-year-old daughter, Emily, live in a New Jersey town that is a forty-five-minute train ride from Manhattan. The couple bought their suburban house in 1996. Unlike many blue-collar people who have spent their working lives dodging layoffs, this white-collar couple seemed bulletproof against hard times. Lisa, who works for Catholic Charities, has a master's degree; and her husband was director of global affairs for a large corporation, making over $75 an hour.

On June 13, 2008, their world changed. Lisa's husband was laid off. That meant a 70 percent drop in income. He got a job at a local supermarket part time, stocking shelves on weekend nights, for $10 an hour. The market kept his schedule under thirty hours so it wouldn't have to pay benefits.

Their house edged toward foreclosure. They bounced checks, something that had never before happened. Yet they earned too much to qualify for food stamps or for help with utility bills.

"There is no ACORN for middle-class people," Lisa said, referring to the group that advocated for the poor. "There is no support for us."

Lisa at the time told *USA Today* reporter Emily Bazar, in a story that was never published, "We're staring into a gaping maw, a big black pit of uncertainty."

A year later, things turned around. Lisa's husband was able to land another well-paying job, only three weeks before the family would have lost its home.

I first talked with Lisa in early 2009, just as things were stabilizing for her family. That did not, however, mean a return to any kind of "normal." This family of three was living a new normal of frugality amid continued economic fear. In Lisa's case, this adjustment was also coupled with a lot of anger.

The last time I was in touch with Lisa, in late 2010, 4.3 million homes nationwide were in foreclosure or had payments more than ninety days past due. Many of these troubled mortgages were prime loans, not the subprime mortgages that had dominated the start of the housing crisis. And more homeowners were perched on the edge of failure. Nearly one fourth, 23.2 percent, of all American homeowners were "underwater," owing more on their loans than their houses were worth in the third quarter of 2010, according to Zillow Real Estate Market Reports. That figure was up from 22.5 percent in the second quarter.

Lisa is representative of millions of suburban Americans who have not ended up homeless but are living lives of economic struggle nonetheless. On the exterior of the homes in the suburbs where people like Lisa reside, all looks well. If only it were so.

Lisa said that the year-long experience of joblessness and almost losing their home had forever changed them.

"For starters, we're trying to be a lot more intentional about how we use our money," Lisa told me. "Our lives here are not sustainable."

Even though her husband once again has a good job, she said the family is bleeding money. Things are tight. She and her husband "have on occasion taken second jobs . . . but it sucks that for all our efforts, we have zero dollars left at the end of the day to go away on vacation or put new tires on our car."

She feels a sense of aloneness compared with some people she knows who use credit cards to go to Broadway shows and take vacations.

"We really never lived that way. We never had the hedonistic lifestyle. A couple of medical bills add up, ones the insurance company decides it won't pay. Quality day care, preschool. . . . We never were extravagant."

The family has stopped doing a number of things: "Going to the movies. Going out to dinner. Buying new clothes. Well, we do get some for our daughter. But we do a lot more with friends in terms of sharing clothing. I always pass on Emily's clothing to friends with smaller kids.

"We haven't used a credit card in three and a half years. It's a trap. The whole system, for it to work, is predicated on you being in debt. If we don't have the money, we don't buy it. We have a budget. It's for necessities: car payment, mortgage, food. We don't have cable."

A big factor driving this family's thrift is soaring property taxes. When they bought the house in 1996, the taxes were $5,400. In 2009, the total was $13,200. In 2010, they paid nearly $15,000. Her town's leaders passed a 19 percent increase for 2011, which means the couple will owe around $18,000.

"It's a regular house. It's not in Montclair. I know people there who are paying thirty thousand dollars in taxes," she said, referring to an exclusive New Jersey town.

Lisa's worldview is as much colored by these staggering tax increases as it is by nearly losing her family's home to foreclosure. New Jersey has the highest property tax rate in the nation, averaging $7,300 per house. This average includes low-cost rural areas; taxes are far higher in communities with good schools and proximity to jobs in New York City.

Anger over these ever-rising taxes led the heavily Democratic state to elect Chris Christie, a Republican, as governor in 2008. Christie has made reducing taxes into a crusade. In 2011, a 2 percent cap on annual increases will go into effect. But it is riddled with loopholes.

"The newly-passed bill mandating the 2-percent property tax cap will have NO impact," Lisa wrote me in late 2010, the capitalized letters emphasizing the kind of anger she harbors. "Left out of the cap was salaries/benefits of public employees." In other words, there is a lot of room for increases way beyond the cap, including the 19 percent jump in her town slated for 2011.

A tenet of conservatism is to be against taxes. Even though this is a major issue for Lisa, she does not consider herself conservative. She worries deeply about the far right feeding on the anger of Americans and what this may lead to politically.

"I'm a liberal. I qualify by saying I'm not a capital 'L' liberal," Lisa explained. "I do not follow lockstep any liberal ideology." She defined herself as a Democrat. She said she supports "legalizing marijuana, gay marriage." She also supports providing food stamps for the needy. However, she was quick to add: "I do resent the entitlement philosophy of some who believe the government 'owes' them, but these are not the unemployed or indigent. These 'entitlement queens' are public employees."

With her family's reduced income and recent rises in what they must pay for health insurance, it galls her that public employees in New Jersey keep getting raises and still contribute almost nothing toward their health care. The head of the sanitation department for her tiny city is paid $98,000 a year and yet contributes only $24 a month toward his health care costs, she said. She feels it is fundamentally unfair that government workers continue to live as middle-class Americans did in the 1950s through the 1970s, while taxpayers like her are subsidizing them in the tough economic times of the 2010s. In 2009, her salary increased by 1 percent; her husband's remained flat.

"While those in the private sector continue to experience salary freezes and hikes in our health care benefit contribution—or, worse, job losses—teachers, police, and others in the public sector demand annual cost-of-living increases . . . one example: our school district raised taxes 7-percent last year to give teachers a 4-year contract with annual increases." In order to keep the tax increase from being even higher, Lisa added, the district had to cut teaching positions and eliminate buying new books. "Are students the priority?" she asked.

"Government is a big, bloated tick," she declared. When I later e-mailed to ask her what she meant by this, Lisa replied, "The 'bloated tick' I referred to is government at all levels, uncontrolled, irresponsible spending that drives up my taxes. . . . I have no choice of how much I pay for garbage collection, leaf pickup, local police, public schools."

Lisa would like to move her family to a rural region where they could live more simply and get away from higher property taxes. But that may be a long time in the future. There is a 10 percent foreclosure rate in her area, which means that selling the house would be difficult.

"I can't move. No one in their right mind would buy a house in my town. If we could find a seller—oh, my God, I'd be gone." Speaking of herself and many of her neighbors, Lisa added, "We cannot sell our homes because the assessed value outstrips the market, and the guarantee of double-digit annual tax increases ensures that foreclosure is just an eventuality. . . . I hate being so angry. I used to be a free spirit and really easy-going but feel trapped."

Over and over, Lisa apologized for her anger as we communicated by phone and e-mail in late 2010. "Sorry to rant," she wrote in one message. "It's just so intractable."

She is struggling to keep a positive attitude and look to a better life in the future.

"I think there's something going on," she said about the reaction of middle-class people like her family to these hard economic times. She feels there is an awakening.

"We're now going way, way back, to the era of our grandparents. I used to make fun of them because they never threw anything away. They even darned socks. Other cultures have a saying, 'Don't spend tomorrow's money.' You appreciate things better when you have to save to get them, have to wait."

Her family has a garden of tomatoes, herbs, peppers. She likes the idea of community agriculture. "You're not a victim of some corporation." Unfortunately, she says, her city just passed a law forbidding residents to keep chickens, contrary to many other cities that are liberalizing such rules. This bugs her.

Her experience has taught her family this: they have to control their own lives.

"I won't entrust my well-being with the state," she asserted. "I'm more comfortable with individualism. You have to take care of yourself. I teach my daughter to think like this. Don't expect the cavalry to come in. Government at all levels bails out the special interests . . . but not the rest of us. We are just their revenue stream. At the end of the day, you can barely cover your basic living expenses. . . . I think it's a broken system that forces you to work just to have a roof over your head and food and nothing more. We're two people with advanced degrees, and we don't have time or money to do much else than we are doing."

In early 2011, Lisa emailed with bad news: her husband had been laid off from the job that had saved them from foreclosure. Once again they faced losing the house.

"Dylan Thomas wrote that 'after the first death, there is no other,' and I don't doubt his sincerity and heartbreak, but this constant job loss thing kills you over and over."

I listened to Lisa's anger with keen interest. There is so much of it out there in the United States.

In 2010, the Tea Party and those far to the right dominated the airwaves, newspapers, and websites. Because of this, the faces of anger that most of us saw were those of men wearing goofy-looking hats from the 1700s; the voices most of us heard were screaming the word "Nazi" or "Hitler" to decry modest policies that even Richard Nixon strongly supported, such as national health care or regulation of industries to prevent harm to workers and citizens. The various media focused on these cartoon characters, not the broader anger found in someone like Lisa and the millions of others in homes they are about to lose or may lose in the coming few years. Lisa is scared of what she calls the "mean-spirited illiterate Tea Party candidates." Yet those relatively few people get the headlines, while a multitude of others suffer quietly. As Professor John Russo pointed out to us in Youngstown, Democrats did well in the suburbs in 2008. But they didn't do so well there in 2010. The 2008 crop of Democrats failed the Lisas of this nation. Someone must speak for Lisa and people like her to give them a reason for hope, an alternative to the forces of rage and hate. Who will that be?

PART 6 REBUILDING OURSELVES, THEN TAKING AMERICA ON A JOURNEY TO SOMEWHERE NEW

It's a war . . . It's like when Hitler invaded Poland in 1939.

—Stephen A. Schwarzman, CEO of the Blackstone Group, an individual whose net worth is $8 billion, on President Barack Obama's proposal to have hedge fund managers pay their fair share of taxes

We have the right to get rid of this government by any means necessary. Violence is part of the scenario. The option is on the table. But it is not the first option.

—Texas Republican and Tea Party candidate for Congress Stephen Broden, October 21, 2010

The single most important thing we want to achieve is for President Obama to be a one-term president.

—Mitch McConnell, Republican minority leader of the U.S. Senate, on the eve of the midterm election, October 29, 2010

More than half (55%) of all adults in the labor force say that since the Great Recession began 30 months ago, they have suffered a spell of unemployment, a cut in pay, a reduction in hours or have become involuntary part-time workers. . . . The survey also finds that the recession has led to a new frugality in Americans' spending and borrowing habits.

—Pew Research Center's Social and Demographic Trends Project, June 2010

Virtually everything on the fiscal policy side will be off the table in the deadlocked partisan world we face in 2011 and 2012. This greatly increases the probability of a Japanese-style lost decade that would span the decade 2007–2017.
—Robert J. Gordon, Northwestern University economist

Robert Reich, former secretary of labor, wrote in July 2009: "On one side are the V-shapers who look back at prior recessions and conclude that the faster an economy drops, the faster it gets back on track. And because this economy fell off a cliff late last fall, they expect it to roar to life early next year. Hence the V shape. Unfortunately, V-shapers are looking back at the wrong recessions. Focus on those that started with the bursting of a giant speculative bubble and you see slow recoveries . . . investor confidence returns only gradually. That's where the more sober U-shapers come in. They predict a more gradual recovery, as investors slowly tiptoe back into the market. . . .

"My prediction, then? Not a V, not a U. But an X. This economy can't get back on track because the track we were on for years—featuring flat or declining median wages, mounting consumer debt, and widening insecurity, not to mention increasing carbon in the atmosphere—simply cannot be sustained.

"The X marks a brand new track—a new economy. What will it look like? Nobody knows. All we know is the current economy can't 'recover' because it can't go back to where it was before the crash. So instead of asking when the recovery will start, we should be asking when and how the new economy will begin."

24 ZEN IN A CRIPPLED NEW HAMPSHIRE MILL TOWN

You journey to Berlin, New Hampshire, by dropping over "The Notch," as Franconia Notch in the White Mountains is called by locals. The Notch separates the two worlds of this state, the wild North Country from the populated south. Berlin, pronounced as one syllable and said rapidly, isn't technically at the end of the road. But in a de facto manner it is: two-lane blacktop ribbons, bisecting a wilderness of birch and fir infested with moose, deer, and not much else, go to the sparsely settled Canadian frontier and the unpeopled forests of Maine. Few travelers have any reason to come through. You have to want to end up in Berlin.

Michael, filmmaker Ron Wyman, and I entered the nearby town of Gorham on a day when the snow was blinding white and the actual air temperature was 4 degrees above zero. The wind chill was something like minus 25 degrees. A billowing plume of white steam rose against the bluest of skies.

The Cascade Flats mill, owned by Fraser Papers Inc., which produces hand towels, paper for business use, and other products, is situated on the bank of the Androscoggin River. If we hadn't read the newspapers, we might have been fooled by that steam and the sound of machinery rumbling in the arctic air into thinking that all was well with the 240 people employed here. But Fraser was in bankruptcy, and it had been announced just the previous week that the mill was for sale and that, if no buyer was forthcoming, it would be shut down. The plant, in a conservative calculation by the mill's manager, contributed about $80 million to the economy in the greater Berlin area. (Later, in October 2010, Fraser did close the mill. Two buyers then came forward, but the deals fell through. Then, in December, a third buyer stepped in and won approval from a bankruptcy court. If this deal is completed, the buyer has indicated that the mill may reopen in early 2011. The plant would be the last paper mill left in the North Country.)

The mill closing would be the latest blow to "The City That Trees Built." Berlin became an epicenter for paper making in the 1850s when the steep drop in the river was harnessed to make electricity. In 1888 and 1892, the Brown Company built huge plants—a mill in Berlin to make pulp from wood chips and the factory in Gorham that turned that pulp into paper. At their peak, the two plants employed some 2,000 workers. Even as recently as 2001, there were 850 jobs.

In 2006, the pulp mill in Berlin closed. In 2007, the plant was leveled, save for one smokestack that remained as part of a plan for a small plant that would make electricity from wood chips. It would employ just a few dozen workers. What was left was a blank spot in the center of the city—and that lone stack rising like a nasty middle finger that mockingly reminds residents of what had once been.

There was an exodus. The city's population, once 22,000, fell to fewer than 10,000 as homes and apartments emptied. But these units didn't remain vacant for long: an influx of poor people from southern New Hampshire began coming. The newcomers were fleeing the high rents of what was then the housing boom; they were desperate for lower-cost rentals, especially those that would accept federal Section 8 vouchers. Work was scarce for these new arrivals; at best, they got part-time jobs like those in the Wal-Mart SuperCenter that had opened a few years ago. In 2008, the last big grocery store closed, and with it went 185 better-paying jobs. On the plus side, several hundred new jobs came in the form of a federal prison, in addition to employment at a state prison that was already here.

Amid this economic turmoil, an arsonist or arsonists set to work. Thirty-four buildings, most abandoned multifamily structures, have been torched in the last few years. The fires come in the night. Sue Watson, with the Family Resource Center, a nonprofit agency that helps a thousand economically troubled families each year access services, says children are terrified of dying in a fire and sleep on the floor in their parents' bedrooms.

The charred ruins from the arsons visibly illustrate the anxiety that infects the city. Berlin and surrounding Coos County have the highest per capita rates in the state for suicides, drug dealing, and domestic violence, said Watson.

Berlin is a microcosm of America. Save for its vastly diminished manufacturing base, it has an unsustainable economy built on prison jobs and part-time work at stores selling goods made in China. Some see hope in a proposal for a casino, which has thus far been turned down in close votes by state lawmakers, though it may yet get approval. It would mean more part-time jobs and perhaps the attendant side attractions such as strip clubs. Girls could grow up aspiring to be pole dancers, while boys might plan on becoming prison guards, if poverty doesn't drive them to crime and cause them to end up as inmates.

But there's more. Berlin is a microcosm in another way. The town's decline can be traced to all the usual reasons—union jobs that cannot compete with what is essentially slave labor overseas, the cost of materials, U.S. environmental regulations versus the toxic horror allowed in Third World nations, and so on—the same reasons found in former steel cities such as Youngstown, Ohio.

One other reason is also ubiquitous: Wall Street greed. You know this story. A company is bought and leveraged with debt. Money dealers walk away with multimillions. The company then cannot compete because of the debt load. The dealmakers luxuriate in the Hamptons or sail yachts in the Caribbean, enjoying the spoils gained from ruining the lives of the thousands of workers who are left behind.

In the case of Berlin, James River Corporation spun off the mills as Crown

Vantage, with a $400 million debt load, in 1995. At the time, the stock traded at $24 per share. The debt made profit impossible, and the stock price had fallen to $2.50 by the time the company was again sold.

The penultimate buyer was one Mehdi Gabayzadeh, who bought the distressed operation with its six valuable hydroelectric dams, which have 31 megawatts of generating capacity, for $45 million in 1999. His American Tissue company took on Crown Vantage's debt. Through cooking the books at the Berlin mills and other troubled paper mills that he acquired on the cheap, he cost lenders and bondholders about $300 million. Gabayzadeh was convicted of fraud in federal court and sentenced to fifteen years in prison. The Berlin mills closed.

Yet it wasn't the final death knell for the pulp mill in Berlin. Fraser bought it and the Gorham works in a 2003 bankruptcy sale for $31.5 million. The company ran the Berlin pulp mill until 2006, when it was closed for good.

We stopped in for a tour of the Cascade Flats mill given by the manager, who took us to vats that held 30 tons of pulp being spun into a white goop. It emerged from one of the vats as a glutinous sheet, wide as a cottage and 99 percent water. This sheet was then fed through steel rollers that squeezed out the liquid and compressed the fiber, drying it until it came out as office paper on the other side of a machine long as a city block.

The manager, who had worked in paper mills all over the Midwest and the East since 1962, was desperately trying to save the plant. He had plans to make it profitable by switching to tissue paper. He told us that the workers were highly motivated, setting production records in the previous months. The workers had fire under their asses because they knew what would happen if they weren't productive—they would wind up like their neighbors who had lost jobs. The manager had seen too many shutdowns. He told us that one importer was selling finished paper for what it cost an American company to buy the raw pulp.

The manager was a well-read man who quoted economic theory. He shook his head and wondered aloud: To have jobs, we have to make things. But how can we do that against the economic headwinds that assail us in a "world economy"?

I looked at the manager and shook my head. Both of us pondered. *What do we do? Just what do we do?*

I felt like Tolstoy uttering the same question as he agonized over the poverty he saw in the Khitrov Market, "the saddest spot in all of Moscow." I remembered reading how he had been driven to a form of madness by this.

It was a question that had been gnawing at me for three decades, and it continued to do so as we set out to work on this book: what can people do?

It was in Berlin, finally, that I came to understand the first part of the multifaceted answer. It took form at the home of Tim Lapointe, a third-generation mill worker. His grandfather had worked in the pulp mill, his father put in forty years there, and Tim had twenty-two years in when the plant went down.

As Michael, Ron, and I drove out of the Androscoggin River Valley toward Tim's house, looking down on the town and the vast blank patch of snow where the pulp mill once stood, I told my companions that I expected to find an angry man at the house atop the hill.

Instead, we found something else.

Tim answered the door. He was balding but looked more youthful than his fifty-one years. The house was well kept; Tim had rebuilt most of it when he and his wife bought the dwelling years before. We sat in the kitchen with the nice wainscoting he had installed. I noticed the view of famed Mount Washington out the window.

Tim began to tell us the story of his life. He tried for a job at the mill when he graduated from high school, he said, but it was a bad time. So he went into the U.S. Army. When he got out, he went to college, studied industrial arts, and became a machinist. The early 1980s recession was raging. He went over The Notch and got a job in Manchester. He was laid off. He got another job in that town and was again laid off. He came back home and landed a job in a local machine shop. The owner died.

At this point in his life, he was about to get married and raise a family. "I made a promise to myself: I was going to work in the mill, if it was the last thing I did," Tim said. "It was security."

He was hired and had a few good years. Then the ownership began changing hands. There was no money to keep up the equipment. Finally, in 2001, the mills closed. Tim got another job for half the wages. When Fraser reopened the pulp mill in 2003, Tim came back, but things never really gelled, and morale was low. When the plant closed in 2006, Tim got into a federal program that funded an employer to hire and retrain him. The job was over The Notch, and he commuted 100 miles round trip each day. The employer never trained him, and when the program ended, he was let go. By then, he had two sons in college.

"I put myself to work to find a job. I'm usually pretty good at it. I left no stone unturned. I got lucky, found another job, crossing The Notch again, at another machine shop."

The owner actually retrained him, without any federal funding. But orders fell, and Tim had been laid off a few months ago, in September. It was now December.

"And here I am."

"You've been through the wringer," I said.

"I'm still going through the wringer. I know it's going to work out eventually. But the quality of life that was there back when the pulp mill was running, it's gone. I accept the change that's in front of me. But it hasn't happened yet. What is it? I don't know what it's turning out to be. I caught a glimpse of Jesse Ventura last night, and he said it's a plot to take over the world."

Tim laughed. It's hard not to at least half-believe the conspiracy people. "It's going to be the rich, and it's going to be us. That's it."

"Are you angry?"

"I'm beyond angry. It's—I have to survive, alone. I don't get what's going on in the country right now. It is—" He paused. "I don't know how to deal with it. I'm dealing with it right here with my own government in my own little home. There won't be any help, I feel. There's really no help now."

"That's wrong."

"Yes, it's wrong."

Rather than being depressed, Tim said, he decided he needed to find community. Being alone was not good. He studied different groups in town—church organizations, the Knights of Columbus, the Lions Club.

"I grabbed Free Masonry. I'm trying to get together with other men and people and be part of a group. Because, I think, we're going to need that later on—community."

He had recently joined. There were only three Masons in the group when he went to the first meeting. Other newcomers soon showed up with the same goal of finding community. "We're getting eight to nine people now," Tim said. "They're helpful, and they're encouraging. And I can get out there and be helpful also."

They're planning how they can assist nonmembers in need.

On the job front, Tim has given up on manufacturing. He's studying for his commercial driver's license, which might allow him to get a job driving a school bus. His wife works as a cook for a school. "This morning, I had a bus driving class. Tomorrow, I've got another one."

He is very upbeat about bus driving. I noted that he has a positive attitude for someone who has been through so much.

"I try. My other side is pretty negative. I'm grateful. I have to count my blessings every day. I'm so grateful that I didn't buy a big home. I bought a home that was very inexpensive, and I put in my time and effort to fix it up. There's no mortgage. So I just pay high taxes, which is like rent. I have to heat it. But we're able to have shelter, a roof over our head.

"We have no credit card debt. We have to live within our means. That's the problem with America now. We've lived beyond our means. We don't have a boat, an in-ground pool, or a big house. I'm hoping to just get by until I retire. I'm going to survive. Like I say, I'm counting my blessings about what I don't have. I have to have patience. If I don't have patience, I get all nerved up and worked up. It's a rotten feeling getting out of bed in the morning, I tell you right now, when you have no job, no nothing—"

Tim fell silent. "Okay, you're getting me into it right now. The negative side. It's real."

"How do you get over that, when you get out of bed in the morning?" I asked.

Tim took a deep breath. "I have a thing—

"I studied martial arts for several years. It was with a Native American fellow who came over this way from Montana. He started his own school. He's a shaman. You go to this school, you always felt good. He'd exercise you, he'd get you to read. He taught me a lot of things."

The shaman was vague about what he was teaching. Tim discovered that it was Reiki, a Japanese form of meditation that reduces stress.

"And so when I get up in the morning, I do Reiki. And this energy, it's in a lot of healing. The Chinese have it, the Tibetans have it, the Indians have it. It's just a form of meditation, and it helps clear my head. It helps me to stay connected and not shoot off somewhere and get depressed. It's kind of embarrassing—"

I urged him not to be embarrassed.

"Some people think it's a whacky thing," Tim acknowledged. "Up here, since we're Catholic and we were taught certain things, it's taboo—"

"Those people who say that are the ones who probably need it the most," Ron interjected.

"It's all attitude," Tim said. In addition to Reiki, he finds peace in the plentiful woods around him.

"I walk up the street here, just two, three properties away, hit the woods. I'll walk three, four miles up, all the way back. You're in your own Zen. It's quiet."

Tim has gained mastery over what could have been consuming anger. Not long after we saw him, he landed a job as a custodian a quarter mile away from his home. He also traveled to Boston to attend a leadership/mentoring seminar, hoping to learn ways to expand membership in the Masons so the group can more effectively help others in the city of Berlin.

25 A WOMAN OF THE SOIL IN KANSAS CITY

Sherri Harvel was hoeing around her purple-hulled peas in a community garden in Kansas City. Her teenage children were at home. Sherri sometimes sang gospel songs as she worked. Suddenly, a voice rose above the corn in a nearby patch.

"It's the devil!" a woman shouted. Sherri looked up and saw the woman was holding a weed aloft. "Weeds, they're the devil!" the woman explained. Sherri laughed.

It was the early 1990s, and Sherri had just joined the garden. An African American resident of the inner city, she worked hard as a single mom, and she was stressed by her job as a loan-processing officer for a bank. The garden most evenings was a refuge, for at least an hour of relaxation.

One day a few summers later, Sherri was in the patch, complaining about her job, wishing she could be in the garden all the time. One of the other community gardeners suggested that Sherri sell some of the excess produce at a farmers market.

The next weekend, Sherri took some tomatoes and beans to the market, and they rapidly sold. She wondered: is it possible to become a for-profit farmer in the city?

Then Sherri heard about Kansas City selling abandoned lots. She put in a bid on four adjoining ones, totaling a quarter acre, and she got all four for a bargain. The major cost was getting a water line put in for irrigation, a few thousand dollars. In 2003, she quit her banking job to become an urban farmer.

She called the new business Root Deep Urban Farm.

Sherri, a woman who lives modestly and values her connection to the soil and the peace of mind that comes with it, is the opposite of Wall Street's Big Boys. I'd first interviewed Sherri by phone in early 2008. Her story stuck with me. I wondered: could some of us find a way to live through hard times by growing our own food, not only surviving but finding some peace amid economic chaos?

Kansas City is at the forefront of the urban farming movement. In some places, such as New York City, land is just too expensive for such an enterprise to really thrive, though in 2010 a 1-acre rooftop farm called the Brooklyn Grange began operating, and there were plans for more such "sky" farms. But in many cities—Detroit, Pittsburgh, Los Angeles, and others—urban farming on empty lots is booming.

What some people are doing is creating what Robert Reich has termed "X"—"a brand new track—a new economy." These are individuals one might call "Xsumers." They have cut back and changed their ways. They're growing their own food, selling the surplus, shopping for secondhand goods, and abandoning credit cards. It doesn't mean that they're leading lives of want. Some, like Sally in Michigan, a woman we encountered early in this book in "Snapshots from the Road," are taking the first baby steps into a new life. Others, like Sherri, are farther along.

Sherri became active in the nonprofit Kansas City Center for Urban Agriculture, which "helped me to look at it from more of a business standpoint." KCCUA, founded in 2004, runs a 2-acre demonstration city farm. Funding comes from the U.S. Department of Agriculture, grants, and income from the farm.

At a KCCUA meeting in early 2008, the news was both good and bad: they could accept no more CSA (community-supported agriculture) members, who contract for weekly supplies of produce, because there weren't enough urban farmers to meet the exploding demand. But fifty urban farmers did show up to talk about the next steps they'd take to grow even more food in the city. One man wanted to raise tilapia. Others included Erika Wright, disabled from muscular dystrophy, who earns as much as $100 each Saturday at a farmers market; and John Kaiahua, a Hawaii-born Vietnam veteran who farms some 2 acres of land in the city. And there's Pov Hun, Chaxamone Lor, and their four children, who grow bitter melon, used as part of an organic green tea mixture they sell. And there is a group of Somali refugee women who farm on a Catholic church's property.

I finally got to visit Sherri. We met at the KCCUA demonstration farm. I found her in one of the warehouse-size greenhouses on the property, tending to hundreds of plant starts, some of which she'd sell at the farmers market and some of which would go into the ground at her urban farm.

She proudly showed off her rainbow mix Swiss chard and seven varieties of tomatoes, including one called a "white cherry," her favorite. She also had purple Russian kale, basil, peppers hot and sweet, oregano, sage, and thyme.

We shook hands. Hers were spotted by earth, and she seemed a bit self-conscious.

"That's not dirt," I said. "That's soil."

"Exactly! I tell people that all the time!" Sherri exclaimed. The plants were beautiful. I remarked that "it's always a miracle" to see things growing.

"Yes," Sherri said, with contentment, over the whirring of a giant ventilation fan.

Sherri estimates that a little less than half her annual income comes from farming. She took on a part-time job at Target to pick up the slack. She cuts back hours at the store in the growing season. In the winter, she puts in more time at Target.

Sherri has become adept at marketing. A surprise best-seller has been purple-hulled peas—traditional African American food. That's good, she says, because they're the easiest to grow, and the plants are good producers.

"After a while, I knew this is where I needed to be. It would take all the stress away. You can think out there. It turned into one of the biggest changes in my life," Sherri said. "I had the stress of an eight-to-five job. Farming is a seven-day-a-week job. I try to take Sunday off, but there is always something that needs doing.

"I don't make a lot of money on a yearly basis. I'll bet I don't even make minimum wage. My income level dropped quite a bit. I've had to cut some things out. You know, it's okay. For me, it was worth it to have peace of mind, peace of my soul for something that I love, makes me relax. It's very labor intensive. I don't have a tractor and things like that to help me out. I have a small Rototiller, five horsepower.

I'd love a ten horsepower. I wish I could afford it. They work the soil better. It's a lot smoother. I'm pushing the limits. I would love another full acre.

"It's not that farming doesn't have its own craziness. But it's a good craziness. I cry sometimes thinking about the transition I've made. It's made such a change in my life—taking control, making decisions that in the long run are better for you."

She will never go back.

"What I do feeds me spiritually. I eat better than most people. I know the nutritional value of what I grow. I can go out the door, pick a tomato, harvest carrots and beans. To me, I have the advantage." She also trades with other farmers who grow chickens and raise other crops that she does not. She lives in a world of an underground and organic economy. She cannot calculate what she personally saves on food out of her cash budget, but it doesn't matter that she can't quantify a figure. It's priceless.

I walked up to a house, the KCCUA office, on the 2-acre property. Behind it, a crew washed fresh-picked spinach that was robust and dark green—a Muhammad-Ali-in-his-prime vegetable, compared to the pale weakling variety found in big supermarkets. Katherine Kelly, whose title is KCUAA executive director/farmer, ran spinach under water in a tub as she said, "We've got this vibrant, growing food movement. It's in expansion mode. And then there's the economy, that is in a shrinking mode. In some ways, they're working against each other. In other ways, the work we do actually becomes more important because we're promoting self-sufficiency. Sherri is a good example. You get somebody growing in a neighborhood, and they become a role model.

"I grew up with an uncle who gardened; that's how you learned. There's a generation that hasn't had that. You put somebody in there who's a role model, and all of a sudden, gardening isn't scary, it becomes possible. Sherri will have someone stop and say, 'Can I have an extra tomato plant for my porch?' And she'll give them one. So in that way, what we are doing becomes part of the response to hunger and poverty, because it's self-sufficiency tools that we're giving people.

"We've got some people in the greenhouse, they're going to make fifty dollars a week. But they'll have food for their own family. It will generate a little extra cash. Other people will make a couple hundred a week. Our demonstration farm, which is quite large, we've grossed, two years in a row, over a hundred thousand dollars."

The farm is not subsidized. It's run as a for-profit component of the nonprofit enterprise. KCCUA wants it to be a true demonstration project, to show small urban farmers how they can make it. Of the farm's budget, Katherine said, "I want them to look at it and have it be meaningful to them and their operations."

We went inside her office. Katherine commented that what is happening in

America right now really is our going back to the future. She told the story of a very old man who approached her after a talk she gave on the KCCUA.

"He grew up in a truck farming family," Katherine said, invoking a term I had not heard in years. Truck farming was local agriculture, small farmers who grew "truck," local food.

"He was telling me his father's schedule. They sold at the city market. They would be out in the fields at seven o'clock, they would work all the way through, mother, father, son, and one hired hand. Eat lunch, have dinner in the field."

The father would nap. Then "he'd go to the city market and sell the produce, from midnight till four A.M. or five whatever, till they sold out. Catch a nap. Then go back out in the field. We're not working hard at all!" she laughed, thinking of the comparison.

"I asked him how much of the produce that Kansas City needed came from around here. He said probably ninety percent. Some of it was shipped northward. There was this thing—when Arkansas and Oklahoma started getting produce, they would sell locally, and then they would send it northward, by rail, to catch the price. When Kansas City got produce, it would sell northward to get a good price."

Thus in the south-to-north region, fresh produce was available for a big part of the year. Then came refrigerated trucks.

"All the grocery stores he used to sell to, he said, 'They wanted a twelve-month supply, and so they stopped buying from us.' He was really clear. 'We fed Kansas City.' That just blows my mind. We get this 'Oh, we can't do that, this whole local food movement. We need our corporate farms.'"

Perhaps the old-style truck farms won't return because consumers want a constant supply of a wide variety of produce, but things are happening. Seed companies report that sales have increased: the D. Landreth Seed Company in Philadelphia told a *Washington Post* reporter in 2009 that sales were up 75 percent from the previous year; at Wal-Mart, seed sales went up 30 percent. Backyard chickens are becoming popular: the U.S. Postal Service shipped 1.2 million pounds of packages containing mostly chicks, but also baby ducks and turkeys, in the first six months of 2009, a 7 percent increase from a year earlier, which means millions more birds.

Many people are starting to take care of their own lives in a very fundamental manner—growing and raising some of what they eat. And something even larger is going on, something I didn't really think about until I talked with Daniel Dermitzel, associate director/farmer at the KCCUA.

As Dermitzel washed scallions that day I visited, he asked about what I'd been learning in my research. I told him about the Alexander family and how they were finding power and hope in family and in relying on themselves. I mused that urban farming was part of how people might take control of their lives.

Daniel listened politely. When I had finished speaking, he said, "There is a tendency among people just starting this to overemphasize the individual self-sufficiency aspect. One of the things we have to understand is that we are not alone. We can say to ourselves we are on our own."

But we are not.

What happens, Daniel said, is that people begin growing food and, as they do so, they begin to discover they are part of a community as they meet others like them. They begin trading with fellow gardeners and, in the process, make friends.

Daniel mused that it could be the start of some kind of collective awakening.

"I think we're all on that journey," he said. "We're just learning."

It was an elemental aspect of growing food that I had not fully considered.

This spontaneous creation of community is where our strongest hope lies.

26 THE PHOENIX?

Youngstown is a difficult place to find hope. Like many cities in the Steel Belt, it's never been the kind of town where most residents drink their morning coffee bright with optimism for the new day, even in the best economic times. If defeat is a possibility in any endeavor of life, it tends to be embraced as the inevitable result. Growing up in Cleveland, I called this the "can't do" mentality. Mill towns are just that way.

Of course, in the days of my youth, there were, relatively speaking, few real problems. So when a true crisis occurred, with the shutdowns and layoffs, this defeatism matured into something far more debilitating. This is true not only in Youngstown but also in much of steel country. An excellent description comes from Abigail Wendle, twenty-three years old, who grew up in Youngstown and wrote this e-mail to me in the summer of 2009:

> My grandfather worked in the steel mills his whole life in Youngstown. He recently passed away and spent his last 20–25 years in pain because his knees were totally shot from crawling on frozen ground in the darkness of the pipes at the mills for some 50 years. I "interviewed" him once and asked what his greatest fear was. His answer was "the devil." Springsteen sings in "Youngstown" about going to the fiery furnaces of hell and having no place in Heaven. That's a really dark but on-point thing for him to sing. My grandfather seemed to never allow himself to find joy in anything. He would just wave his hand and accompany the gesture with the comment, "It's a bunch of shit." Didn't matter so much what the "it" was.

One has to understand this attitude to comprehend the world into which Ian Beniston was born on February 5, 1983, on the north side of Youngstown. His father, William J. Beniston, was one of the thirty-five hundred workers, along with Joe Marshall and his son, who lost their jobs at U.S. Steel's Ohio Works. William, who worked in the blast furnace department, had only thirteen years in at the mill and didn't get much in the way of severance.

William became a truck driver and a member of the Teamsters union. Ian's mother, Martha, was a nurse. With these jobs, the Benistons and their three children were able to remain in the city.

But it was a city beset by wrenching violence and tension resulting from so much joblessness. There were record numbers of murders and arson. This reality came close to the Beniston home on September 22, 1987. At 4 A.M., at the foot of the family's driveway, Youngstown police officer Paul Durkin, thirty-four, stopped a man who appeared to be holding items stolen from automobiles. The suspect shot Durkin twice in the chest with a .22-caliber weapon. The wounded Durkin fired six shots back but missed. The officer died at the scene. The suspect was convicted for the murder.

Ian was four. He stood in the door with his mother and older brother watching the flashing lights of police cars. The incident became part of his childhood, as did the sight of smoke on the horizon. The smoke wasn't from the mills; it came from burning houses, arson that occurred almost daily.

"I never saw the steel mills," Ian said. "I don't have any memory of the mills. Growing up, I watched the city falling apart."

Most searing was the sense of defeat that defined many adults in his world. The collective mentality was that everything was a bunch of shit.

Ian went to Youngstown State University and earned a degree in sociology. He moved to Columbus, Ohio, and began working at ACP Visioning + Planning, a consulting firm. He did planning work for urban renewal efforts in communities across the United States. He also studied for a master's degree in city and regional planning at the Austin E. Knowlton School of Architecture at Ohio State University.

"I didn't really understand that there were vibrant cities," he said. "The more I studied, the more I saw that Youngstown was really fucked up."

After graduating from Ohio State in 2008, he didn't move on to New York, Atlanta, or a European city—he came home to Youngstown. That summer, he began working for the Mahoning Valley Organizing Collaborative, a nonprofit with a goal of improving the neighborhoods of Youngstown and the surrounding area.

He'd returned to the city of his birth in the hope of changing it. He was twenty-six and eager to dig in. He had a lot of energy—his face was bright, with brows like tildes splashed in heavy ink over intense eyes, and an infectious smile. He looked at decay and saw opportunity. Ian had a vision.

When we first met Ian in early 2009, some months after his return home, he sat with his colleague Damareo Cooper in a second-floor office in downtown Youngstown. On the wall was a big map, which identified (in green, red, and orange shading) all the empty property in Youngstown—nearly 44 percent of all the property in the city was vacant. There were 4,578 abandoned structures and 22,804 vacant lots, as well as an estimated 37,000 occupied homes. The map had been researched in late 2008 by 150 volunteers who walked and drove each street in this city, which once had a population of 170,000 but was now just under 73,000, according to a 2008 U.S. Census estimate, and still falling.

Ian explained that the Mahoning Valley Organizing Collaborative had to first identify blight before anything could be proposed to fix it.

The nonprofit's aim was to tear down the ruin and create something new. They were not quite certain what that new should be: the collaborative had been in existence for only nine months. But the members were clear that change had to start with getting rid of the eyesores that affect the psychology of the city. Some of the land could be returned to nature, and some could be used to grow food.

Aside from the collaborative's goals, the city of Youngstown was examining what could be done to save money in the shrunken town. Officials were studying the notion of working block by block: if a block has just one occupied home, that owner could be offered a buyout incentive; perhaps another block with a half dozen homes would be preserved. In Flint, Michigan, officials have proposed shutting down entire sections of the city so that other neighborhoods can survive. Besides aesthetics, such contraction means that less money would be spent on cops, garbage pickup, snow plowing, and other services. Both Flint and New Orleans officials have looked at Youngstown as a model of what might be done.

Taking big parts of cities off the grid defies nearly three centuries of the American belief in expansion. Growth has always been seen as good.

Ian and Damareo had difficulty explaining the specifics of a possible end result, but they were passionate about the process of reinvention. For now, they said, they believe in demolition. "We have five thousand houses that need to be torn down," Damareo noted. What will follow must include neighborhood stabilization, giving residents a sense of pride.

Ian described what he saw as three kinds of people in his hometown: the defeated; those in denial, mostly older residents who believe that industry will return; and the young, like him, who hunger for a new path. He admitted that it would be difficult to convince those in the first category that anything could be done. As for the second group, Ian laughed about the possibility of the mills being rebuilt.

"I'm just looking forward," he said. "I don't know what they know. Some people are stuck in the past. A whole new generation, not as large—most of them are gone—has a whole different view of reality."

Ian paused. "I'm a realist. Some people don't want to hear that."

The members of the collaborative were not trying to dictate what residents should do. Instead, they were listening and asking questions, trying to formulate a new tomorrow as they went along.

Said Damareo, "People are beaten down. There's a sense of hopelessness. There's a distrust of outsiders. We have to show them we're here for the long term. That goes back to when they were going to get a blimp factory. They're not forgiving."

Said Ian, "We've been in a recession for thirty years. There are a lot of similarities between New Orleans and Youngstown. They got that way by a natural disaster; they got it all at once. Ours happened over thirty years. I don't think the citizens of Youngstown are any more responsible for their situation than the citizens of New Orleans are."

Ian had no illusions that Youngstown as a whole could be saved. But he believed it was realistic to try and reclaim some neighborhoods, piece by piece. The collaborative wanted to work on Saul Alinsky's model of helping people find a way to help themselves. People needed to relearn how to dream.

"Our job is reinstilling that hope."

I left the office wondering about Ian's passion and idealism. It was a wonderful thing, that kind of energy. But could they accomplish anything tangible? Over the years, I'd covered a lot of empowerment efforts and found that they often fizzled. Talking Alinsky and making it happen are two different things.

Months later, when I got back in touch with Ian, he had switched jobs and was now assistant director of the nonprofit Youngstown Neighborhood Development Corporation. He was translating hope into action much faster than I could have imagined. He was about to officially announce some big news: around $2 million in grants, with more money possibly coming, to kick off a neighborhood salvation demonstration project. It would cover more than thirty square blocks, an area known as the Idora neighborhood, a north-south corridor thirteen blocks long and three to four blocks wide.

"The neighborhood that we are looking at is at a tipping point. The vacancy rate is not extremely high. We will take what is vacant and fix it up."

There were one hundred vacant lots in the Idora area. "A lot of them are now dumping grounds. They don't look owned," Ian said. Local people will be hired to clean and fix up the lots, making some lots into parks and open space, with amenities like split-rail fences; planting others with native vegetation that absorbs contaminants in the soil; and turning yet others into urban farms. By the end of 2009, the initiative had obtained grant funding from six organizations to "conduct food access work, so a neighborhood market garden and work to introduce fresh food will be included."

"With a team put in place from the neighborhood, that in itself will foster a sense of ownership," Ian said. The name for the revitalized area will be the Idora EcoDistrict.

Further, there will be rehabilitation of abandoned or decaying houses. An ownership plan would create incentives for people to move into the neighborhood. In the commercial corridor, efforts were under way to open a grocery store.

As the summer of 2010 neared, six homes were being rehabilitated to green standards. Thirty homes had been torn down. Some were being "deconstructed" to recycle wood and other materials to be used locally.

Maurice Small, whom Ian describes as a "legend" of the urban farming movement, was now on staff. Small had created 250 community gardens in the greater Cleveland area through an organization called City Fresh, a nonprofit part of the New Agrarian Center. City Fresh develops and teaches urban residents how to farm, while also providing nutrition education. (At the end of 2010, a report by the development corporation showed that 115 parcels of vacant land, some 14.5 acres, had been redeveloped into greenspace and five community gardens. Eighty-four residents were farming the gardens, producing "over 3,200 pounds of fruits and vegetables.")

Ian knew that even all this would not be enough to save the city. Rather, he saw it as the start of a process of showing people what could be done.

Part of the process is jobs. The August 2009 cover story of *Entrepreneur* was titled "The Ten Best Cities to Start a Business (Youngstown, Ohio, Anyone?)." The magazine cited the nonprofit Youngstown Business Incubator, which had brought some homegrown high-tech jobs to the city. This nonprofit provides free or low-cost office space, and it helped propel Mike Broderick and his company, Turning Technologies, into business. The firm, with 130 employees, makes audience response systems "used in college lectures, corporate events, and even game shows." *Entrepreneur* quoted Broderick as citing the affordability of Youngstown—especially rent and taxes—as well as the eagerness of officials to help.

"Things are moving pretty fast," Ian said of the demonstration project. "We're hoping this can be translated into other neighborhoods. Already, other neighborhoods are lobbying for similar projects."

27 LOOKING FORWARD—AND BACK

"We are all caught up in the middle of insanity," Velma Hart told *Washington Post* writer Michelle Singletary not long after Hart had expressed her economic worries to President Barack Obama at a town hall meeting on the eve of the 2010 midterm elections. "My husband and I joked for years that we thought we were well beyond the hot-dogs-and-beans era of our lives," Hart told Obama. "But quite frankly, it's starting to knock on our door and ring true that that might be where we're headed again. . . . Mr. President, I need you to answer this honestly: Is this my new reality?"

About a month later, Hart was laid off from her job as a chief financial officer for AMVETS, a nonprofit that provides services to veterans. Her boss told Singletary that Hart "got bit by the same snake that has bit a lot of people. It was a move to cut our bottom line."

As 2010 came to a close, the insanity began to sink in for millions of Americans. Throughout that November and December, each day's newspapers brought more disconcerting reports.

Obama caved in to Republican demands without a fight and extended tax cuts for multimillionaires, which meant that the richest 0.1 percent of Americans each received an average tax cut of $370,000. "It's a huge giveaway to the super-rich in tough economic times," said Representative Jim McDermott, a Democrat from Washington; he deemed the cuts "craziness." To secure these tax cuts for the wealthy, Republicans had held hostage the unemployment benefits for the 2 million jobless who were about to fall off the rolls, claiming that helping the jobless would increase the national debt—a debt that hadn't existed when Bill Clinton left office, a debt that had originally ballooned in part as a result of those same tax cuts for the extremely rich.

Republicans were keen on destroying health care reform, even though "for the ninth year in a row, the number of Americans under age 65 covered by employer-sponsored health insurance . . . declined," the Economic Policy Institute reported; those with job-related health insurance fell from 61.9 percent of that age group in 2008 to 58.9 percent in 2009.

As Republicans prepared to take control of the House of Representatives in 2011, Republican Spencer Bachus of Alabama was picked to chair the House Financial Services Committee, which has power over Wall Street and banks. He told the *Birmingham News,* "In Washington, the view is that the banks are to be regulated, and my view is that Washington and the regulators are there to serve the banks."

Wall Street was back to partying. A thousand people crammed into the Good Units night club in Manhattan for a Halloween bash sponsored by Josh Koplewicz, an investment analyst at Goldman Sachs. Headlining was Lil' Kim, the hip-hop singer. The *New York Times* reported a "substantially larger crowd than the last several years" as Kim "performed dressed in a black cat costume." Bankers and traders were again engaging in bidding wars for summer beach rentals in the trendy Hamptons; three of them bid more than $400,000 for one rental in Southampton.

Bankers and traders were expected to reap $144 billion in bonuses and pay as the year ended. Corporate profits were at record levels, nearly $1.7 trillion annually, the U.S. Commerce Department reported. Profits had grown for seven consecutive quarters, among the fastest rates in history. Yet companies continued not to hire.

Meanwhile, 17 million families had found it difficult to eat for at least some period of time in the previous year, according to a report by the U.S. Department of Agriculture.

There were 26.6 million Americans who lacked full-time jobs, counting those who had grown discouraged and those who were involuntarily working part time—a jobless rate of 17 percent. Only the 15.1 million Americans who had not given up or had not gotten part-time jobs were counted in the official rate of 9.8 percent.

The Federal Reserve predicted that unemployment would remain high for years to come.

New York Times columnist Nicholas D. Kristof wrote, "If you want to see rapacious income inequality, you no longer need to visit a banana republic"—instead, he advised simply looking around at our nation. Readers protested, on the grounds that he'd wronged banana republics: many Latin American countries now have less income inequality than the United States.

Where does this insanity take us?

I surely cannot predict what will happen. But I can raise questions and provide some possibilities based on history and on what I know from thirty years of listening to Americans.

THE 1930s COLLIDE WITH THE 2010s

As we head into a precarious economic future, it's vital to keep in mind where we've been. Perhaps the most important decade we can learn from is the 1930s, the era of the Great Depression.

Like many Americans, I'd grown up hearing about how communism was a force to be reckoned with in those hard times. But in fact, American communists were not that plentiful. In 1935, *The Nation* magazine estimated that there were only about thirty thousand party members in the United States.

They were, however, certainly visible, with the result that their perceived power, especially in the wake of the Bolshevik revolution in Russia and the fears it engendered, was much greater than their actual power. Witness, for example, the events of "Red Thursday," a round-the-world rally against unemployment, held on March 6, 1930. New York City's demonstration on Union Square, with two thousand communists and thousands more onlookers, was the largest in America. Singing the "Internationale," party members marched down Broadway in defiance of police orders. Communists were eager for confrontation and hoped the cops would overreact. The *New York Times* reported that hundreds of officers rushed in, "swinging nightsticks, blackjacks and bare fists . . . hitting out at all with whom they came in contact."

In *My America,* Louis Adamic wrote,

> Well-to-do and wealthy people are afraid. . . . [They] seem to actually believe that the unemployed and the "proletariat" generally are about to heave up and annihilate them. . . . The riots on Union Square frighten them; to read the morning papers brings well-to-do people to the verge of nervous collapse; for they do not know that the occurrences on Union Square are not spontaneous mass-revolutionary demonstrations, but only organized "revolutionary" theatricalism.

The "Red Thursday" demonstrations failed to convert the working class to communism or to produce a sustained mass movement. Revolution was not coming. Nevertheless, Adamic made an important observation:

> No newspaper or person of any importance in the United States had manifested the slightest awareness of the national unemployment situation. The demonstrations had become sensational front-page news . . . because they had produced bleeding heads; and I gave the Communist party a sort of left-handed credit for starting the country toward unemployment-consciousness, which finally—in the autumn of 1930—forced even President Hoover to draw his ostrich head out of the sandpile and admit the existence of a social emergency . . . the worker is not news when he quietly starves. . . . Threatening "revolution," they—unwittingly—frightened great numbers of the naturally conservative but uninformed middle-class people into supporting, however half-heartedly, the New Deal reforms and the immense relief expenditures during 1934–37.

Demanding jobs, unemployment benefits, union rights, and an end to foreclosures, in addition to their agitation for revolution, the communists held the energy at the start of the decade. But by the late 1930s, the right had gained momentum. Conservatives viewed the New Deal as communistic, and the most extreme among them began turning to fascism. Anger caused some to seek scapegoats, much as some Germans had done in embracing Hitler's anti-Semitism.

Leading them was a Catholic priest. Father Charles E. Coughlin was America's first right-wing radio personality. In 1934, he had 10 million listeners, a greater proportion of the population than Rush Limbaugh draws today.

Early on, Coughlin appeared somewhat liberal. But a shift to the hard right came in his broadcast of November 20, 1938, in which he cited anti-Jewish Nazi propaganda and made other false claims. In New York City, radio station WMCA declared that it would no longer broadcast Coughlin unless he provided an advance script. He refused. In Germany, the Nazi press rose to Coughlin's defense, and a headline in the newspaper *Zwoelfuhrblatt* blared, "Americans Not Allowed to Hear the Truth."

A new organization had begun to form, dubbed the "Christian Front," in opposition to the "popular front" organizations of the left. The Christian Front attracted anti-Semites. On December 15, 1938, six thousand people gathered in a New York City auditorium to cheer Coughlin and boo Roosevelt. On December 18, the Christian Front organized two thousand "Coughlinites" to march on WMCA.

Up to this point in the Great Depression, observers had warned of an emerging fascist trend in the United States, but there had been little evidence of mobilization. Now, violence began.

Coughlin called for the formation of "platoons." On May 21, 1939, pro-Coughlin picketers, who maintained a daily vigil at WMCA, marched to Times Square, where they started a "series of running fist fights," according to the *New York Times,* targeting people who were selling anti-Coughlin publications. By mid-1939, the thuggery had spread. Writer Dale Kramer reported that "gangs of young hoodlums rove subway platforms late at night insulting Jews. A favorite tactic is to make jibes at a Jewish girl in the presence of her escort; the swain, thus provoked, attacks and is beaten by superior numbers. One youth, Irving Berger by name, was dangerously stabbed in such a fight in Grand Central Station."

The Christian Front was dealt a blow on January 13, 1940, when the FBI arrested seventeen members on charges of trying to overthrow the U.S. government, including leader John Cassidy, who was called "Fuehrer." A stash of weapons was found, along with fifteen partly assembled bombs. According to the FBI, the suspects had been plotting to kill a dozen congressmen, bomb Jewish newspapers, and take over National Guard armories.

Although the case fell apart, and the defendants walked, the publicity shattered the Christian Front. With the arrival of World War II, the government banned Coughlin's newspaper, *Social Justice,* from the U.S. mail in 1942 as "seditious." That same year, Coughlin's church superiors ordered the cessation of his radio show.

American fascism lost its energy during the war and the prosperity that followed, as its prime causative factor—economic disenfranchisement among white people—lessened. (Many black Americans were certainly in bad straits both in the

1930s and in later decades. But, as is the case today, they were not major actors in far-right movements; more often, they were the targets of the extreme right.)

Summing up his view of American fascism, Kramer wrote in 1940: "It will take time for a powerful [fascist] movement to organize itself out of the confusion caused by the [coming] war. But the technique of prejudice politics has been so well learned that should economic insecurity continue there can be no doubt that the American people during the next decade will be forced to deal with powerful 'hate movements.'"

Kramer was correct—he was just off in his timing. His warning would apply less to the 1950s, despite that decade's McCarthyism, and more to decades hence, when the white working class would again be stressed. As I argued in my book *Homeland,* the emergence of right-wing talk radio in the 1980s did not happen because the hosts created an audience; instead, it was a free-market response that capitalized on already existing anger, based on growing economic insecurity.

Today's right wing has its fringe, and there are dozens of Coughlins. They use modern communications such as e-mail and Twitter as well as talk radio to send their followers to disrupt town hall meetings and, in some cases, to openly carry loaded assault rifles and pistols outside events where the Democratic president and members of Congress are speaking. Sarah Palin was telling them, "Don't Retreat, Instead—RELOAD." They cranked up the volume after health care legislation passed in 2010, subjecting Democratic members of Congress to racial and anti-gay slurs and even death threats; some were spat upon. Bricks were hurled through the windows of regional Democratic Party headquarters. *New York Times* columnist Frank Rich wrote, "How curious that a mob fond of likening President Obama to Hitler knows so little about history that it doesn't recognize its own small-scale mimicry of *Kristallnacht.*"

Just as Adamic posited back in the 1930s that "the worker is not news when he quietly starves," many Americans have been quietly struggling for the past three decades. The majority are quietly frustrated. But today's Coughlinites, who are likely as few in number as were the communists of the 1930s, are not quiet about their anger. Some of them, a very small number, turn violent.

A report by the U.S. Department of Homeland Security, which was leaked in 2009, warned, "The consequences of a prolonged economic downturn—including real estate foreclosures, unemployment, and an inability to obtain credit—could create a fertile recruiting environment for rightwing extremists. . . . Rightwing extremist chatter on the Internet continues to focus on the economy, the perceived loss of U.S. jobs in the manufacturing and construction sectors, and home foreclosures. Anti-Semitic extremists attribute these losses to a deliberate conspiracy conducted by a cabal of Jewish 'financial elites.'"

At this point, violence comes with frightening regularity from lone gunmen who invoke neofascist beliefs. Examples include Richard Poplawski, a fan of Alex Jones and Glenn Beck, who killed three Pittsburgh police officers on April 4, 2009. He believed that President Barack Obama would outlaw guns. He feared a "Jewish-controlled one-world government." Then, on June 10, 2009, white supremacist James von Brunn killed a guard at the U.S. Holocaust Memorial Museum. He left a note: "You want my weapons—this is how you'll get them. The Holocaust is a lie. Obama was created by Jews."

On July 18, 2010, Glenn Beck fan Byron Williams filled his mother's Toyota Tundra with guns and headed the three hours west to San Francisco, intent on killing progressives at an office of the American Civil Liberties Union and at the Tides Foundation, the target of more than two dozen of Beck's rants. Williams, who was wearing body armor, was stopped for driving erratically by the California Highway Patrol on Interstate 580 in Oakland. A twelve-minute gun battle ensued in which Williams fired a 9 mm pistol, a shotgun, and a .308-caliber rifle loaded with armor-piercing bullets. Two officers and Williams were wounded.

Williams told journalist John Hamilton in a jailhouse interview, "I'm a revolutionary. . . . You know, when you become unemployed, desperate, you can no longer pay your bills, when your society has come to a standstill . . . companies are moving overseas, what do you think is gonna happen?"

All of these individuals believed that they were front-line soldiers at the dawn of a revolution, as did Timothy McVeigh in 1995, when he blew up the Alfred P. Murrah Federal Building in Oklahoma City, killing 168; and as did the Christian Front in 1939.

Then, in early 2011, six were killed when Congresswoman Gabrielle Giffords was shot and thirteen others were wounded in Tucson. Jared Loughner was charged. Some deemed it the act of a lone nutcase. But rightwing rhetoric is what inspires lone nutcases. Pima County sheriff Clarence W. Dupnik addressed this, lambasting the "vitriol that comes out of certain mouths about tearing down the government" and decrying how "unbalanced people" respond to it. "The anger, the hatred, the bigotry that goes on in this country is getting to be outrageous."

I can't get the turmoil of the 1930s out of my head. I've wondered endless nights: what lessons can we learn from those times? I keep thinking of Franklin Roosevelt's 1933 inauguration speech and this line: "the only thing we have to fear is fear itself."

These words came to be heard by generations of schoolchildren watching grainy newsreel footage, becoming something of a platitude. Yet no one back in 1933 had any certainty about how the future would unfold. Would there ever be an economic turnaround? Would democracy be preserved? Communists had rioted at Union Square; fascism was ascendant in Europe. One wonders how the Coughlinite anger would have played out in America had World War II not ended the hard times and turned the public solidly against fascism. Certainly the outcome was not preordained.

Today, there is no game-changing energy coming from the left. But on the right, there is loud and visible agitation from the various Tea Party organizations as well as radio and television personalities such as Glenn Beck. At the extreme right, there are all those lone gunmen. And credence was added to the Department of Homeland Security's warning of neofascist homegrown terrorism: in early 2010, the FBI and the ATF busted members of Hutaree, a Christian militia group in Michigan, who had planned to kill a police officer and then kill other cops at the funeral, hoping to spark a general uprising against the government.

The economy is key to the outcome. Will we have a "new normal" of 9 to 10 percent official unemployment? Will there be another financial crisis that plunges us into a 1929-style crash, making an already bad situation much worse? If unemployment remains high for years to come, as predicted by the Federal Reserve, the resulting anger could lead to more Hutaree-like groups; some surely will succeed at terrorist attacks.

We don't know how bad or how widespread those acts of violence might be. What is certain is that organized violence would cause popular fear akin to or even greater than the public reaction against the "rioting" communists in 1930. These neofascists might begin to appear more powerful than their numbers would warrant.

In this context, FDR's line about fear takes on new meaning for today. When they are afraid, otherwise smart people do stupid things; stupid people do even stupider things. In the face of potential violence, Americans need to think about how to deal with their fears, how best to oppose violence, how to defend against it.

I see two possible outcomes. In one scenario, the government cracks down on militia groups, and the nation becomes extremely repressive. Terrified voters elect get-tough politicians, and we give up even more civil liberties in the process. In the end, a police state is created, which could result in a dangerous Weimar-like era.

Another scenario imagines a liberal response rather than a fascist one. Recall the reaction of many white Americans to the fiery uprisings of African Americans in the inner cities during the 1960s. Motivated by fear that the violence would spread, some adults in the community where I grew up, a very white suburb of Cleveland, believed that welfare and social programs were "buying off" black anger and thus came to support such reforms, albeit in a sometimes grudging fashion. They wanted order, not chaos.

In the 1930s, a majority of Americans wanted a return to normalcy, not a Soviet-style dictatorship, not Italian- or German-style fascism. Writers like Adamic, an immigrant who understood Americans better than most native-born citizens did, grasped this elemental fact. That is why Roosevelt succeeded in the end, overcoming the Tea Party sentiment of his day. I don't think anything has changed in our culture. If violence occurs, a majority of Americans will want a return to peace. The question is how we would get there: through repression or through dealing with working-class despair by concrete actions that could create a more egalitarian society.

History, of course, does not provide an exact model. In terms of their own ultimate aims, it was not in the long-term interests of the 1930s communists to have Roosevelt succeed—if he prevailed, it would end their hope for revolution. But their agitation and activist work bolstered the efforts of union organizers and other progressives. This larger and less radical movement is what really made the New Deal work. Today, that active coalition of the left is moribund—for now. Will it reemerge to agitate for positive change, even in an environment of fear? And where is the leader of today, akin to FDR, who could help make this happen? In his first two years in office, Barack Obama has not proven to be that president.

On the right, there is no organizing for any kind of positive change. The message has simply been "no" to everything other than the failed bromides of calling for more tax cuts and less government.

If we as a society fail to deal with the anger that is building in America, who knows what will occur? All bets will be off in a country beset by fear and violence. So, for me, a central question remains: why do we have to wait until things degenerate into violence before we address the fundamental unfairness of our economy?

RECLAIMING THE SPIRIT OF THE 1930s

In 2010, the Tea Party movement became the face of anger in America. The media have been blamed for overcovering the Tea Party, and indeed many Americans see it as a widespread mass movement. (A great number of my friends in New York City believe a majority of people in the center of the country are Tea Party converts.) The reality is that just a small percentage of those Michael and I met in our travels can be counted in its corner. Tea Partiers are actually a very narrow and elite slice of the rightward-leaning portion of the country, wealthier on average than most Americans. The Tea Party organizations are in fact secretly funded in part by billionaire conservatives, and they are composed of basically the same percentage and type of people who opposed FDR in the 1930s.

There is currently no left movement comparable to the Tea Party to act as a counterbalance. Those who are politically liberal, moderate, or independent are feeling a similar amount of fear and anger, but they have not yet found voice in any group or political party. There are myriad reasons why, but I believe that one of the most important is how we view ourselves in terms of class.

Sometime between the middle of the last century and the present day, the term "working class" became a pejorative, even though most of the nation was made up of working-class citizens. We all began to consider ourselves "middle class," "rich" (or soon to be rich)—a message drummed into us by the forces that drove American culture, from advertising to television to glossy magazines to what we saw on the big screens at the theaters. Politicians and conservative academics who demonized the poor contributed to the creation of this belief.

By the 1960s and 1970s, the people who had survived the 1930s Depression had children (or grandchildren) in college. I was one of them. Many of us came from blue-collar families. Enmeshed in our newly developing "middle-class" identity, we were part of the great wave of upward mobility in the postwar era. Most of us were white, but some blacks and Latinos were also included. Menial work was for summers and maybe part time during the school year, but our collars became very white after graduation. Blue-collar work was passé.

We laughed at Archie Bunker when he showed up on our televisions during the Nixon years in the pioneering show *All in the Family,* about the rift between working-class Archie and his upwardly mobile daughter, Gloria, and son-in-law Michael, whom Archie called "Meathead." Gloria and Meathead were our role models. We were better and smarter than Archie, who had a daytime blue-collar job and moonlighted at night driving a taxi. We dealt with information, first on paper and later on computer screens. We had heard our parents' mantra as we grew up, that we'd turn out "better" than they did, and we were sure it was true. In our self-absorption, we focused on "me," while we forgot about "us."

But during these days, as neoliberal notions about free trade and neoconservative ones about free-market economy emerged and took root, a noose began closing around the necks of the Archie Bunker class.

Nixon was there to point out that the rope was chafing. But Reagan, he was the pro. Reagan reminded the Archies that their faces were turning purple because the rope was so tight and that it was wielded by those profligate and "liberal" children of the Great Depression generation. In reality, the rope was being twisted by the velvet-gloved hands of the acolytes of Ayn Rand—those with fat bank accounts and their enablers in academia and politics.

Reagan told the Archies that there were two classes in America: the poor (blacks) and the rich (whites). Reagan didn't put it this directly, but the coded language was clear. And he made sure they knew that the Republicans were the party of the rich (and the white workers who aspired to be rich) and that the Democrats, in this crafted false universe, were the party of the poor (that is, nonworkers and minorities).

The money to maintain this illusion of wealth and middle-class status began to require two incomes, as more and more women entered the workforce. Then, when that wasn't enough, long after Reagan was gone, we funded the fantasy with second mortgages and maxed-out credit cards. And then that ended.

Now we are here, facing the truth: we are not all rich. And we won't soon be.

It will take time for us to be educated to this fact. But reality has a curious way of focusing one's attention. Whether that education entails furloughs and pay cuts, job loss, foreclosures and evictions, or bankruptcy from medical bills, Americans will slowly rediscover that most of us are working class, white or blue collar.

I know from life experience that people are capable of change. As we go deeper into the hard times ahead, perhaps it will cease to be a negative to be "just" working class. Maybe when that day comes, be it 2019 or 2029, there will be enough anger among us to agitate for change in order to level the playing field and to make wages fair once again, to finally deal with all the jobs that have left the country by focusing on ways to reemploy Americans, and to stop coddling the big-money interests. Maybe then a modern New Deal mentality will take root in the United States.

We are at the start of a long journey back to a political and cultural sensibility from the past—the 1930s.

THE ROLE OF THE INDIVIDUAL AND THE GOVERNMENT

So what do we do? Just what do we do?

The answer, in the short term, is that no one is going to save you but yourself. That's the message from the Alexander family, Sally, Maggie Fonseca, Sherri Harvel, Tim Lapointe, Ken Platt, Lisa Martucci—just about everyone in this book and many others I interviewed whose stories are not included here. We cannot expect the change that must occur to be a top-down process. Right now, the top in this country means money. Big money. And big money takes care of itself.

That leaves us to take care of ourselves. As Jim Alexander said, we need to do as much as possible with our own hands. When Ken Platt talked about how we might have to find "different satisfactions," he meant that we have to change how we live. Sally is on this journey and has no illusions about returning to the house on the hill. Tim Lapointe has accepted that he and his wife will have to get by with less income, yet appreciate what they do have.

Many of the people we found in our travels believe that they are alone. In fact, they are part of a new awakening in America, as Lisa and others told me. Some people are growing their own food and cutting back on consumption. Others are building more closely knit families. We have to count on each other—this is what Ian Beniston is trying to foster with the Idora ecovillage in Youngstown. In this search for community, Tim in New Hampshire is connected to Sherri in Missouri, just as Sally in Michigan is linked to Lisa in New Jersey.

At this point in the cultural/political landscape, we can rely only on ourselves and our communities. If someone had told me back in 1980 that I'd be writing these quasi-libertarian (in reality, anarchist) words, I would have been incredulous, for it seemed inconceivable that we would ever be left so vulnerable as a society.

We need to regain a sense of civic engagement to move forward. At the most elemental, this means voting and holding politicians accountable, from City Hall to the U.S. Capitol. It's true that action beyond simply voting is often much easier said than done—I think of Maggie, working three jobs, raising two children, and relying on a food bank, with barely enough time to sleep—but being active can mean many things. In today's America, simply engaging our neighbors, being aware of those around us, is itself a revolutionary act. The process of rebuilding ourselves and our communities is ground zero for positive transformation. From small acts large changes can emerge, including the creation of a mindset that could help to reshape our economy.

As today's economic devastation continues to unfold, I keep reading about how Wall Street is waiting for American consumer spending to kick in so that the market can soar and things can return to "normal." Any sign, no matter how feeble, sends stocks higher. The so-called experts don't come out and openly say that we should go back to the time a few years ago when people earning Wal-Mart wages took out second mortgages and ran up $20,000 or more in credit card debt they could never repay. But that's their real message. It's the only way consumers will be able to spend unless they are paid higher wages.

In the early 1980s, the average household credit card debt, in 2008 dollars, was about $2,000. In 2008, it was $8,539, according to Moody's Investors Service. Consumer debt has become so high that people won't be able to resume spending in the same way, as they have done after other downturns.

Given a chance, of course, many Americans would resume the binge, future personal bankruptcy be damned. Critics point out that a new era of frugality has been declared in recent previous recessions, only to end soon as these downturns are over.

This time is different because of the gravity of the economic hit and the level of personal debt. Perhaps history is murmuring. A generation was seared by the Great Depression. Both sets of my grandparents, and my father, to a large degree, were typical: profoundly frugal, eschewing consumerism. Dimitro, my paternal grandfather, saved pulled nails and hammered them straight for reuse. My father used items until they were worn out. Dad owned a collection of frayed electrical extension cords held together by duct tape that was of dubious efficacy—the cords sparked, yet he was loathe to spend money to replace them. My maternal grandparents, Robert and Frances Kopfstein, simply never bought anything new. Their house was an unchanged personal museum to furniture from the 1930s and 1940s, which they used until their deaths in the 1980s.

Each generation, of course, forgets. By the 1950s, a new crop of consumers emerged, to be sold new wants and desires, as Vance Packard documented in *The Hidden Persuaders.* By the 1980s and 1990s, bankers who never could have peddled a second mortgage to Robert and Frances Kopfstein had fresh targets with no memory of the Great Depression.

But some of the people in this book have in fact begun to restructure their lives, asking themselves questions such as these: Do we really need 6,000-square-foot trophy homes that require sky-high purchase prices, excessive costs for heating and cooling, soaring taxes, and a huge amount of time to clean and maintain? Why not have "only" 2,000 square feet of living space and use the extra 4,000 square feet of earth to grow food?

The value of urban or suburban farming cannot be measured simply in pounds of carrots and spinach. Growing our own produce and maybe keeping backyard hens for eggs not only saves us cash; we earn psychological income, empower ourselves, and create community when we barter what we have harvested for products or services from our neighbors. There's something about working the soil that makes you see other parts of your life more clearly. Emma Goldman, a feminist and anarchist active in the early 1900s, famously said, "If I can't dance, I don't want to be part of your revolution." For me, revolution means growing carrots and tomatoes; I would substitute "garden" for the word "dance" in her quote.

Some of this may sound like conservative ideology, and it is: individuals must take responsibility to live within their means, applying old-fashioned thrift along with hard work. But it's coupled with the idea that the government must play a role in helping citizens, creating jobs, restructuring the economic game so that working Americans share in its rewards—which is liberal ideology.

What I write about in this book is neither liberal nor conservative. It's human.

Yet many Americans have a strong distrust of the federal government. It's a sentiment as old as the republic: it varies from mild cynicism to rage. Most of us, however, are happy when the government builds and maintains roads, controls air traffic, protects national parks, and ensures the safety of the food we eat, among many other tasks. Libertarians feel otherwise—about the only use they see for government is to provide military protection; anything beyond is viewed as socialism.

So it was among 1930s conservatives who saw FDR as the socialist anti-Christ. Even then, these fossils in the flesh were unmoved by the suffering in America. But by the time the New Deal was in full swing in the late 1930s, all but the most hard-core conservatives had come to realize that the U.S. government had a role in helping its citizens. The bedrock conservatives fought for decades to destroy the New Deal. They gained traction only after 1980, when memories had faded enough for them to strip away many of its protections, particularly by attacking financial regulation and the social safety net. As a result, we've lived through the greatest upward redistribution of wealth since Coolidge.

We are essentially struggling to relearn the lessons of the 1930s. We are also reliving a version of its political and economic battles, as well as fighting new ones.

While this book is focused on people, I want to point out three significant areas in which I believe government must play a key role. My analysis is purposefully brief—I am a journalist, not a policy wonk, and others have written excellent books that tackle these issues in depth. In particular, I recommend the work of William Greider, Paul Krugman, Robert Reich, and the late Chalmers Johnson for more thorough analyses.

Sharing the Wealth

In 1988, when I was living in Cambridge, Massachusetts, I had dinner with Harry Fleischman, who in 1944 had been the campaign manager for Norman Thomas, Socialist Party candidate for president who ran against FDR. Harry, born in 1914, had begun union organizing as a teenager and was a long-time member of the Socialist Party USA. He told me stories about his activism in the 1930s, and then we began talking about the economy. Harry scrawled a chart on his paper napkin that showed how a depression was triggered when 1 percent of Americans amassed a large share of the wealth, as happened in the 1930s. He pointed out that there are only so many dollars in an economy and that if the rich hoard them, money does not circulate. It was nothing more than simple math, he insisted. With great excitement, Harry made a new chart showing that we were on a similar course for a new depression, with a growing concentration of wealth in fewer hands.

The numbers Harry cited are commonly known. In 1928, 23.9 percent of all income in America went to just 1 percent of its citizens. This percentage had been edging up all through the 1920s.

By the 1970s, as Robert Reich has noted, only between 8 and 9 percent of total income went to the top 1 percent of the population, because of the effects of the New Deal, which redistributed wealth, and later the impact of the GI Bill and the Great Society. But the pendulum began to swing back as "trickle-down" economics came into vogue. In 1982, the top 1 percent was collecting 12.8 percent of all income. When I met Harry in 1988, the wealthy's share had risen to 16.6 percent. By 2007, 23.5 percent of income was taken in by that 1 percent.

Trickle-down prosperity remains a myth. A 2009 Census Bureau report showed that median U.S. income, adjusted for inflation, was lower in 2008 than in 1998. Among the poor and the middle class, the poverty rate rose and wages stagnated or declined. Yet between 2002 and 2007—when President George W. Bush pushed through his tax cuts for the wealthy—households in the top 1 percent, earning more than $400,000 annually, raked in two-thirds of the country's total income gains.

In late 2010, on ABC's *This Week* with Christiane Amanpour, a few of America's wealthiest said that this was wrong. Warren Buffett, Bill and Melinda Gates, and Ted Turner all agreed that they should pay higher taxes.

"I think that you should raise taxes on the very rich," Buffett said. He had surveyed his office staff and noted, "I had the lowest tax rate of the sixteen." The average rate paid was 32 percent, while he paid just over 16 percent. "I didn't have any tax shelters. I didn't have any tax planner. It was all courtesy of the U.S. Congress. I mean, they did my tax planning for me."

Amanpour pointed out that some critics still call for tax cuts to boost the economy. Buffet replied, "Well, the rich are always going to say that, you know, 'just give us more money and we'll all go out and spend more, and then it will all trickle down to the rest of you.' But that has not worked the last ten years, and I hope the American public is catching on."

Wealth must be diffused more widely in order for our society to have a middle class.

Is it socialism when the government, through laws and policies, spreads these dollars around? Or is it simply saving capitalism, as Roosevelt did, from its worst excesses? This is not money distributed as welfare. Rather, it should be considered an investment, used to fund job programs, education, and perhaps even tax breaks for the working class. People who work should be rewarded, and there should be a safety net for those who are left out of the American dream.

Creating Jobs

The Federal Reserve and many politicians view boosting the U.S. gross domestic product as the best way to jump-start the economy. But Robert J. Shiller, a professor of economics and finance at Yale University, has challenged that notion, arguing instead that we should use government policy to directly create "labor-intensive service jobs in fields like education, public health and safety, urban infrastructure maintenance, youth programs, elder care, conservation, arts and letters, and scientific research." He cites the success of 1930s-era programs such as the Works Progress Administration and the Civilian Conservation Corps. This proposal certainly would put more money in working people's hands than trying to get it to them via bailing out bankers and then waiting for the trickle-down that never really happens.

Creating new programs along the lines of the WPA and the CCC would help one group in particular. A stunning report released in 2010 by the U.S. Bureau of Labor Statistics shows that 37 percent of individuals between the ages of eighteen and twenty-nine are jobless—nearly the same rate as in the 1930s Great Depression. Among those in this category, 23 percent have stopped looking for work because they are discouraged.

We are losing a generation of workers. As *New York Times* columnist Bob Herbert wrote in 2009, "Young men and women who remain unemployed for substantial periods of time find it very difficult to make up that ground. They lose the experience and training they would have gained by working." Young people have to get in the habit of waking each morning to head off to a job—something that is learned only by doing. The skills young people would acquire through a modern WPA or CCC would be an investment in their—and our—future.

I have firsthand evidence. My father's older brother was jobless in the Great Depression, and he found work through the CCC. He went to Idaho, built roads and walls, and learned construction, which became his lifelong trade. As a result, he made good wages after the war and until he retired in the 1980s. The investment in my uncle by the government came back many times over. He paid vastly more in taxes over his lifetime than the piddling amount spent on him in the Cs.

It's true that the WPA and the CCC didn't end the Great Depression. But what would have occurred had they not existed? In the case of my uncle, I know the answer. The programs gave young people hope and training and made ordinary Americans feel that something was being done for them. In 1960, John Steinbeck wrote that the WPA's workers "built many of the airports we still use, hundreds of schools, post offices, [stadiums], together with the great and permanent matters like the stately Lake Shore Drive in Chicago." A half century after Steinbeck wrote these words, many of these things are still functioning. They were an investment in our people, our infrastructure, and our environment.

Cutting Back on Military Spending

The U.S. military budget in fiscal year 2010 was $680 billion, double what it was in 2000. In this last decade, we've been fighting two unwinnable wars, with costs of ultimately several trillion dollars, and we've been doing it with money borrowed from China. Of the total budgets spent on the military by all nations on earth combined, the United States expends 43 percent. Chalmers Johnson, the author of *Blowback* and other books on the cost of the U.S. military, notes that America has some eight hundred Defense Department installations scattered across the globe.

This kind of empire is very, very expensive to maintain. We no longer have the money for it.

Like the British after World War II, we still don't realize that we can't afford to be a superpower. It took the 1956 Suez Crisis for the United Kingdom to recognize that its military and colonial glory days were over. The British controlled the Suez Canal as part of their dwindling empire. But when Egyptian president Abdel Nasser nationalized the canal, the tens of thousands of British troops garrisoned on its banks were impotent. The British government was broke, and the United States held the purse strings. So when the Americans told the British to withdraw, they had no choice. It was an emasculating moment for the island nation after a long run as a global power—but a necessary one.

We haven't yet had our Suez moment. The sooner it comes, the better.

Every time I hear that there's no money for Social Security or health care or a new WPA, I realize that of course we would have the money—and plenty of it—if we were to cut back on our military adventuring. Most politicians don't want to admit to this reality; they'd rather sustain the illusion that we still can afford to be the world's superpower while fighting two wars at once without raising taxes. (One exception is Rep. Alan Grayson [D-Fla.], who introduced a bill titled "The War Is Making You Poor" in 2010.)

We spend trillions of dollars creating high-tech weapons systems to fight enemies that don't exist. Many politicians on both sides of the aisle argue that making these weapons creates jobs in their districts. But if these trillions were put into developing alternative energy, more useful jobs would result. And if we are able to cut our dependence on foreign oil because of this, trillions of dollars would remain in this country rather than being sent to the Middle East to pay for our oil addiction. Some of that money finds its way into the bank accounts of those who want to kill us. The cessation of that terrorism subsidy would be an added bonus.

I believe nation building begins at home. It is long overdue.

CODA

Sacramento may be the capital of California, but the city has a long history of a hardscrabble underbelly. Beginning with the 1849 Gold Rush and continuing after the last spike had been driven for the transcontinental railroad in 1869, the city has been one end of the road for migrants, especially those who are living on the margins. To the present day, when they can't make a go of it, some end up homeless.

Among the attractions are the waterways that run through the city—the clear American and the muddy Sacramento rivers join near downtown. The draw isn't the presence of water in rare quantity for parched California, but the riverbanks thick with vegetation that conceals the camps of the homeless "river people." Michael and I spent a lot of time in these camps back in the 1980s. It's fitting to end this book in the place where it began—Sacramento and the surrounding Central Valley.

Thirty years after I first set eyes on the Sacramento and American rivers, I stood atop a levee that was the backdrop for some of Dorothea Lange's photographs when she snapped her shutter in 1936, documenting the Great Depression for the Farm Security Administration. She photographed two major homeless camps on the American River where, by her count, 110 families lived. In one picture, a little girl clutches a ragged and dirty doll as she stares blankly into the lens; the girl is a living version of what she holds in her arms. Lange's photographs capture images ubiquitous to the Central Valley—levees in the background, live oaks, mistletoe clumped in the branches of ash trees.

The camps Michael and I found in the early 1980s weren't as elaborate as those

Lange photographed. Most were in secret places deep in the jungle of greenery. One camp later grew in size, a village of shanties belonging to Montana Blackie and his hobo buddies Shorty and Woody. (Their neighbors were the Murrays, a homeless family whose boys are pictured in the second section of Michael's photographs.) The cops eventually made Blackie and his pals move on.

The cops kept the river people cowering in the shadows through the 1980s. I wrote stories about most of those sweeps, for the newspaper and in a book about Blackie, *The Last Great American Hobo.* Then I left town.

I wiped my brow as I stood on the levee that day in mid-2009. The summer sun was powerfully hot.

John Kraintz approached on a rickety bicycle; we'd arranged to meet. If I hadn't known better, I might have dismissed the man coming toward me. Most pronounced was his gray straggle of beard, tied in a ponytail below his chin. (He had stopped cutting his hair and beard to protest the wars in Iraq and Afghanistan.) He wore a ball cap with a car dashboard lamp attached to the top night and day. At age fifty-five, his face was deeply lined.

John enjoys political and cultural conversation. When we first met, he talked about the American economy and paraphrased a quote he attributed to Thomas Jefferson: "'I am a farmer so my son can be a businessman, and his son can be an artist.' Jefferson understood how it works."

John grew excited talking about how the U.S. economic system was off kilter and how we had to start thinking about each other and not just about money.

"The economy has to be for the people! It's not now!"

"You should be in Congress," I noted.

"I wouldn't like the company I'd have to keep. I'll stick with river people."

John is an Edge Man. He'd become one eight years ago.

"I was working at a sheet metal shop," he said. "I was working on this piece of metal. I realized, 'What the hell am I doing this for? I'm barely making ends meet. I'm wasting all my time here.' They take your time away from you. And that's more precious than any amount of money. That can't be replaced."

All John's pay went for rent; nothing remained for food. "Real estate speculation caused rents to rise at the same time we were cutting jobs and pay. Real estate values have to come down to match wages," he argued.

So John quit and came to the river. In those early years, he had been "just" a homeless guy living in the brush.

Then, in 2007, Loaves and Fishes, a local nonprofit that provides many services for the homeless, along with the Sacramento Homeless Organizing Committee and

Francis House, became plaintiffs in a lawsuit against the city and Sacramento County, contesting laws that prohibited camping and had been used against the homeless. City officials quietly placed a moratorium on enforcing those laws. Homeless people began to gather in a field near the railroad tracks and the Blue Diamond almond plant at the northern edge of midtown. They no longer needed to hide in the brush. Over a period of months, the camp grew to become a tent city with some two hundred residents. The camp was not a political protest—it was merely a community that formed organically. Members organized themselves into committees to decide matters of importance, and John emerged as a leader and spokesperson.

In early 2009, the tent city was featured on the *Oprah Winfrey Show*. This publicity created a centrifugal pull that drew media from all over the world. Many American journalists had tent cities close to home, which they had typically ignored. But now Sacramento's tent city became America's tent city.

Some reporters tried to make it something that it was not, a place filled with the recently unemployed. In fact, at that point, most residents were the chronically homeless, Edge Men like John; it was too soon for families such as the Alexanders to show up. Desperation and homelessness run in cycles. When *Life* magazine sent Michael and me out looking for homeless families in 1982, we couldn't find anyone like the Alexanders, but by 1983 they were there. In early 2009, the majority of economically distressed families were still hanging on in foreclosed houses or staying with relatives, short-term solutions that would soon run out. (By the time this book is published, they will be out there, as new timers.)

What had really happened was that America had nudged closer to being like Mumbai, as journalist Scott Bransford noted in a 2009 article for *High Country News*. He argued that it is misleading to call these encampments tent cities; they have more in common with shantytowns. The headline of his story said it all: "Tarp Nation."

Post-Oprah, Sacramento's leaders were unhappy with the attention. Governor Arnold Schwarzenegger got involved. There ensued the usual process. Officials said they'd find shelter beds and thus would be able to close the tent city, skirting (on paper) any charge of being heartless. Everyone familiar with the homeless, however, understands that many will never go to a shelter. I would not. Most shelters have more in common with prisons. They're havens for disease, and I'm scared of the crazy and violent people found in them. For the working homeless, the restricted hours and required sign-in times of a shelter mean they'd lose jobs. A tent on the river is preferable.

"They promised they would find housing for forty to eighty of the people at the tent city," said Joan Burke, a director at Loaves and Fishes. "But they closed it down long before the housing was in place."

In other words, officials lied. I'd witnessed this same ruse used in the 1980s with smaller sweeps of the homeless.

The camp was forced to disband, and, on top of that, the city was scheduled to close a shelter with 150 beds on July 1, casting even more people out onto the street.

The homeless and their advocates were angry enough to plan to do something that would have been unimaginable in the 1980s: they'd march in protest and occupy city-owned land in defiance of the anti-camping ordinance. On July 1, 2009, John led the march to agitate for a legal camp for the river people. Advocates dubbed it the "Safe Ground" campaign. Its model was the sanctioned camping areas in Portland, Oregon, and Ontario, California. Organizers said no taxpayer money would be needed; in fact, in an inverse of free-market enterprise, leaders told me they could run the camp for about $2 a person per night, not the $70 a person the city paid for shelters.

There was historical precedent. In notes to one of her pictures taken in November 1936, Dorothea Lange wrote of the eighty families in a camp on the American River: "They pay one dollar and twenty five cents a month ground rent." The families had to build their own shanties.

As I stood talking with John atop the levee, I couldn't get Lange's images out of my head—from the lesser-known pictures she took here in Sacramento to those more famous, among them the migrant mother with her children in the California town of Nipomo, which became an iconic image from that era. The past suddenly felt very close, a continuum between that old Depression and this new one.

John explained that after being evicted from the tent city, most residents went to the riverbanks in violation of the law—but they stayed out of sight. Not far from the levee where we stood was John's tent, one among some thirty-five others. Other camps were along different sections of the river.

As we walked a well-worn path through a blackberry bramble, John said that there were new timers on the river, though not in his camp.

"It's chronics there," he said.

"Chronics?"

"I'm using their definition in terms of people who have been out here over a year and have some sort of disability," he said, referring to what county officials had told him. "A lot of folks lack coping skills. It's more than just 'I lost my job, I worked all my life.'" He pointed to the forest. "These people out here, understand, they're never going to fit into society."

The canopy was thick with birds that were loud in protest of our presence. A few tents materialized amid the tree trunks. All were spaced to give maximum room between sites. John told me that even some of the most mentally ill people had formed a community in the tent city and again here in the illegal camp.

"That's what separates us from animals. We don't have the claws of the cat or the teeth of the wolf, but we do have social skills. We had to survive in the wilderness back in the day before we had all this technology. We'd have a hard time if all we had was our fingernails and our—well, I don't have mine. I would be dead because I wouldn't be able to chew my food."

I recalled our earlier conversation about wealth in America, about how everything has been skewed to provide for those on top.

"And in the world, for that matter," John said. "Most of the world has a five or ten percent upper echelon, about an eighty percent middle, and ten percent in abject poverty. I don't think, personally, that we have that last problem here—there's just too much around. Just what we can find in the dumpsters keeps us above that. I consider myself rich. I live in a nice place. I have plenty of food. I don't have any cash in my pocket, but it's just worthless paper anyhow. I have what I need, when I need it."

I arrived early at Loaves and Fishes for the July 1 rally. I'd written about the organization when it opened in 1983, and I marveled at how it had grown.

I met with a new timer, Jim Gibson, an unemployed construction worker. Jim currently had a day job, working for a company that hires the homeless to hold signs on street corners to advertise closing sales. He'd held signs for Circuit City, the bankrupt national chain, and bankrupt regional retailers Mervyns and Gottschalks.

"The person who runs it is a great lady," Jim said of American Sign Holders. "If it wasn't for her, I'd be in a world of hurt. That, and Loaves and Fishes. There's lots of stores closing; I make a living off that. That's perverse, isn't it? But if someone wants to mismanage a multimillion-dollar business into the ground, I'll stand there for seven dollars an hour."

A crowd—of mixed race, ethnicity, and class—grew in size. It included the foul smelling, the finely cologned, the poorly clothed, the well dressed, some with gray hair, and others who were pierced and/or tattooed. Speeches were made, by John Kraintz and Sister Libby Fernandez, the executive director of Loaves and Fishes, among others. After about an hour of crowd pumping, the march began. People filed out of the parking lot. Signs sprouted over their heads: HOW MANY PAYCHECKS AWAY ARE YOU? and JESUS WAS HOMELESS.

I counted 250 people marching in a line that stretched about a quarter mile along Richards Boulevard. John ran in front, yelling encouragement through a bullhorn.

"How's it going?" I asked.

"It's a little scary," he whispered.

I paid attention to citizens driving by—truck drivers, businesspeople, retirees, and blue-collar workers. There were waves of approval, thumbs-up gestures, peace signs, honking horns, smiling faces. I waited for raised middle fingers or shouts of "Get a job!" But there was no negativity. In the 1980s, there surely would have been naysayers. Perhaps citizens are scared today, fearing that they or someone they know could end up on the bottom.

Maybe we were getting closer to Steinbeck's 1939, that moment when we started caring about each other.

The first marcher arrived at a sun-baked lot where some of the group intended to erect tents. "Ah, there's no place like home!" this homeless man said as he studied the graveled ground rippling heat.

I ran into National Public Radio reporter Richard Gonzalez, whom I've known for years. After a brief reunion, he pointed to a man holding up a bicycle who would be a good interview. I went over to David, who was in his forties.

David told me, "I'm a welder. I worked in the same shop for the last twenty years, in Colorado. Then they started laying people off. I lost my house. My car. Everything."

He came to California on Greyhound.

"California is a big state. I figured, 'I can get a job.'"

He figured wrong. He goes out every day looking for work. "I hold a sign. I do dishwashing jobs. Anything. To me, it's a shock to my system. If you told me a year ago that I'd be homeless, I'd say, 'No way.' This is ridiculous."

When the tent city was shut, David spent some time at the shelter that was slated to be closed. Today, he had marched but wouldn't camp with the protesters. "I'm going back to the river."

"What have you learned from what's happened to you?"

"I've learned it's as bad as it was in the thirties."

I bade him farewell. As I walked off, David yelled, "Hey, say something to the spirit out there for me." I gave him a thumbs-up.

I sought out Richard in the crowd. He told me that he'd interviewed David for NPR all through the tent city story. The last time Richard saw him, David had grown angry.

"He said, 'You are part of the problem.' And he's right."

What Richard was talking about is this: does the media spotlight really do anything? Richard felt the frustration that I had carried for decades.

I wanted to say, "Yes, what we've done has mattered. That's one of the things I've learned in all the years of doing this. I really do think that what we've documented is really starting to sink in. We have made a difference." But I didn't speak these words. I simply shrugged; there was no time to explain. Richard was on deadline and had to run off.

I was told on the Q.T. that the homeless would not camp on the bleak lot after all.

Instead, they were headed over to a tree-shaded, city-owned property next to the old Southern Pacific railroad yard, where they intended to set up a surprise camp.

Late that afternoon, I showed up at the guerilla camp. John Kraintz and about two dozen others had pitched tents. A woman pounded stakes for the signs.

"We'll try to obey the law," John said. If the police came to throw them out, they'd simply move to another spot and declare it Safe Ground. Then another, and so on. John noted that about ten people had used similar tactics to push the city of Portland to create Dignity Village on city-owned land.

"It was just like pulling teeth out of a crocodile, but they did it," John said. "We're trying to prevent a problem. We're trying to present a solution—if we can hold this group together."

In 2010, as the calendar rolled toward the one-year anniversary of the march, I returned to Sacramento. John was still pulling teeth from the crocodile's mouth. The city was resisting. All over the nation, save for a few cities, it was the same story: people don't want the homeless near them, even though the dispossessed live on the streets of the neighborhood anyway. Yet it goes deeper, I believe. The truth is that we don't want to codify the reality that we have a permanent underclass of Edge Men and Edge Women. We consider ourselves the "classless" society. To allow a tent city is to abandon this myth.

It is to admit that we are Mumbai.

In the past months, John and an ever-changing band of some thirty to forty homeless people had been forging ahead with the guerilla camps. At the same time, the Safe Ground campaign worked political levers, meeting with city officials to hammer out a report. In the open comments section of each council meeting, the homeless spoke of the need for Safe Ground. (Later, at the end of 2010, Sacramento mayor Kevin Johnson would affirm that an "outdoor transitional facility" was needed and that authorities were seeking a site that could provide basic shelter with shared bath and kitchen facilities for sixty to one hundred people.)

"We didn't go away," John said. "They didn't expect that. They thought we'd vanish after the march."

Joan Burke expects that the city will eventually relent. "The key words in a report we produced with council members state that this is not a 'tent city,'" she said. "It will be a real community for people who have been living outside in Third World conditions."

John believes the city will give in strictly for economic reasons. "State and local governments are broke. They're letting meth cookers and other people who have done serious crimes out of jail. They can't afford to keep them in. If they can't hold someone who is a serious threat, how are they going to hold someone for camping?"

We were reading the usual clichés in the newspapers from the powerbrokers who peddle securities: "The fundamentals are strong," and so on. A *New York Times* headline had recently proclaimed: "Hedge Fund Pay Roars Back." The top twenty-five hedge fund managers had averaged $1 billion each the previous year. To make his money, David Tepper, the head of Appaloosa Management, who had racked up a record $4 billion take in the Wall Street casino, wagered that the federal government would bail out the banks. Tepper had profited hugely from this welfare for the wealthy.

Standing outside the Safe Ground office at Loaves and Fishes, however, I found no one who had been bailed out. Signs of revival were bleak. There were many fresh faces in the crowd, huddling from a late spring rain. Joblessness, at least according to the lowball official rate, held steady at just under 10 percent. A Pew Economic Policy Group study found that more than four out of ten jobless citizens had been unemployed for six months or more, a record in post–World War II America. A quarter of them had not worked in more than a year.

"We are in the most interesting of depressions," John said of the so-called jobless recovery. "We have an economy in which robots are producing cars and other things. But robots don't buy anything. There's a depression of overproduction. People have become redundant in this economy. We can't deal with it the same way we've dealt with previous depressions. It's a whole new way to think about an economy. We have to change how we treat people."

These were the wisest words about America I'd heard from anyone in the thirty years of work that went into this book.

Later that summer of 2010, Michael and I were back in the Central Valley, at the old hobo jungle in Oroville. The sun burned exposed skin. Central Valley heat is different from the heat felt in the Deep South or the East, and not just because the air lacks humidity. It's a quiet inferno. You don't hear the cries of as many insects and birds as you do in other regions.

We stood in a thicket of digger pine, approximately where we'd jungled up for the night in 1982 on our first hobo ride. WP Jim, an old hobo at the nearby rescue mission, had warned us that the rail yard bull was prowling, so we dared not reveal ourselves. We peered north to the spot, about 300 feet distant, where No Thumbs and his campmates had been slain. I'd brought an empty wine bottle to show filmmaker Ron Wyman the "hobo microwave" taught to me by No Thumbs. As the paper burned down and Ron filmed us making coffee, I figured it was a memorial ceremony of sorts for the old hobo.

Things now seemed even more dangerous. The previous day, while we were shooting footage in the Sacramento yard 68 miles to the south, two homeguards, local homeless men, who had been jungled up in abandoned boxcars stalked us. They were mostly hidden, though we could see their legs dashing beneath boxcars and the occasional flash of a knife blade, held low, glistening in the sunlight as they screamed, "WE'RE GONNA FUCKIN' KILL YOU!" It felt like shadowy demons from our hobo past, like those I see in the nightmares that sometimes cause me to awaken howling in terror, were out to get us.

The Oroville jungle was empty of hobos, yet there were signs that this camp had been recently used. Some hobos were still riding, including the writer William T. Vollmann, who, as I was finishing this book, told me that it was a whole lot more difficult to be a hobo these days. The yards were hotter than ever, save for distant places such as Montana, yet he was still riding. "Dale . . . you should come train hopping with me one of these days," Bill suggested. He added, speaking of today's economic depression, "This one's going to be worse" than the 1930s. "It's going to be more violent."

As I mulled over this dark forecast from a writer I greatly respect, I thought this: I don't know if I have it in me to be out there with the ghosts of No Thumbs, Shorty, and all the others now dead. But there are moments, like the intense nights as I was writing the last words of this book, when Bill might have convinced me to get back out on that road that would take us everywhere. If I were to ride again, however, it would not be to find new timer hobos. Things have changed since the early 1980s—trains no longer carry twenty-five to thirty job-seekers. Michael and I had a hunch why this was so, and it wasn't just because the yards were hotter and scarier—

I spotted movement in the distance, far from the tracks. I squinted. A lone figure, distorted by heat rippling off the rocky ground, hobbled with apparent difficulty. The person vanished into another stand of dusty olive-green digger pine.

Barking dogs announced our presence as we neared that pine thicket. Inside the sheltering fog of drab needles were two elaborate and well-maintained camps—

one had a desk-size propane-powered cooking grill, the kind found in suburban backyards. The occupant was not present. In the other camp, we found Carolyn, in her fifties, who looked oddly familiar.

She was no hobo. Carolyn told us that she and her husband had owned a double-wide mobile home on 20 acres about an hour distant. Her husband had had a stroke and been hospitalized; even with health insurance, the co-payments had been devastating. After he died, Carolyn fell behind on her mortgage because of the hospital bills, and she lost the land to foreclosure.

She'd spent last winter out here. It was stormy. This tent was her third—the other two had been torn apart by wind. Carolyn had been a home health nurse, but her knees had given out, and she became unable to lift the injured or elderly, which meant that she could no longer work. Walking was painful. She was trying to get federal disability, but the process is designed to delay; it could be another year or two before she is approved. She had just come from the hospital, where she had an MRI in an attempt to prove her case.

"I don't want to spend another winter out here," she announced.

She is proud. Carolyn talked about the life she had once led on that piece of land, where the couple had gardens that fed them. Her eyes wandered 180 degrees around and then stopped at some unseen point, as she stared long and hard at her present desolate world. There was a gulf of silence.

The men who dwell in the village of sorts in the surrounding scrub land, many of whom have lost jobs, are of great assistance to her. There are about a dozen such camps. The men call her "Ma." I realized why she seemed so familiar—she was evocative of "Ma Joad" from the 1940 film version of *The Grapes of Wrath*.

One of these men lovingly brought this Ma Joad, version 2010, a big tumbler of ice water, the ice coming from the cooler of a man named Randy in a nearby camp. The man knew she'd had a difficult time making it to and from the hospital, and he wanted to comfort her.

As Ma drank the cooling water, she told us how this village in the brush had celebrated the previous Thanksgiving: she and the men had cooked a turkey on that suburban-style grill. She had made pumpkin pies from scratch.

We paid a visit to Randy Duncan's camp. His old Buick sedan was parked beneath a cottonwood with leaves shimmering and sparkling in the sun. I'd seen a lot of homeless camps in the last thirty years, but this one was singular—it was beyond clean. Randy had a 40-gallon garbage can with a black plastic liner. "I take it to the dump every day," Randy, a twenty-year U.S. Navy man, said. He explained that he cleaned up debris in the surrounding area, too. He even lugged an abandoned refrigerator into a thicket to get it out of sight. He also plays de facto cop and chases away "tweakers," drug users, and people who come to dump trash.

Randy is maintaining standards. He's no bum. Nor is he a Joad—he has none of the edge of a hard-lived working-class life. If you saw Randy walking down a crowded sidewalk, he would be among the last people you'd guess to be homeless. He is well-groomed, and his clothes are freshly laundered.

His downfall? He left a business he ran in Missouri to come to nearby Yuba City to care for his dying mother. Hers was a long and slow illness. Randy lost the business and found himself with money troubles—a lot of debt. After his mother died, he sought work, but he discovered what so many in his age bracket have learned: today jobs are not easy to come by for people in their fifties, no matter how hard a worker you may be. Additionally, we'd heard from others that even fast-food chains now run credit checks on applicants. If you've lost your home or compiled a bad credit report, many companies won't hire you, even to flip burgers or swab a floor.

"But I'd do it again, to take care of my mother," Randy said.

This is how it was in America those last days we worked on this project. A year earlier, we had not commonly seen people like Ma and Randy. What would the coming year bring?

When Michael returned home to Washington, the newspaper sent him to cover a story about homeless people receiving free dental care. When he arrived at the site, all he saw were white-collar, well-dressed people—they could have been shoppers at Tyson's Corner or any of the region's other big malls. He went to the director of the program and asked, "Where are the homeless people?" The director pointed and replied, "*Those* are the homeless people." Michael learned that many had lost their homes to foreclosure and had ruined credit.

One difference from the 1980s is that today homelessness and economic upheaval have spread more widely, including to white-collar Americans. And there was another change as well.

Back in the early 1980s, the newly jobless had hope of finding work in other regions. They traveled, as Sam had done, believing that there would be opportunity in another city. This was also true in the 1930s. In James Rorty's book *Where Life Is Better: An Unsentimental American Journey,* published in 1936, he found Americans chasing dreams: "Thousands of unorganized men, women and children thumb the passing cars going east, west, north, and south, going nowhere in particular." And John Steinbeck captured the story of the migrant Dust Bowl refugees who saw California as a promised land.

In the early 2010s, desperate people are not moving the way they did in the

1930s and 1980s. A few are traveling, such as David, whom I met in Sacramento, but most are not. They know that life is not better somewhere else. Randy told us he wasn't even thinking of going back to Missouri. He's the kind of guy we found on the trains three decades ago, but today he knew not to waste energy on that. His hope was to get lucky in the nearby college town of Chico, which he was blanketing with applications.

Twain's river has stopped flowing. Steinbeck's Mother Road is dead. Running is not an option.

In the summer of 2010, men and women were not on a journey to nowhere. They were simply staying put, everywhere—an entirely different kind of nowhere.

Because we can't run, things have to be made to work where we are now. Home, wherever we live, is the frontier we face.

As Michael shot photos that summer in the Central Valley, many of the people in his prints, especially the white women, had Dorothea Lange faces—drawn, with the wear lines of hard-lived lives. They are unique Central Valley faces. Although Mexicans were also present in the Central Valley back then—and Latinos constitute a major portion of the population today—Lange's photographs are dominated by whites. For them, maybe it's the impact of the sun, the genetic stock of those who came here in the 1930s, or some combination of both. They looked like this seventy-four years ago when Lange took her pictures, and thirty years ago when Michael made images for our first book. They will likely be the same in another thirty and seventy-four years.

The test will be in how we treat them and all Americans living precarious lives. Even if you are wealthy or secure, those less fortunate are reflections of all of us. We are all workers. You may never find yourself on the street with nowhere to go. But the people we met are signs of so much that is wrong, an economy and a government that cater to Wall Street and not your street, whether you live in a trailer court or a fine suburb.

I recall my interview with David Davenport, the CEO of the Capital Area Food Bank in Austin, Texas, who is filled with hope.

"I think there is a shift that's occurring," David said. "It's a generational shift. The baby boomers, they're still a powerful force in America, but are moving on. The echo generation is coming up, and even the generation behind that. They have a very different view. They don't accept things as inevitable. I've got high hopes for that generation because, in a lot of ways, I'm disappointed in my own.

"There was a time slavery was accepted in the United States. And if not slavery, segregation was viewed as inevitable. Disease in our cities was seen as inevitable. Things were never going to change. From time to time in our country, the younger generation has questioned things that were considered inevitable. And through that, we eradicated slavery. We dealt with the issue of civil rights and segregation to the extent that we have an African American president. We dealt with disease by building sewers. Things that just seem insane now were considered the norm at one time.

"I'm an optimist. Sometime in my lifetime, and I hope it's soon, community by community, we will embrace the belief that hunger is unacceptable in this country. Now everybody sees it could be us, it could be our family—it's not just the guy living under the bridge. They recognize that hunger doesn't care what your bank account used to look like. It doesn't care what the color of your skin is.

"Is it acceptable that a nation as strong and powerful as the United States, with the capacity to feed just about the entire world, has such a large number of people—we're looking at thirty million right now—hungry? The chance of that number becoming more staggering is frightening. We have to, as a nation, figure out our priorities. We've faced bigger challenges in this country."

Back in New Orleans, I had a conversation over beers with Shamus Rohn and Mike Miller about tent cities. Shamus defended them. Mike cut in and said, "Like, *dude,* this is America! We need housing. It becomes an excuse, a dumping ground of the lowest rung of society. We *camp* in tents. We don't *live* in them."

Shamus's point was this: What can people with no other options do in the short term? In the long term, he and I agree with Mike. We should all be living in real homes.

Are John Kraintz, Mike Miller, Shamus Rohn, David Davenport, and I all fools? Do we really think that we are living in someplace like America?

And so we go on, like hobos on a night train, hurtling through darkness to another town, another desperate dawn.

I think of all those I've met in the past thirty years, guys like Edge Man Ed. In late 2010, Michael visited Nashville, which had experienced record flooding that spring. Ed's shanty was lying in ruins hundreds of feet from its original location, the tarp with the hand of Ron White and the cigar torn and flapping in a breeze, as if it might have been an exit hole from which Ed had tried to escape the violence of the flash flood from the Cumberland River gone wild. Other huts from the camp were suspended thirty feet up in trees. Homeless people told Michael that they had seen two people they couldn't identify swept away and presumably drowned, their bodies never found. No one had seen Ed since the deluge. Perhaps he is alive—we hope, but who knows?

And there was Crazy Red. I ran into him last in 1991, near the fig tree in Santa Barbara, six years after our first meeting. He was far more haggard then. In 2010, a social worker who knew Crazy Red back in the 1980s told me she didn't know what had happened to him. Is he still alive? The street takes them early. If he's moved on, I hope he's found America on the other side.

For the majority of people we met, their fates remain these kind of unsettling mysteries.

Of those I know: Maggie hangs on, through hard work and with hope for her two daughters, in her Habitat for Humanity home in Austin. I remember her asking, nearly in tears, "Do you think I'm doing the right thing?" Jim Alexander essentially asked the same question about ending up in a tent with his family. Are any of us doing the right thing as we muddle through this grim era? What is the right thing?

Matthew Alexander is recently back home after being stationed for six months in the Afghan desert, at a base that was often hit by mortar rounds. He will have to go back to war in the near future, to support his family. I think of the eleven-year-old boy we met back in Texas so long ago. Why did it have to come to this for that homeless kid? Jennifer, his sister, e-mailed me: "Everyone always says how strong I am . . . truthfully, I'm a scared girl huddling in a tent in the middle of a tornado." For her father, Jim, Vietnam still haunts, as does the experience of being homeless. Jim is alone in that house that he built in the woods of northern Michigan, missing Bonnie, filled with worry for his son. Sam is in that Midwest town, living a life unknown to us, but I must have faith that he and his children are doing well. Sally is raising her children in Michigan, adapting to a new way of living. In Youngstown, Joe Marshall Jr. and Ken Platt look at their children and grandchildren and wonder what kind of world they will inherit. And the others—

What I want to tell all of them is this: we don't have to be a Tarp Nation. We overcame that kind of desperation and lack of caring for our fellow citizens in the 1930s. We can do it again. No little girl in this country should have to grow up with the memory of huddling homeless and terrified in a tent as a tornado blows in. We will at long last relearn what is truly too big to fail—the lives and hopes of working men and women.

We must become someplace like America.

Dale Maharidge
New York City
February 4, 2011

ACKNOWLEDGMENTS AND CREDITS

Many thanks to the following people and institutions:

All the working people in America who allowed us into their lives over the past thirty years, including (not in order of importance) the Alexander family: Jim, Jennifer, Matthew, and Bonnie; Sam; Maggie Fonseca and her daughters, Mary Frances and Irene; the Marshall family, Joe Sr., Kay, Joe Jr., and Ellen; Ken Platt and Ken Jr.; Sally; Sherri Harvel; Edge Man Ed; Jazz and Trent; Frank and Frances; Linda and Obie Butler; John Kraintz; Tim Lapointe; Leo Arteaga; B.T.; George, Lou, and their son, Michael; the citizens of Celina, Tennessee; Lisa Martucci; Edge Man George; Randy Duncan; Carolyn; Hector; J.J. Johnston; Crazy Red; Yvonne; Robert Morris; Dolores Johnson; the members of Local 1375 of the United Steelworkers of America in Warren, Ohio; and so many more. There are hundreds of others who are not quoted or pictured in these pages. We are humbled by those who were willing to share their lives with us so that others can learn from what has happened to them.

The Open Society Institute, which gave Michael and me a Katrina Media Fellowship to fund a novel, *Child of the Flood.* This work, still being completed, tells in words and interpretive pictures a story about New Orleans and a much larger story of America. Much of the research from this project led to the material in this book about the Crescent City. Some of the pictures are also used here.

The Corporation of Yaddo and the MacDowell Colony, for support in my development as a writer. The nascent concept that became this book was spawned during my residency at Yaddo.

The *Washington Post,* for allowing Michael to use some of the photographs published here. Michael is indebted to his former editors, Joe Elbert and Bonnie Jo Mount, and to his current editor, Michel du Cille.

John Russo and Sherry Linkon at the Center for Working-Class Studies at Youngstown State University.

Ian Beniston, of the Youngstown Neighborhood Development Corporation, and Damareo Cooper, at the Mahoning Valley Organizing Collaborative.

Martha Kegel at UNITY in New Orleans, and the homeless outreach team of Shamus Rohn and Mike Miller. UNITY was extremely generous in providing help.

Katherine Kelly and Daniel Dermitzel at the Kansas City Center for Urban Agriculture.

Mark Morris, director of photography, at the *Sacramento Bee,* for providing a photo of No Thumbs.

Mona Gonzalez, executive director, and Sue Cole, coordinator of the mentoring program, at the River City Youth Foundation in Austin, Texas.

Michael Foley, executive director of the Casa Esperanza Homeless Shelter in Santa Barbara, California.

Susan Watson, family support director, and Tom Austin, executive director, of the Family Resource Center in Gorham, New Hampshire. And Katie Paine who opened her home to us when we stayed in nearby Berlin.

Reporters Amy B. Wang and J.J. Hensley at the *Arizona Republic,* and, at the American Civil Liberties Union in Phoenix, executive director Alessandra Soler Meetze and staff attorney Annie Lai.

Various editors we've worked with over the years for our stories and books on the working class: the late Bob Forsyth, who hired me at the *Sacramento Bee;* Bill Moore, formerly of the *Bee,* who sent us to ride the rails in 1982 and without whom this book would not exist; the late Mike Flanagan, a *Bee* editor who wisely sent us to Santa Barbara in 1984 to cover the homeless sweeps, where we met Crazy Red; *Bee* editors Mort Saltzman and Terry Hennessy; James W. Fitzgerald Jr. and Allen H. Peacock, who published *Journey to Nowhere,* our first book, when they were at the Dial Press; Frank Lalli at the now-defunct *George* magazine; Micah Sifry, when he was at *The Nation;* Jeffrey Klein, formerly of *Mother Jones* magazine, who always urged me to challenge readers' notions of what it means to be a progressive.

Bruce Springsteen; those at Jon Landau Management: Jon Landau, Barbara Carr, Jan Stabile, and Alison Oscar; and Mary Mac.

Joan Burke, Sister Libby Fernandez, and the Reverend David Moss at Sacramento's Loaves and Fishes.

Feeding America, the nation's largest food bank, for all its help over the years, particularly its regional food banks in Knoxville, Tennessee, and Grand Rapids, Michigan. And special thanks to the Capital Area Food Bank in Austin, Texas, and its CEO, David Davenport; former executive director Judy Carter; and others in the organization.

In Houston, the organization SEARCH, which helps the homeless.

Many friends, too numerous to all be mentioned here, who have supported us over the years. Foremost among them are Dick Schmidt, Michael's mentor and friend, and his partner, Jan Haag. Jan has not only provided emotional support to us for decades; we also turned to the research she did for her master's thesis on our work and relied on her 1991 transcript based on twenty-five hours of interviews to fill in memory blanks for the first part of this book.

The many individuals who have tried over the years to make a feature film on our early work on the new homeless: television writer David Levinson; director John Longenecker; producers Karen Spiegel and Christopher T. Olsen; the late screenwriter Dick Cusack; and our executive at HBO, Kary Antholis. Their heroic efforts in three different attempts involved many thousands of hours of labor. Making a film about workers is not an easy task against the headwinds of what is seen as commercial in Hollywood, and we cannot thank them enough, even though the attempts were in vain. The latest team is the independent company Either/Or Films. We thank executive producer Buzz McLaughlin and director Aaron Wiederspahn—along with Ann Cusack, Tom Koranda, Deborah Wettstein, Kris McLaughlin, and our film manager, Carey Nelson-Burch, for what may be the film that actually gets made.

Documentary filmmaker Ron Wyman, who was with us to witness and record some of our travels around America for more than two years; he is a brother-in-arms.

Finally, a trio of editors at the University of California Press: Naomi Schneider, who offered excellent guidance and support while I was still working in the field and who also helped to shape the book editorially; Dore Brown, who provided both high-concept advice and editing skills as the manuscript was being finalized; and a special thanks to Mary Renaud, whose keen eye caught numerous small glitches, while she also considered the big picture and asked the questions that caused me to home in on exactly what I meant to say in key places in this book. And I also thank others in the design and acquisitions departments at the press: Sandy Drooker, Kalicia Pivirotto, and Stacy Eisenstark.

All the photographs in this book were taken by Michael Williamson, with the exception of the sixteen that are scattered in the chapter text (which were taken by Dale Maharidge). Some photographs appeared earlier in *Journey to Nowhere: The Saga of the New Underclass* and in the *Sacramento Bee,* the *Washington Post,* and *George* magazine. Some parts of the text appeared in different form in *Journey to Nowhere* and in *George* magazine.

Grateful acknowledgment is made to the following for permission to reprint song lyrics: To Bruce Springsteen for lyrics from "Youngstown," from *The Ghost of Tom Joad.* Copyright 1995 Bruce Springsteen (ASCAP). All rights reserved. Lyrics reprinted by permission. To Duncan Phillips (son of the late Utah Phillips) and the Long Memory Project, for lyrics from "Bridges," by Utah Phillips. Copyright 1996 Bruce "Utah" Phillips. All rights reserved. Lyrics reprinted by permission. And for lyrics from "Annie Is Back," by James W. Alexander, John Anderson, and Janet Regier, © 1964 (Renewed) ABKCO Music Inc. All rights reserved. Used by permission of Alfred Publishing Co. Inc.

Grateful acknowledgment also to the *Sacramento Bee* for permission to reproduce excerpts from "Detox Center Is Home to Winos," by Dale Maharidge, published January 17, 1981; and "They Rode the Rails to Death," by Paul Avery, published August 22, 1982. Copyright 1981 and 1982, *Sacramento Bee.* Reprinted by permission.

NOTES

page 1 The murder of Kenneth Burr and the homeless sweeps: Dale Maharidge, "Santa Barbara Leans Hard on Transients," photographs by Michael Williamson, *Sacramento Bee,* December 16, 1984.

page 4 Michael Williamson's 2009 travel: Many of Michael's 2009 trips were taken as part of a *Washington Post* project titled "Half a Tank: Along Recession Road," with staff writer Theresa Vargas, http://voices.washingtonpost.com/recession-road.

page 5 Landmarks from Steinbeck's work in the Central Valley: Dale Maharidge, "*Grapes of Wrath* Revisited—And the Rural Poor Get Poorer," *The Nation,* January 6/13, 1992, pp. 10–12.

page 5 Lillian Counts Dunn: Dale Maharidge, "Can We All Get Along?" *Mother Jones,* November/December 1993, pp. 22–27.

page 5 Books by Anderson, Rorty, Wilson, and Dos Passos: Sherwood Anderson, *Puzzled America* (New York: Scribner, 1935); James Rorty, *Where Life Is Better: An Unsentimental American Journey* (New York: Reynal and Hitchcock, 1936); Edmund Wilson, *The American Earthquake: A Documentary of the Twenties and Thirties* (New York: Doubleday, 1958); John Dos Passos, *The Big Money* (New York: Harcourt, Brace, 1936), the final book in the *U.S.A.* trilogy and the one that most applies to the 1930s.

page 5 Wolfe's "Theory of Everything": Paul Gray and Andrea Sachs, "Tom Wolfe: A Man in Full," *Time,* November 2, 1998.

page 5 Steinbeck's phalanx theory: This theory of the "group-man" emerged in letters that Steinbeck wrote to friends and in an essay; see, for example, *Steinbeck: A Life in Letters,* edited by Elaine Steinbeck and Robert Wallsten (New York: Viking Press, 1975), pp. 79–81.

page 6 Wall Street traders leaping from windows: In his book *The Great Crash: 1929* (New York: Houghton Mifflin, 1955), John Kenneth Galbraith debunked this myth of stockbrokers committing suicide by jumping from office windows (p. 30). There were no jumpers, though later some traders did kill themselves by sticking their heads in unlit ovens and by other means, Galbraith notes.

page 6 The 1930s Great Depression as two recessions: Alan S. Blinder, "It's No Time to Stop This Train," *New York Times,* May 16, 2009; and Randal E. Parker, *The Economics of the Great Depression: A Twenty-First-Century Look Back at the Economics of the Interwar Era* (Cheltenham, U.K.: Edward Elgar Publishing, 2007), pp. 6, 17, 26.

page 11 2009 U.S. job losses of 740,000 and 660,000 per month: The numbers quoted by the radio announcer were official at the time of our travel, although they were later revised by the U.S. Department of Labor's Bureau of Labor Statistics. In its final analysis, the bureau reported essentially equal figures for those two months: February saw a loss of 651,000 jobs, with 663,000 lost in March. See www.bls.gov/news.release/archives/empsit_03062009.pdf; and www.bls.gov/news.release/archives/empsit_04032009.pdf.

page 15 Infant mortality rivaling that of Haiti: Dale Maharidge, "Rich Man, Poor Man: Two Worlds of Detroit," photographs by Michael Williamson, *Sacramento Bee,* September 30, 1984.

page 19 2.2 million homes foreclosed in 2008: Christopher Mayer, senior vice dean of the Columbia Business School, testimony before the U.S. House of Representatives, Committee on the Judiciary, *Hearing on H.R. 200, The Helping Families Save Their Homes in Bankruptcy Act of 2009, and H.R. 225, The Emergency Homeownership and Equity Protection Act,* January 22, 2009; see www4.gsb.columbia.edu/null?&exclusive=filemgr.download&file_id=5850.

page 23 Adamic diary entry: Louis Adamic, "From My Diary," in *My America, 1928–1938* (New York: Harper and Brothers, 1938), p. 298.

page 24 Joblessness in central Tennessee: Dale Maharidge, "This American Is Hungry," photographs by Michael S. Williamson, *George,* October 2000; Associated Press, "Furniture Maker Berkline Moving Upholstery Division to Mississippi," May 4, 2007. On the Clay County website, the local Chamber of Commerce lists 2,053 employed in 2003, the most recent data; see www.dalehollowlake.org/index.php?option=com_content&task=view&id=12&Itemid=26.

page 31 Wal-Mart employment in 1979: Wal-Mart website, "History Timeline," http://walmartstores.com/AboutUs/7603.aspx.

page 31 General Motors employment in 1979: Tim Reid, "The Day the Music Died for General Motors: The Symbol of a Proud Nation, The Fall of General Motors Has Stunned America," *Times of London,* June 2, 2009.

page 31 Forbes 400 in 1982: *Forbes,* September 13, 1982.

page 31 CEO pay in 1978: Lawrence Mishel, Jared Bernstein, and Heidi Shierholz, *The State of Working America 2008/2009,* An Economic Policy Institute Book (Ithaca, N.Y.: Cornell University Press, ILR Press, 2009). This information was further clarified in an e-mail exchange between Mishel and the author, 2009.

page 31 Unemployment rate, 1982: Seth S. King, "U.S. Jobless Rate Climbs to 10.8%, A Postwar Record," *New York Times,* December 4, 1982.

page 40 Youngstown described as a "necropolis": James M. Perry, "Idle Mills, a Dearth of Hope Are Features of Ohio's Steel Towns," *Wall Street Journal,* January 20, 1983.

page 44 A peak of 21 percent unemployment: United Press International, "Youngstown Remains at Top in Unemployment Rate, 18.7 Percent," November 15, 1982. The article noted that the jobless rate had peaked the previous August, at 21 percent.

page 44 Increases in child abuse, mental health caseload, and suicide attempts: Larry Green, "Rust Bowl Steel Mills Waste Away," *Los Angeles Times,* April 23, 1983.

page 45 Bankruptcies and rising crime rate: Dale Maharidge, *Journey to Nowhere: The Saga of the New Underclass,* photographs by Michael Williamson (New York: Dial Press, 1985), p. 35.

page 49 Times Beach and dioxin: Wayne Biddle, "Toxic Chemicals Imperil Flooded Town in Missouri," *New York Times,* December 16, 1982. The abandoned town was later turned into Route 66 State Park.

page 71 Wal-Mart employment in 1992: "Wal-Mart Stores Raise Over $8.2 million for Children's Hospitals," *PR Newswire,* June 1, 1992.

page 71 General Motors employment in 1992: Associated Press, "Here Are Some Statistics on Employment, Job Cuts, Financial Losses," March 13, 1993.

page 71 Forbes 400 in 1990 and 1995: *Forbes,* October 22, 1990; *Forbes,* October 16, 1995.

page 71 CEO pay in 1989: Lawrence Mishel, Jared Bernstein, and Heidi Shierholz, *The State of Working America 2008/2009,* An Economic Policy Institute Book (Ithaca, N.Y.: Cornell University Press, ILR Press, 2009). This information was further clarified in an e-mail exchange between Mishel and the author, 2009.

page 73 On writing about poverty: Kathleen J. Edgar, ed., *Contemporary Authors* (Farmington Hills, Mich.: Gale Research, 1996), vol. 148, pp. 274–276.

page 76 Labor unrest at WCI Steel: Thomas W. Gerdel, "Town Rallies around WCI Workers," *Cleveland Plain Dealer,* October 8, 1995; Rick Teaff, "WCI Steel Shows Union to the Door; Brings in Replacement Staff to Run Plant," *American Metal Market,* September 4, 1995.

page 81 CBS interview: The *CBS Morning News* segment with Bruce Springsteen aired on January 22, 1996. The CBS crew had filmed us in Youngstown on January 13, 1996.

page 86 Elias quoted: David Elias, "All Roads Lead Up," *Financial Services Advisor,* March 1, 2000.

page 86 Tate on labor unions: Broadcast on ABC-TV's *Good Morning America,* January 31, 2008. The report was based on tapes obtained from Flagler Productions, a Kansas company that once worked for Wal-Mart recording its events and meetings.

page 87 Citi's "Live Richly" campaign and the boom in second mortgages: Louise Story, "Home Equity Frenzy Was a Bank Ad Come True," *New York Times,* August 15, 2008. The specific ad slogans cited are only a few found amid hundreds of pictures from the campaign posted on Flickr and other websites, easily accessed through an Internet search.

page 87 Wal-Mart wages: Arindrajit Dube, Dave Graham-Squire, Ken Jacobs, and Stephanie Luce, "Living Wage Policies and Wal-Mart: How a Higher Wage Standard Would Impact Wal-Mart Workers and Shoppers," UC Berkeley Center for Labor Research and Education, Research Brief, December 2007, http://laborcenter.berkeley.edu/retail/walmart_livingwage_policies07.pdf.

page 87 Walton family wealth: *Forbes,* September 24, 2004.

page 87 Wal-Mart employment in 2000: "Wal-Mart Stores Inc. to Open 46 Clubs and Stores in Three Days," *PR Newswire,* January 22, 2001.

page 87 General Motors employment in 2000: "General Motors 2009–2014 Restructuring Plan," presented to the U.S. Department of the Treasury, December 31, 2008, http://preprodha.ecomm.gm.com:8221/us/gm/en/news/govt/docs/plan.pdf.

page 87 Forbes 400 in 2000: *Forbes,* September 21, 2000.

page 87 CEO pay in 2000: Lawrence Mishel, Jared Bernstein, and Heidi Shierholz, *The State of Working America 2008/2009,* An Economic Policy Institute Book (Ithaca, N.Y.: Cornell University Press, ILR Press, 2009). This information was further clarified in an e-mail exchange between Mishel and the author, 2009.

page 89 Our article on child poverty and hunger: Dale Maharidge, "This American Is Hungry," photographs by Michael Williamson, *George,* October 2000.

page 89 13.5 million children in poverty: *The State of America's Children: A Report from the Children's Defense Fund* (Boston: Beacon Press, 1998).

page 89 Inadequacy of the federal minimum wage: Author's interview with Jen Kern, director of the Living Wage Campaign for the Association of Community Organizations for Reform Now (ACORN), summer 2000.

page 89 Rents skyrocketing far from high-tech jobs: Author's interview with Sheila Crowley, president of the National Low Income Housing Coalition, May 19, 2000.

page 89 5.4 million households paying high rent or living in severely distressed housing: "Strategic Plan FY 2001–FY 2006," U.S. Department of Housing and Urban Development, July 21, 2000, http://archives.hud.gov/budget/fy01/strategic721.pdf.

page 90 Austin rent affordability: R. Michelle Breyer, "A Hard Hunt for Homes: Austin Apartment Market among Tightest in Nation," *Austin American-Statesman,* July 8, 2000.

page 90 Wages needed to afford housing: Jennifer G. Twombly, "Out of Reach: The Growing Gap between Housing Costs and Income of Poor People in the United States," National Low Income Housing Coalition, 2000, www.nlihc.org/oor/oor2000.

page 90 Feeding America food distribution, 1990 and 1999: Author's interview with Maurice Weaver, media relations director of Feeding America, summer 2000.

page 90 Welfare data: "HHS Reports All States Meet Overall Welfare to Work Participation Rates; New Record of Parents Working," U.S. Department of Health and Human Services report, August 22, 2000, http://archive.hhs.gov/news/press/2000pres/20000822.html.

page 91 44 million Americans without health insurance: U.S. Census Bureau, *Current Population Survey,* 2000. In 2009, the Census Bureau reported that 50.7 million Americans were uninsured; see "Income, Poverty, and Health Insurance Coverage in the United States: 2009," issued in September 2010, www.census.gov/prod/2010pubs/p60–238.pdf.

page 94 University of Texas workers on food stamps: Author's interview with Peg Kramer, president of the University of Texas Staff Association, March 30, 2000.

page 97 Description of Charles Murray: Jason DeParle, "The Most Dangerous Conservative," *New York Times Magazine,* October 9, 1994.

page 97 Murray's book as the "intellectual foundation" for welfare reform: American Enterprise Institute for Public Policy Research, "Scholars and Fellows: Charles Murray," www.aei.org/scholar/43.

page 101 Sanford Weill's wealth: Forbes 400 list, *Forbes,* September 17, 2008.

page 101 Citigroup's bailout: David Enrich et al., "U.S. Agrees to Rescue Struggling Citigroup," *Wall Street Journal,* November 24, 2008.

page 101 Wal-Mart employment in 2008: Wal-Mart Inc., "Corporate Facts: Walmart by the Numbers," March 2010, www.walmartstores.com/download/2230.pdf.

page 101 General Motors employment in 2008 and projection for 2014: "General Motors 2009–2014 Restructuring Plan," presented to the U.S. Department of the Treasury, December 31, 2008, http://preprodha.ecomm.gm.com:8221/us/gm/en/news/govt/docs/plan.pdf.

page 101 Forbes 400 in 2008: *Forbes,* September 17, 2008.

page 101 CEO pay in 2007: Lawrence Mishel, Jared Bernstein, and Heidi Shierholz, *The State of Working America 2008/2009,* An Economic Policy Institute Book (Ithaca, N.Y.: Cornell

University Press, ILR Press, 2009). This information was further clarified in an e-mail exchange between Mishel and the author, 2009.

page 104 Bierce's final letter and movements: Jacob Silverstein, "The Devil and Ambrose Bierce," *Harper's,* February 2002, pp. 50–58.

page 105 Fuentes imagines Bierce's last days: Carlos Fuentes, *The Old Gringo* (New York: Farrar, Straus and Giroux, 1985).

page 106 Steinbeck's uncle and the WPA: John Steinbeck, "A Primer on the Thirties," *Esquire,* June 1960, p. 89.

page 106 Film rights for *The Grapes of Wrath:* "Fox Gets Steinbeck Book," *New York Times,* April 21, 1939.

page 107 Steinbeck on government being responsible for its citizens: Steinbeck, "A Primer on the Thirties," p. 85.

page 117 Heisenberg's Uncertainty Principle: Werner Heisenberg (1901–1976), a German theoretical physicist, was a pioneer in quantum mechanics. He posited that in order to observe an electron, one has to shine a light on it, which disturbs its velocity; thus one cannot be sure of its natural state. This principle has now taken on a wider meaning. "The social corollary of this Uncertainty Principle is that the act of observing an event changes the nature of that event, and for two reasons: (1) the event immediately becomes relative to the observer; and (2) observing the behavior of people who know they are being observed changes their behavior. This principle has become well-known owing to its many applications in literature and journalism," wrote Jon Tuttle in "How You Get That Story: Heisenberg's Uncertainty Principle and the Literature of the Vietnam War," *Journal of Popular Culture* 38, no. 6 (November 2005): 1088–1098.

page 130 Feeding America food distribution, 1999 and 2009: Author's interview with Ross Fraser, national media relations manager of Feeding America, May 2009.

page 135 Boehner's remark: "If Senate OKs Bank Bill, Expect a Year of Debate," *Marketwatch,* March 17, 2010.

page 135 Low-paying future jobs: "Where the Jobs Are," editorial, *New York Times,* July 23, 2009.

page 135 Wall Street bonuses according to Johnson Associates: Gina Chon and Brett Philbin, "Wall Street Bonuses Get 17 Percent Bounce," *Wall Street Journal,* February 24, 2010.

page 135 Average pay for senior Wall Street traders: Eric Dash, "Some Year End Bonuses Could Hit Pre-Downturn Highs," *New York Times,* November 5, 2009; Chon and Philbin, "Wall Street Bonuses Get 17 Percent Bounce."

page 135 Tepper's $4 billion payday: Nelson D. Schwartz and Louise Story, "Hedge Fund Pay Roars Back," *New York Times,* April 1, 2010.

page 135 Profitable companies laying off workers: Nelson D. Schwartz, "Industries Find Surging Profits in Deeper Cuts," *New York Times,* July 26, 2010.

page 135 1.4 million long-term unemployed workers: "Unemployment Situation Summary," U.S. Department of Labor's Bureau of Labor Statistics, press release, January 8, 2010.

page 135 Beck's company revenues: Lacey Rose, "Glenn Beck Inc.," *Forbes,* April 26, 2010.

page 151 Details of the Angela Ball homicide: See these three stories in the *New Orleans Times-Picayune,* by reporter Ramon Antonio Vargas: "Dead Woman Found inside Vacant City Hall Annex Appears to Have Killed Herself, Though Coroner Hasn't Classified Death," July 24, 2009; "A Stripper's Turbulent Life Ends in an Abandoned Building in New Orleans, and Troubling Questions Linger," August 7, 2009; "Coroner Rules Dancer's Death a Homicide," January 6, 2010.

page 154 Sweeps and arrests by Maricopa County sheriffs, 2007–2009: Associated Press, "Civil Rights Advocate Uses Text Messages to Warn Residents about Arizona Crime Sweeps," January 4, 2010.

page 154 American Freedom Riders motorcycle club assisting in arrests: *Ortega Melendres, et al. v. Arpaio, et al.,* U.S. District Court for Arizona, filed July 16, 2008; also see the Discussions tab on the group's Facebook page: www.facebook.com/topic.php?uid=128617880491116&topic=131.

page 154 Sheriff's department brags of arrests: On the Maricopa County Sheriff's Department website, www.mcso.org, a search for "illegal immigrant" details these activities. Nine months after my visit, the number of arrests was 36,983.

page 154 Class action lawsuit against Sheriff Joe Arpaio and the Maricopa County Sheriff's Department: *Ortega Melendres, et al. v. Arpaio, et al.,* U.S. District Court for Arizona, filed July 16, 2008.

page 155 Maricopa County population growth: William Finnegan, "Sheriff Joe," *New Yorker,* July 20, 2009, pp. 42, 44.

page 155 History of Joe Arpaio: Maricopa County Sheriff's Department website, www.mcso.org/index.php?a=GetModule&mn=Sheriff_Bio.

page 156 The death of Scott Norberg and other torture inside the Maricopa County jail: Barry Graham, "Star of Justice—Letter from Phoenix," *Harper's,* April 2001; Anya Lockert, "Family Sues over Man's Death in Jail," Associated Press, March 28, 1997.

page 156 *Phoenix New Times* reports on lawsuits against the sheriff: These reports began with an article by Tony Ortega, "Paying the Price," *Phoenix New Times,* August 28, 1998. The newspaper has published numerous articles since then updating the costs.

page 156 Arrest of five people for clapping at a public meeting: Associated Press, "Five Arrested at Maricopa County Meeting Acquitted," September 1, 2009.

page 156 Hayes-Bautista's theory of "Quakers" and "Puritans": Dale Maharidge, "In California, the Numbers Tell the Story," *New York Times,* March 29, 1999.

page 157 Army reservist making a citizen's arrest: "Pulling Guns on Illegals?" editorial, *Santa Fe New Mexican,* April 14, 2005.

page 157 Arrest of Shawna Forde and her associates: Kim Smith, "Three Accused of Killing Girl, Dad in Arivaca Likely to Have Two Trials," *Arizona Daily Star,* November 24, 2009; Mary Sanchez, "Minuteman's 15 Minutes Are About Up," *Salt Lake Tribune,* July 11, 2009.

page 157 Suffolk County, N.Y., teenagers attack Latinos: Manny Fernandez, "L.I. Teenagers Hunted Latinos for 'Sport,' Prosecutor Says," *New York Times,* March 19, 2010.

page 158 *East Valley Tribune*'s Pulitzer-winning series: Ryan Gabrielson and Paul Giblin, "Reasonable Doubt," which ran from July 9 to July 13, 2008.

page 158 Ward on anti-immigrant organizations: Author's phone interview with Eric Ward, August 18, 2009, followed by an e-mail exchange.

page 159 Mayor Phil Gordon on Arpaio's "reign of terror": Finnegan, "Sheriff Joe," pp. 42–53.

page 160 Newspaper coverage of Phoenix protest march: "10,000 Marchers, 5 Arrests at Immigration Protest," *Arizona Republic,* January 15, 2010.

page 164 Arrest of Puente leader: Stephen Lemens, "Joe Arpaio's Goons Grab Salvador Reza off the Street and Arrest Him, Again," *Phoenix New Times,* July 30, 2010.

page 164 Arpaio endorsing Tea Party candidates: Associated Press, "Arizona Sheriff Joe Arpaio Fires Up Tea Party Base at Las Vegas Tea Party Express Bus Stop," October 20, 2010.

page 164 Governor Jan Brewer's remarks about S.B. 1070: Randal C. Archibold, "Arizona Enacts Stringent Law on Immigration," *New York Times,* April 24, 2010.

page 164 The top 1 percent collecting 80 percent of U.S. income increase: Timothy Noah, "The United States of Inequality: Introducing the Great Divergence," *Slate,* September 3, 2010.

page 164 Brookings Institution report on American poverty: Elizabeth Kneebone and Emily Garr, "The Suburbanization of Poverty: Trends in Metropolitan America, 2000 to 2008," Brookings Institution, January 20, 2010, www.brookings.edu/~/media/Files/rc/papers/2010/0120_poverty_kneebone/0120_poverty_paper.pdf.

page 165 Tax Day Tea Party rally: Dana Milbank, "Free the Forbes 400," *Washington Post,* April 18, 2010.

page 166 Kondratiev's theory: Vincent Barnett, *Kondratiev and the Dynamics of Economic Development: Long Cycles and Industrial Growth in Historical Context* (London: Macmillan, 1998), pp. 105–115.

page 168 Emanuel's lobbying to weaken the Sarbanes-Oxley Act: Victoria McGrane, "Kanjorski Snipes at Emanuel," *Politico,* November 3, 2009. The Sarbox reform that Emanuel sought was passed by the House and later was folded into the Dodd-Frank Financial Regulation Bill, passed by the U.S. Senate in July 2010.

page 168 Levitt quoted: Frank Rich, "The Night They Drove the Tea Partiers Down," *New York Times,* November 8, 2009.

page 168 Emanuel's history: Elisabeth Bumiller, "The Brothers Emanuel," *New York Times,* June 15, 1997; Ken Dilanian, "Emanuel Brings White House Wall Street Savvy," *USA Today,* November 7, 2008.

page 169 Volcker gives financial reform legislation a B grade: Louis Uchitelle, "Volcker Pushes for Reform, Regretting Past Silence," *New York Times,* July 10, 2010.

page 169 No large bank bailouts between the 1930s and the 1980s: Paul Krugman, "The Fire Next Time," *New York Times,* April 16, 2010.

page 169 Hoenig on the role of the Federal Reserve: Thomas Hoenig, "Keep the Fed on Main Street," *New York Times,* April 17, 2010.

page 169 Leaked IMF memo: Paul Krugman, "Don't Cry for Wall Street," *New York Times,* April 23, 2010.

page 170 Blankfein's comments: Robert Watts, "Goldman Boss: We Do God's Work," *Sunday Times of London,* November 8, 2009.

page 170 Goldman Sachs salaries: Louise Story and Eric Dash, "For Top Bonuses on Wall Street, 7 Figures or 8?" *New York Times,* January 10, 2010; Graham Bowley, "Strong Year for Goldman as It Trims Bonus Pool," *New York Times,* January 22, 2010.

page 171 Trillin on the new money dealers: Calvin Trillin, "Wall Street Smarts," *New York Times,* October 14, 2009.

page 171 "The best and the brightest": David Halberstam, *The Best and the Brightest,* 25th anniv. ed. (New York: Ballantine, 1992). Halberstam intended his title as irony, to describe the misguided hubris of the Kennedy White House and its involvement in the Vietnam quagmire. In an introduction to the anniversary edition of the book, Halberstam wrote that the phrase "is often misused, failing to carry the tone of irony that the original intended."

page 172 Goldman Sachs employees requesting concealed weapons permits: Alice Schroeder, "Arming Goldman Sachs with Pistols," *Bloomberg News,* December 3, 2009.

page 175 The "Big Boys": John Steinbeck used this term in "A Primer on the Thirties," *Esquire,* June 1960, p. 85; Steinbeck capitalized the words.

page 175 Treatment of women at Goldman Sachs: Peter Lattman, "Three Women Claim Bias at Goldman," *New York Times,* September 16, 2010.

page 177 4.3 million homes in mortgage trouble in 2010: "A More Realistic Outlook," editorial, *National Mortgage News,* November 8, 2010.

page 177 One-fourth of American homeowners underwater: "Home Values Near Unprecedented Decline as Hints of Stabilization Wane in Third Quarter," Zillow.com and *PR Newswire,* November 10, 2010, http://zillow.mediaroom.com/index.php?s=159&item=215.

page 178 Average New Jersey property tax and the recent gubernatorial election: Angela Delli Santi, "NJ Gov Seeks Quicker Action on Bills to Help Stabilize Property Taxes," Associated Press, October 12, 2010.

page 179 Loopholes in New Jersey property tax cap: Shawn Boburg and Dave Sheingold, "Homeowners Take Yet Another Hit," *The Record* (Bergen County, N.J.), November 7, 2010.

page 182 Schwarzman quoted: Jonathan Alter, "A 'Fat Cat' Strikes Back, *Newsweek,* August 15, 2010.

page 182 Gordon quoted: Sewell Chan, "Fearing Fate of Japan, Not Greece," *New York Times,* November 5, 2010.

page 183 Effects of the recession: Pew Research Center, Social and Demographic Trends Project, "How the Great Recession Has Changed Life in America," June 30, 2010, http://pewsocialtrends.org/2010/06/30/how-the-great-recession-has-changed-life-in-america.

page 183 A new economy: Robert Reich, "When Will the Recovery Begin? Never," July 10, 2009, www.alternet.org/economy/141232/when_will_the_recovery_begin_never.

page 185 Recent sale of the Cascade Flats mill: Kathy McCormack, "Fraser Papers Gets Court Approval to Sell Gorham, NH, Paper Mill," Associated Press, December 8, 2010.

page 186 Arson in the Berlin area: Associated Press, "ATF Offering Rewards in North NH Arsons," December 4, 2009.

page 187 Details of the sale of the paper and pulp mills: Nathan Vardi, "Paper Trail; Two Iranian Immigrants Assembled the Nation's Fourth-Largest Tissue Maker. But When Their Company Collapsed, Creditors Couldn't Find Most of the Assets. What Happened?" *Forbes,* November 25, 2002; Frank Eltman, "Former CEO Sentenced to 15 Years in $300 Million American Tissue Fraud," Associated Press, September 25, 2006.

page 187 Tolstoy and the Khitrov market: Leo Tolstoy, *What Then Must We Do?* translated by Aylmer Maude, with an introduction by Jane Addams (Oxford, U.K.: Oxford University Press, 1935), pp. 8–12.

page 191 The Brooklyn Grange: Leigh Remizowski, "Turning a New Leaf: Produce Program Unveils Queens Crop," *New York Daily News,* July 22, 2010.

page 192 Other urban farmers in Kansas City: Information from "Urban Farm Tour," published by the Kansas City Center for Urban Agriculture, 2008.

page 194 Increase in seed sales: Adrian Higgins, "Demand for Vegetables Is Rooted in Recession," *Washington Post,* June 15, 2009.

page 194 Increase in the shipment of baby chickens: William Neuman, "Keeping Their Eggs in Their Backyard Nests," *New York Times,* August 4, 2009.

page 196 Officer Paul Durkin's murder: "Cop Killer Up for Parole," *Tribune-Chronicle* (Warren, Ohio), July 13, 2009.

page 197 Report on vacancies in Youngstown: The Center for Urban and Regional Studies, Youngstown State University, vacant property survey completed by the Mahoning Valley

Organizing Collaborative and Youngstown State University, Mahoning County GIS files, January 23, 2009.

page 199 Success of the Idora neighborhood project: "Lots of Green: 2010 Impact Statement," Youngstown Neighborhood Development Corporation, December 2010.

page 200 Velma Hart: Michelle Singletary, "Woman Who Told Obama Her Financial Fears Has Lost Her Job," *Washington Post,* November 22, 2010.

page 200 $370,000 in tax cuts for the richest Americans: Nicholas D. Kristof, "A Hedge Fund Republic?" *New York Times,* November 17, 2010.

page 200 McDermott quoted: David M. Herszenhorn, "Congress Sends $801 Billion Tax Cut Bill to Obama," *New York Times,* December 16, 2010.

page 200 2 million at risk of losing unemployment benefits: Michael Luo, et al., "Millions Bracing for Cutoff of Unemployment Aid," *New York Times,* December 3, 2010.

page 200 Decline in health care coverage: "Employer-Sponsored Health Insurance Coverage Continues to Decline Sharply," Economic Policy Institute, November 16, 2010, www.epi.org/publications/entry/news_from_epi_employer-sponsored_health_insurance_coverage_continues_to_dec.

page 200 Bachus on serving the banks: Mary Orndorff, "Spencer Bachus Finally Gets His Chairmanship," *Birmingham News,* December 9, 2010.

page 200 Wall Street partying: Susanne Craig and Kevin Roose, "With a Swagger, Wallets Out, Wall Street Dares to Celebrate," *New York Times,* November 24, 2010.

page 201 $144 billion in bonuses and pay for Wall Street: William D. Cohan, "The Power of Failure," *New York Times,* November 27, 2010.

page 201 Rising corporate profits: Catherine Rampell, "Corporate Profits Were Highest on Record Last Quarter," *New York Times,* November 23, 2010.

page 201 17 million families hungry: Kimberly Kindy, "USDA: 17 Million Families Struggled to Get Enough Food in 2009," *Washington Post,* November 15, 2010.

page 201 Unemployment rates in late 2010: "Employment Situation Summary," U.S. Department of Labor, Bureau of Labor Statistics, December 3, 2010, www.bls.gov/news.release/empsit.nr0.htm.

page 201 Federal Reserve predicts high unemployment: Don Lee, "Gloomy Fed Employment Forecast Overshadows Upbeat GDP Data," *Los Angeles Times,* November 24, 2010.

page 201 Kristof on inequality: Kristof, "A Hedge Fund Republic?"

page 201 Number of Communist Party members in the 1930s: Raymond Gram Swing, "Patriotism Dons a Black Shirt," *The Nation,* April 10, 1935, p. 409.

page 202 "Red Thursday": "Onlookers Swept into Melee as 2,000 Reds Start a Parade," *New York Times,* March 7, 1930; "A Hundred Heads Clubbed," *Chicago Daily Tribune,* March 7, 1930.

page 202 Adamic on the "Red Thursday" demonstrations: Louis Adamic, *My America: 1928–1938* (New York: Harper and Brothers, 1938), pp. 93–94, 303, 332.

page 203 Father Coughlin: "WMCA Contradicts Coughlin on Jews," *New York Times,* November 21, 1938; "6,000 Here Cheer Coughlin's Name," *New York Times,* December 16, 1938; "2,000 Picket WMCA, Backing Coughlin," *New York Times,* December 19, 1938; James Wechsler, "The Coughlin Terror," *The Nation,* July 22, 1939, pp. 92–97; Dale Kramer, "The American Fascists," *Harpers,* September 1940, pp. 380–393.

page 203 Christian Front: "G-Men Uncover U.S. Revolt Plot," *Atlanta Journal-Constitution,* January 15, 1940; Associated Press, "12 in Congress Marked for Death, Says Hoover," January 15, 1940; "Sketches of Men Held as Plotters," *New York Times,* January 16, 1940; "U.S. Drops Last 5 of 'Front' Cases," *New York Times,* January 3, 1941.

page 204 Kramer's prediction about American fascism: Kramer, "The American Fascists," p. 393.

page 204 Palin Twitter post: March 23, 2010, http://twitter.com/sarahpalinusa/status/10935548053.

page 204 *Kristallnacht:* Frank Rich, "The Rage Is Not about Health Care," *New York Times,* March 28, 2010.

page 204 Leaked report on domestic terrorism: "(U//FOUO) Rightwing Extremism: Current Economic and Political Climate Fueling Resurgence in Radicalization and Recruitment," U.S. Department of Homeland Security, April 7, 2009, www.fas.org/irp/eprint/rightwing.pdf.

page 205 Recent extremist violence: Eugene Robinson, "The Lone Wolves among Us," *Washington Post,* June 17, 2009; Bob Herbert, "A Threat We Can't Ignore," *New York Times,* June 20, 2009; John Hamilton, "Progressive Hunter: Jailhouse Confession—How the Right-Wing Media and Glenn Beck's Chalkboard Drove Byron Williams to Plot Assassination," Media Matters for America, October 11, 2010, http://mediamatters.org/research/201010110002.

page 206 Hutaree: John Seewer, "Ninth Christian Militia Suspect Accused in Anti-Government Plot to Face Charges," Associated Press, March 30, 2010.

page 207 Secret funding of the Tea Party movement: Jane Mayer, "The Billionaire Brothers Who Are Waging a War against Obama," *New Yorker,* August 30, 2010; Dana Milbank, "A Tea Party of Populist Posers," *Washington Post,* October 20, 2010.

page 210 Average household credit card debt: Eric Dash, "The Last Temptation of Plastic," *New York Times,* December 7, 2008. See chart accompanying this article, "How Credit Cards Came to Rule American Lives," graphic by Bill Marsh.

page 211 1950s advertising and consumer spending: Vance Packard, *The Hidden Persuaders* (New York: Pocket Books, 1957).

page 212 Share of income held by the wealthiest 1 percent: See two reports by Edward N. Wolff, Levy Economics Institute of Bard College: "Working Paper No. 407: Changes in Household Wealth in the 1980s and 1990s in the U.S.," May 2004; and "Working Paper No. 589: Recent Trends in Household Wealth in the United States: Rising Debt and the Middle-Class Squeeze—An Update to 2007," March 2010. Additional data drawn from Robert Reich, "Unjust Spoils," *The Nation,* June 30, 2010.

page 213 Falling median income between 1998 and 2008: U.S. Census Bureau report cited in "A Long Way Down," *New York Times,* editorial, September 15, 2009.

page 213 Buffett on taxing the wealthy: Interview by Christiane Amanpour, *This Week,* ABC, November 28, 2010, transcript, http://abcnews.go.com/ThisWeek/week-transcript-giving-pledge/story?id=12258827.

page 213 Shiller on government job creation: Robert J. Shiller, "What Would Roosevelt Do?" *New York Times,* July 31, 2010.

page 214 High joblessness among youth: Louis Uchitelle, "For a New Generation, an Elusive American Dream," *New York Times,* July 6, 2010.

page 214 Herbert on jobless youth: Bob Herbert, "Even Worse for Young Workers," *New York Times,* February 23, 2009.

page 214 Steinbeck on the WPA: John Steinbeck, "A Primer on the Thirties," *Esquire,* June 1960, p. 89.

page 215 U.S. military budget: "Department of Defense, The Federal Budget, Fiscal Year 2011," Office of Management and Budget, www.whitehouse.gov/omb/factsheet_department_defense.

page 215 World military expenditures: Stockholm International Peace Research Institute, chart, "The 15 Countries with the Highest Military Expenditures in 2009," www.sipri.org.

page 215 U.S. Defense Department installations: Chalmers Johnson, "Blowback: U.S. Actions Abroad Have Repeatedly Led to Unintended, Indefensible Consequences," *The Nation,* October 15, 2001.

page 216 Dorothea Lange: There are numerous websites displaying hundreds of Lange's photographs. Among those that mention the Sacramento camps and the cost of rent, see http://narademo.umiacs.umd.edu/cgi-bin/isadg/viewobject.pl?object=60474. Also see Anne Whiston Spirn, *Daring to Look: Dorothea Lange's Photographs and Reports from the Field* (Chicago: University of Chicago Press, 2008).

page 218 The moratorium and the history leading to the tent city: Denny Walsh and M.S. Enkoji, "Lawsuit Targets Homeless Policy," *Sacramento Bee,* August 2, 2007.

page 218 Oprah Winfrey's show on the tent city: "Tent Cities in America: A Lisa Ling Special Report," air date February 25, 2009, *Oprah Winfrey Show,* ABC. The show was rebroadcast on June 19, 2009; see www.oprah.com/world/Lisa-Ling-Goes-Inside-a-Tent-City_1/5.

page 218 Comparison to Mumbai: Scott Bransford, "Tarp Nation: Squatter Villages Arise from the Ashes of the West's Booms and Busts," *High Country News,* March 16, 2009.

page 218 Governor Arnold Schwarzenegger gets involved in tent city: Loretta Kalb, "Governor, Mayor, Join Forces to Help Capital Homeless," *Sacramento Bee,* March 26, 2009.

page 222 Mayor Kevin Johnson supports tent city: Kathy Locke, "Tent City Envisioned in Sacramento Homeless Plan," *Sacramento Bee,* November 16, 2010.

page 223 Pay for hedge fund managers: Nelson D. Schwartz and Louise Story, "Hedge Fund Pay Roars Back," *New York Times,* April 1, 2010.

page 223 Pew study on unemployment: Pew Economic Policy Group, "A Year or More: The High Cost of Long-Term Unemployment," April 2010, www.pewtrusts.org/uploadedFiles/wwwpewtrustsorg/Reports/Economic_Mobility/PEW-Unemployment%20Final.pdf.

page 224 Vollmann riding the rails: William T. Vollmann, *Riding toward Everywhere* (New York: Ecco, 2008).

page 226 Rorty on 1930s travelers: James Rorty, *Where Life Is Better: An Unsentimental American Journey* (New York: Reynal and Hitchcock, 1936), p. 16.